ORGANIZATIONAL BEHAVIOUR:
Canadian Cases and Exercises
Second Edition

Organizational Behaviour:

Canadian Cases and Exercises

Second Edition

RANDY HOFFMAN
York University

FRED RUEMPER
Georgian College

CAPTUS PRESS

ORGANIZATIONAL BEHAVIOUR:
Canadian Cases and Exercises, Second edition

Canadian Cataloguing in Publication Data

Main entry under title:
Organizational behaviour: Canadian cases and
    exercises

2nd ed.
Includes bibliographical references.
ISBN 1–895712–33–5

1. Organization – Case studies.   2. Organizational
behavior – Canada – Case studies.   I. Hoffman,
Randy, 1944–   II. Ruemper, Fred, 1939–

HD31.074 1994   658   C94–931131–6

0 9 8 7 6 5 4 3 2 1
Printed and bound in Canada

Table of Contents

EXERCISES

Foreword

The managerial profession requires, as do other professions, that practitioners be competent in the application of the skills and knowledge of their field. Your course in organizational behaviour includes case studies and/or experiential exercises because rote learning of theoretical content alone will not create that competence. The purpose of the dynamic learning tools included in this text is to simulate organizational opportunities for utilizing the abstract theories and principles in a controlled manner. In that way, you will be better prepared for the real world administrative issues that will arise in a career in management.

The exercises and cases in this book will therefore provide you with dynamic examples and illustrations of the organizational behaviour theory you are learning. The exercises are each focused upon a single issue that is identified at the beginning of the activity. By following the directions in the book and those from your instructor, you will see how theory may be put into action. Sometimes it is as simple as filling out a form and comparing your results with those of other students, while at other times the activity involves a more complex simulation and more elaborate activities.

The exercises have been grouped according to the organizational context involved, be it the individual, the group, or the entire organization. This is the traditional structure for organizational behaviour courses, and this resource book has been designed to integrate well with a variety of textbooks.

The first part, dealing with the individual, contains exercises that will help you make the connection between principles of psychology and behaviour in the workplace. By showing you how to put the theory in action, we hope that you will avoid the common tendency to fall back solely on the use of "common sense." Psychology can help you develop analytical skills that enable more sophisticated solutions to organizational problems. The first exercise, "Earning Your Mark," is an application of equity theory to a familiar situation. If you have ever worked on a group project for a course and received a group mark for your efforts, you will recognize the potential for forming beliefs that people did not get a mark that reflected their contribution. This exercise builds on this experience.

The section on group behaviour encourages you to employ principles from the field of social psychology. The focus is on the behaviour of individuals as they interact within small groups. Whenever students study in groups or do group projects, it is inevitable that they will also learn something about the way groups operate. In this section we have tried to make the exercises as analytical as possible, so that you understand the principles underlying the superficial aspects of the behaviour of people in groups. For example, in the section on leadership, we have included an exercise which involves measuring how many people a leader can supervise. The exercise results in a fairly precise answer even though you would correctly suspect that such a determination would depend on a great many individual differences among supervisors. The benefit of the exercise is that it does introduce you to the concept of evaluating a number of variables that do make a difference in the number of employees who can be supervised — variables such as geographic proximity or task repetitiveness. The learning goal is a more analytical understanding of the leadership issue.

The third section is centred on the organization and is based on the application of the theories of sociology and anthropology to business life. The activities will help you to come to recognize the formal and informal structure of organizations including the rules, policies, and norms that govern organizational life. The study of organizations is the study of the broad patterns which exist in all organizations.

The cases are organized differently. Since cases are based on real life situations, they seldom illustrate a situation that can fall into a single category or topic like the exercises. The medium-sized and longer cases may be examined for several issues and for different purposes during your course. For that reason we have grouped the cases together neutrally in alphabetical order by title. At the end of each case you will find a series of questions designed to bring out certain salient issues. They have been prepared to help you focus upon those areas of organizational behaviour that are most clearly illustrated in the real life situations depicted. The value in cases is that, over the duration of your course, you will have the opportunity to become acquainted with a more diverse variety of organizational situations than would occur over many years in an administrative career.

Students need some guidance in the method of analysis of cases, so we have provided you with a guide to case analysis. This should be regarded as comprehensive in nature, so, when using it, please feel free to include only those parts that you feel are relevant to your assignment.

Randy Hoffman
Fred Ruemper

Cases

The Purpose of Case Studies and How to Analyze Them

The cases included in this book are designed to help students achieve a deeper understanding of the issues involved in the management of human resources. The cases should give students a feeling of the hard realities of business and the constraints involved in decision making. By exposing himself or herself to a variety of situations involving different types of problems, the student should experience the challenges and dilemmas of the decision maker. The cases presented in this book are based on real situations, and as such they represent what actually took place. For reasons of privacy, the persons, the companies, and the locations involved have been disguised.

It is intended that a student will study the information provided in each case, attempt to diagnose the true nature of the problem or problems involved, search for alternative ways in which the problems can be resolved, and then recommend and justify the most plausible course of action.

Sometimes students feel disappointed because the cases sometimes do not appear to be "dramatic." However, because the cases do represent the realities of an organization, they are likely to be somewhat mundane, at least to the outside observer. Most of the incidents are based on events that were faced by managers and their subordinates on a day-to-day basis. Decisions had to be made about all sorts of problems just as they occurred.

Very often, cases do not contain all the information that the student would like to have. This may be partly the fault of the case writer. However, in real life, the manager must frequently make decisions on the basis of very limited information. Usually, there is insufficient time to collect all the facts.

Essentially, a case study allows the student to experience, to some extent, the realities of a problem situation and to react to the pressures and demands made on the decision maker. It is therefore important for the student to identify closely with the decision maker in the case by trying to put himself or herself in that person's shoes. This is the only way in which he or she will experience the constraints, limitations, and frustrations as well as the joys of effective decision making. As a learning technique, the case method tests the student's ability to diagnose problems and identify, evaluate, and choose the appropriate alternative as the best course of action. Before making a decision, he or she must ideally have considered all the possible alternatives and evaluated the advantages and disadvantages of each. Each alternative must be considered in terms of its "chances" for the best results.

Sometimes students look desperately for the "correct answer" or the "one best solution" without realizing that in case studies, the stress is not on the "right" or "wrong" answer. Instead, the emphasis is on the student's ability to take into account all the variables that might have a bearing on the situation and then find an answer that is feasible. Our experience with the use of cases indicates that only rarely are we likely to have situations for which there is only one solution. Most problems confronted by managers are multifaceted, involving motivational, cultural, structural, technological, communicational, and inter-personal aspects. In dealing with an organizational problem, one has to be able to comprehend all its aspects, including the complex personal interrelationships involved.

The objectives of a case study, as an educational tool, are:

(a) To improve a student's ability to think logically and imaginatively.
(b) To improve his or her ability to communicate.
(c) To provide an opportunity for experiential learning with particular reference to group work and interpersonal skills.
(d) To develop analytical ability and personal involvement in problem solving.
(e) To reinforce previous theoretical learning and to give the opportunity to evaluate critically some of the previously learned theories.
(f) To bring about an awareness of the constraints in decision making.
(g) To integrate the knowledge and skills gained studying the diverse areas within a management or business program.

A METHOD OF CASE ANALYSIS

There are many different methods that can be used to analyze successfully an organizational problem that involves various key issues. However, each would require a comprehensive understanding of the case information and its interrelatedness; a correct decision as to which principles, models, and theories of organizational behaviour should be applied; and competent application of that selected area of knowledge to the problems or issues at hand. Below is outlined one method of incorporating those criteria into a step-by-step procedure for case analysis. It is not the only feasible approach; but it is a method that will work, if applied carefully.

1. **Read the case study two or three times (more, for a long or complex case) in an undirected manner.** "Undirected" means do not think about the questions asked or the method of analysis. The goal here is to become familiar with the management situation that is described without filtering that perception with a premature focus on solutions or answers. If the assigned questions are considered prematurely, the case reader will unavoidably become solutions-oriented from the very first perusal. These solutions are likely to be both superficial and very hard to change as the study of the case proceeds.

2. **During the final reading, make notes regarding salient issues.** These issues will not necessarily conform to those upon which the assigned questions are based. (Although there will most likely be a strong relationship which will eventually become clear.)

3. **Now read and study the assigned question. Record information from the case that appears pertinent to its analysis.** Do not, however, attempt to answer the questions. At this stage the focus is on an organization of the previous impressions of the case in terms of the assigned areas of inquiry. It will usually be necessary to return to the case for further information.

4. **Decide which principles, theories, or models of organizational behaviour, if any, can be applied to the observed data in order to generate solutions.** The key activity is to match the theories, etc. to the case information and assignment. The temptation that must be avoided is to generate solutions based mainly upon intuition and then try to force-fit some handy theoretical rationale to the preconceived answers. Theories of organizational behaviour are to be used in the analysis and solution of organizational problems, not as an afterthought.

5. **Apply the selected general principles, theories, or models and determine what solutions are suggested by this application and select the ones that best deal with assigned problem(s).** Often, more than one answer is supportable for a particular question. A search for additional theoretical rationale and an application of informed judgment will eventually resolve this difficulty. Part of the answer to the case study assignment may require that the rationale for the alternatives and solutions presented also be given. The major strength of any case report cannot reside chiefly in the specific solutions offered, as these are always arguable. Rather, it is the **reasons** for the solutions that will either support or ultimately undermine the student's efforts. They will be correct or incorrect applications of management science and refined judgment.

WHEN SPECIFIC QUESTIONS ARE NOT ASSIGNED

Occasionally, case studies are assigned for analysis without specific questions. The student must then devise a framework that will enable the analytical and/or synthetic treatment of strategic issues. One general approach is as follows.

1. **Follow steps one and two of the procedure given above.**
2. **Identify the salient problems** (no more than three or four can be treated in a typical five- to ten-page case report). The problems may also be divided into symptoms and root causes, thus providing an opportunity later on to suggest measures that might be effective at either or both levels. Notes should now be made categorizing the information in the case according to its relationship with an identified issue.
3. **Employ internal and external constraints and relevant values to establish criteria by which the proposed solutions to the identified problems may be judged.** Wherever possible, ensure that these criteria are objective. Qualitative indicators of success tend to be ambiguous and subject to argument. Too short a list of criteria will result in an incomplete judgment of solutions. Too long a list may be unsatisfiable and unwieldy. Typically, about four to eight criteria will usually do the job for each salient problem. They must however be very carefully chosen to reflect the essential areas that will mean success or failure to the firm's general management.
4. **Follow steps four and five concerning the use of organizational behaviour concepts from the procedure outlined above.** Again, the list of alternative solutions will emerge, and the rationale for the final selection (refer to the criteria) should constitute an important part of the case report.
5. **The final selection of a solution from alternatives is based upon how well it meets the criteria you have established.** Any solution to a strategic problem will be, at best, an optimal approach that satisfies the criteria reasonably well. Sometimes, all that can be found is the lesser among evils. Rarely indeed is any solution a perfect match, meeting or exceeding all criteria. Students are advised to moderate their enthusiasm with a realistic assessment of the merits and drawbacks of their solutions.
6. **Present the chosen solution(s) in detail and realistically.**

Section titles for a case report following this format might then be: "statement of the problem"; "selection of criteria"; "selection and evaluation of solution alternatives"; and "conclusion" (presentation, rationale, and detailed assessment of the chosen solution).

FOUR COMMON PITFALLS

1. Salience of Data and Issues   Most comprehensive cases contain (as do real world situations) much information of little real importance to the main problems or issues that must be confronted. Many problems or issues may themselves be spin-offs of deeper, more important root causes; or perhaps they are incidental and of little consequence to more major concerns. One of the tasks of the case study analyst is to "separate the wheat from the chaff," or identify and focus upon the truly essential elements of the problem at hand. To do otherwise is to become sidetracked by issues of little gravity, and therefore to neglect, in direct proportion, the real goal of the exercise. Often students are asked to take the role of employees, management, upper level executives, or of a consultant to those groups. This viewpoint should form the filter by which the case material is perceived. A careful balance must be struck between the rigorous case report and the scattering and weakening effects of being diverted by too many minor matters.

2. Superficial Solutions   These often arise due to an inadequate analysis of too little data; the failure to establish comprehensive, rather than vague criteria; or some other way in which the case report was not pushed far enough in important directions. For example, suppose the case refers to an ineffective work group — the assignment being to make corrective recommendations. If the case report states, "The managers must improve their leadership skills," that is probably a superficial recommendation. A detailed description of precisely what changes are required and why, and perhaps also, how to carry out these improvements would constitute a proper response. Students should strive to be specific and to include as much detail as possible relevant to the major issues, their analyses, and solutions. The test of a superficial statement is first, does it apply equally well to many firms or specifically relate to the one at hand; and second, would it constitute only vague hints to management, or would it give specific directions or criticisms.

3. The "More Information" Syndrome   It is often a temptation in a case report to "reluctantly" conclude that the data is woefully incomplete, and thus a firm conclusion is impossible. It would be necessary (as the next line usually reads) to get more information before reaching any definite conclusion. In the real world, this sometimes is precisely what happens. In a case study, it is almost always tantamount to ducking the issue. The problem is that the goal of a case study is usually to depict a behavioural or management situation for the purpose of analysis and recommendations; and that cannot be accomplished if the information is said to be incomplete. The student will of course never receive that additional information; and the exercise's aim is thus frustrated. It is therefore important to virtually always complete the case report with the information at hand. If there is legitimate cause to seriously question the quantity or quality of information, then this can be noted as qualifying the competence of the solution. A complete answer should still be attempted.

4. Finally, Answer the Question   Just as the organizational decision-maker must ultimately reach some conclusion, so the preparer of a case report must avoid "waffling" or sitting on the fence when a specific recommendation is requested. Many times it may seem difficult to decide between two or more alternatives. The wisest course is to make the best choice possible and then note that other alternatives may be almost equally attractive.

ACME Corporation

William Talley has been with the ACME Corporation (a crown corporation of the federal government with a high public profile) for three years. During this period Talley had a meteoric rise in the corporation from Director of Public Affairs and Economics to Vice-President of Market Development. Throughout these years Talley worked closely with the President of the Corporation, John Harris. Harris found Talley an able, dedicated, and shrewd manager who was not afraid to speak his mind or get tough with staff, clients, or the media when the occasion required it. Talley's performance assessments were always high, and it was on the personal recommendation of Harris that the Board of Directors agreed to promote Talley to the vice-presidency and to assign him to the demanding responsibilities of market development.

Talley was not afraid of stepping over dead bodies to get to his goal of president of the corporation. Consequently, he had made a number of enemies over the years in the organization. Although Harris was aware of Talley's aggressive personality and high ambitions, he considered him a bright and able colleague and gave him his complete trust and confidence because of their good personal relationship. Then one day Harris got a call from a reporter of a widely circulated and respected newspaper who was doing a profile on Talley.

The reporter asked Harris some seemingly innocuous questions. "Why was Mr. Talley hired initially?" "On who's recommendation was Mr. Talley appointed director and subsequently vice-president?" Then the bombshell hit. "On the ACME Corporation's list of senior officers Mr. Talley has an Hons. B.A. in Economics from the University of Toronto and an M.B.A. from Stanford University beside his name. I checked with Stanford University and they stated that Mr. Talley did not successfully complete his M.B.A. degree. Furthermore, the University of Toronto told me he does not have a honors degree in economics but an honors degree in history." The reporter went on to say, "I have just asked

Mr. Talley whether this is true, and he stated that he has completed the course work for the M.B.A. but that he still has to write his thesis, which he says he can do at any time. He claimed he didn't know why these degrees were listed beside his name in the corporation's official publication."

Mr. Harris was completely stunned by this information. There was a long silence. Then the reporter told Mr. Harris that the story would be printed in the newspaper the next day and asked, "Mr. Harris, can I ask what you are going to do about this employee's misrepresentation of his credentials?"

QUESTIONS

1. What should Mr. Harris tell the reporter?
2. What rights does Mr. Tally now have?
3. If the allegation turns out to be true,
    (a) Is Mr. Harris obligated to take strong action?
    (b) What would you suggest to Harris?

Action Realty Inc. (A)

What was once a small real estate office has evolved into Action Realty Inc., a medium-sized, prestigious brokerage firm specializing in the buying, selling, and management of residential and commercial real estate. It is a young and aggressive company based in Vancouver that started out four years ago as a partnership between two licensed real estate brokers, Harvey and Paul. Beginning in a 800 sq. ft. office, the partners first generated most of the company's sales themselves, and Harvey's wife, Marie, was the entire administrative staff. However, in 1989 they incorporated and moved into a new office with 3,500 sq. ft. of prime office space. This year, the company perceived a need for even more space to accommodate their growing organization and added another 2,000 sq. ft. from next door to accommodate a new commercial real estate division. The company now employs some 200 registered agents, of which 50 are full-time and the rest part-time. An administrative staff of 11 people perform the bookkeeping and clerical functions.

Harvey and Paul are the only shareholders of Action Realty Inc. Even though the company has expanded so rapidly, the two men and Marie still personally oversee the operations of all the staff. Harvey's principal managerial role is to make sure the company reaches or exceeds sales goals. Paul does most of the hiring of new agents, and Marie manages the accounting and clerical personnel. All managerial activities to plan, direct, control, and otherwise administer the firm are performed by the three of them in one capacity or another.

GOALS OF THE COMPANY

The two men's original goal was to establish a large, profitable, and prestigious organization as soon as possible. In other words, making "Big Bucks," with sales volume being the key determinant. But since the real estate environment is of a changeable nature, the company must always try to adapt. Each year, new goals are set according to the economic situation at the time. The two brokers often find it difficult to achieve these goals because in many years survival alone is hard enough to ensure. A current goal is to open a branch office and eventually to establish a multibranch brokerage business. According to the agents and the office staff, "we'll have to see it to believe it."

POLICIES

Action Realty has issued a booklet describing company policies and setting out the rules and regulations which the agents should follow when pursuing business. These policies, rules, and regulations, which the company enforces, are concerned mainly with business ethics — that is, standards of business practice. Employees must abide by these policies to maintain the company's reputation. Agents join the company in order to benefit from the firm's name and to promote personal sales through the use of the firm's image. It is not the goals of the company that concern agents, but the reaching of personal objectives. Often, few agents are really sure what the company's current goals are. Sometimes, whoever attends the company meetings tries to pass the word around.

It would be difficult for Paul and Harvey to enforce other rules and regulations concerning work practices with their prevalent management style — which can be described as relaxed. Probably, this style was adopted because all agents work strictly on a commission basis and develop their own clientele. Action Realty's goal-setting philosophy for individual agents is to "do your best," and agents are responsible for their own productivity. It is essential that they enjoy working for the company, however, for they could leave at any time. The company cannot afford an agent staff that consists only of transients. All agents registered with the company incur overhead expenses regardless of whether or not they produce any sales. That expense can sometimes be kept minimal if they do not occupy a permanent desk within the office. If an agent generates commission revenue of over $25,000/yr., he/she is considered a full-time agent and has the privilege of occupying a desk. Those who do not maintain that quota are considered part-time. The latter group do not have any minimum sales level; they are only required to maintain their licence by paying an annual fee to the provincial government and the local real estate board.

STRUCTURE

The organizational structure of the firm appears to be simple and somewhat flat. The agents all report to the two brokers, Paul and Harvey; the administrative staff reports to Marie. Figure 1 shows the structure.

The personnel are divided into four separate groups. The first is the administrative department, composed of 5 secretaries and 2 accountants, all salaried. They take care of general office duties to ensure that the administration of the company is running effectively and efficiently. The secretaries are constantly barraged with work from the agents, which often causes their own office work to be neglected. The second department is the property management division, which consists of only one agent and his own personal secretary. The

FIGURE 1   ORGANIZATION CHART OF ACTION REALTY INC.

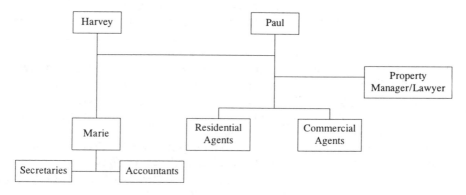

property manager also acts (at times) as the company's lawyer. He is paid by salary and is responsible solely to the Brokers. His job responsibility is to look after the company's real estate investments and to manage properties for clients of the company. He was hired because he was a close friend of the Brokers.

The third department is the residential department which consists of 50 full-time agents. This department contains 50 desks, all separated by partitions to ensure privacy. Out of these 50 agents, approximately 25% work at their full capacity, while the other 75% work at moderate levels to "just getting by." Sometimes, during the evening and occasionally during the afternoons, full-time agents get together to play cards in the office, have a meal outside, or sit around a local pub.

The fourth department is the commercial real estate division, which is the most important department because it generates the highest sales per agent. This department is comprised of small individual rooms restricted to those who deal only in commercial real estate. This poses a problem because all agents would like private rooms. However, even the top salesmen who deal in residential and some commercial real estate do not have their own rooms. Dealing solely in commercial real estate is quite difficult without the right connections and the "know how." It is considered the "gravy" of the business, while selling residential is the "bread and butter." At times, the "commercial only" agents do tend to list and sell residential property, and this upsets the other agents immensely. This places management in a very awkward position. There are so many agents with different needs and desires that it is difficult for the two Brokers to please everyone.

MANAGEMENT

Marie manages the administrative department in a highly centralized way. She tries to control staff and impose certain restrictions upon them. For example, she does not want her staff to socialize too much or to have lunch with the agents. Everything must be done according to the way she wants it done. She feels that her way is the one best way to do the job. There is no room for staff input. Anything done out of the normal procedure must be cleared with her first, yet she is not even present half the time. As a result, there are many complaints within this department. The staff occasionally find their jobs very disorganized and frustrating, and the office does not run as efficiently as it should.

Supplies are locked up after Marie leaves for the evening to prevent "vandalism." Since she is the only one who holds the key, the administrative staff feel as though they are being treated like children or possibly criminals. The morale in this department appears to be quite poor. Marie does not have the formal education of prior job experience to qualify her for this position. The staff find it very difficult to complain or voice their opinions in order to effect any changes because Marie is Harvey's wife. On a personal level, in non-business related matters, the administrative staff gets along very well with Marie and the Brokers. When staff meetings are held (which is very seldom), it is always at staff's request. Management is doing them a favour by holding the meeting, and staff complaints are not taken seriously. Bonuses and promotions are very seldomly awarded in this department, and salaries are increased only with the cost of living.

With respect to the agents, Paul and Harvey practically run the entire organization themselves. They do all the hiring, supervision, and make all the business decisions concerning the company. They do not like delegating authority to members of the sales staff regarding non-routine matters. The main operating policy is to hire as many agents as possible because of the belief that more sales agents registered with the company will result in more sales. The hiring of agents is performed almost indiscriminately rather than on merit. All agents work on a commission basis. The Brokers feel that the best way to manage them is to give them free rein to come and go as they please. Harvey and Paul are extremely active themselves, but they try to accommodate the agents in whatever way they can. New agents are encouraged to come to them whenever help is needed. Yet the Brokers are often very busy with company operations, promotion, and their own sales. General meetings and sales training classes for new agents are held by the brokers every Saturday morning. Since they are obviously so busy at other times, agents do not wish to bother Paul or Harvey. Instead, agents tend to form partnerships of three or four persons working together to help one another on deals. As a result, several persons working together end up doing the normal workload of one person. Productivity actually decreases, and overall performance of the company is lower. Management officially discourages these informal work groups. They prefer agents to work on their own and to only come to management for help.

The agents at Action Realty are hired personally by the Brokers. Everyone seems to have some connection with the Brokers either through social contact or family ties. Hiring decisions are solely based on the personal references of the prospective employees. Management tries to operate the system on an impersonal basis so that decisions regarding employees can be made fairly. Yet the agents feel a close affiliation with the Brokers because of the company's cultural homogeneity and family relationships. Therefore, it is hard for management to maintain a very impersonal approach, however much they try. The Brokers are known for being open, honest, and straightforward with employees. It seems everyone gets along with management. Yet there is still a high rate of agent turnover.

WORKING CONDITIONS

The Brokers motivate their sales staff by, in part, working hard and generating sales themselves. Action Realty's profits at this time are mainly generated by the number and amount of deals the company makes. The agents must be relied upon to produce a large volume of sales in order for the company to cover their overhead and to realize any profits. The "open board," where all the agents' property listings and sales are compiled, covers an entire wall for all to view. Management feels that when agents see how well their associates are doing, it motivates them to work harder.

Overall company morale is very good, and the agents seem to enjoy working there. The office is spacious, comfortable, and pleasantly designed to facilitate good working conditions, which management feels is important for motivating staff to work harder. At times agents arrive ready to work but end up just socializing all day. Management does not seem to mind. They feel that the agents will mainly socialize only temporarily. In the long run, they are expected to motivate themselves to generate increased sales. The company has an "open door policy" which they encourage. Agents are free to talk to the Brokers at any time. It is hoped that this will help resolve any work problems. According to the company, "For people to work together effectively, there must be a friendly, congenial atmosphere based on mutual trust and respect." Informal groups are well established, and rarely does any worker feel alienated. Social gatherings outside of work are encouraged. An Action Realty house newspaper called "Action Times" has been set up to keep employees and outsiders informed as to what is happening within the organization.

To ensure that agents are kept up to date, announcements are placed on bulletins, and letters to each agent are put into their message slots. Policy meetings are held every month on the first Monday morning. Company objectives and new policies are discussed there, giving agents the opportunity to voice freely their opinions and to relate problems. Management is very proud of these meetings as they are evidence of the open communication that exists within the firm. Sometimes guest speakers are invited to these meetings to enlighten the agents on various business-related fields. Since attendance is not mandatory, full-time agents attend whenever they feel like it, or not at all. As for the part-time agents, many are not even aware of the time and date of the meetings.

The company also offers and arranges a variety of planned social activities such as a bowling league every Tuesday evening and a soccer league every Saturday afternoon. Either Harvey or Paul attempts to be present at all these activities. Two major social events are held every year. The management hopes that all of these activities will give staff a sense of belonging.

Management believes that they are doing the best they can to motivate employees by providing great working conditions and by establishing excellent interpersonal relations between them and their staff. However, it seems that employees are still not motivated to work to their full potential. At least, this is the case with 75% of the agents who do not even generate at least one sale per year. Some agents are seen constantly to go in and out of the office daily, yet accomplish next to nothing. Every year profits do increase; but expenses increase as well.

QUESTIONS

1. Describe and compare the motivational states of the agents and the office staff.
2. Are these states the result of the leadership styles employed and the organizational structure? Why or why not?
3. Analyze the reward system at Action Realty with respect to:
    (a) part-time agents
    (b) full-time agents
    (c) commercial agents
    (d) office workers
4. What changes would you suggest to ensure continuing growth in the future?

Action Realty Inc. (B)

By late 1990, the Vancouver real estate market in both residential and commercial business came down from the generally buoyant levels of the late 1980s. Sales became sluggish and commissions to both brokers and sales agents fell substantially. Poor sales expectations among the public meant that properties were withheld from the market. There was increasingly fierce competition among agents for both listings and clients. The only positive sign was that, at long last, mortgage rates were beginning to show signs of a long-awaited decline.

Action Realty seemed to be feeling the effect of the depressed state of the market more severely than many other firms. In response, it had not only shelved its plans to establish branch offices, but management began to worry about whether the present level of business could support even the existing size of the firm.

To make matters worse, one of the two owners, Paul, had developed severe bronchitis during the wet fall weather. He was advised by his doctor to drastically reduce his work hours until his condition improved. Possibly, he would be incapacitated for a few months. Since the poor market conditions were already causing a number of the less productive employees to seek other work, the hiring activities that Paul was now not able to carry out were, at first, much missed. Harvey realized that now there might not be enough business even to keep a part-time agent interested. From a total of over 200 agents at its peak, the firm now had a complement of about 120.

As a barometer for this deteriorating state of affairs, the office atmosphere became decidedly dour. Even the part-time agents, many of whom had previously seemed content to socialize or travel around in groups, were dispirited and frequently complained about business in the office. This was puzzling to the brokers, since most of that group had never been dependant on their commissions to maintain their life styles. The productive section of the full-time agents in both the residential and commercial fields, who previously had rarely been seen idle, now often sat in their offices seemingly waiting for the telephone to ring. Arguments in the office were becoming frequent — especially between full-time and part-time agents. Relations between secretarial support staff and agents, never without friction, were now coming close to the point of breakdown. This was also puzzling since the low volume of business should have made for an easier administrative work flow. Even the informal but very popular company bowling league now consisted mainly of only a few bowling fanatics, whose primary reason for coming out had not been social.

With the burden of management responsibilities almost totally on his shoulders for the present, Harvey became increasingly concerned about the declining income and poor morale of the employees of Action Realty. Other firms, he noted, had all lost some people, but most were managing to survive with a more modest level of sales and a committed core of professionally oriented agents. Harvey was traditionally responsible for setting and attaining performance goals and for occasionally supervising administration, but not hiring. Therefore, he had not questioned or interfered with Paul's practice of bringing in any acquaintance with agent certification as a new employee. Harvey had simply done his best with the staff as it existed. Although it had never mattered in the past, he was now beginning to wonder whether this nearly random method of hiring was creating difficulties in the current situation.

With sales and commissions declining even faster than the number of agents, Harvey knew that effective measures had better be taken quickly. Options he was considering included: immediately terminate all employees whose previous year's commissions were less than $12,000 and move the firm into smaller premises; set realistic sales goals for the next two months and terminate those who did not attain them; or simply try to carry on and hope business improves. He gave himself until the next Saturday morning meeting to reach a decision. He had let the word out that important announcements would be made and he expected a big turnout of staff. That was all to the good, he felt, since his own business activities had always been an important source of income for the firm, and his present preoccupation with this problem was causing him to neglect them.

QUESTIONS

1. Do you believe that hiring practices were responsible for the performance of Action Realty being worse than many other firms during the market downturn? Explain your answer.
2. What other aspects of the firm's management and policies might have contributed to the problem?
3. Evaluate Harvey's measures to alleviate poor performance. Which is likely to be most effective? Do you recommend either option to downsize the firm be adopted?
4. Suggest a solution that you feel would be optimal in alleviating the motivational problems and improving performance. Provide an implementation plan including the outline of what Harvey should say at the meeting.

Affirmative Action at the University of Selkirk

The University of Selkirk is a medium-sized institution situated in a prairie province. During the first half of 1989, it conducted an audit of its faculty members with the intention of determining the degree to which males were overrepresented among faculty members. The conclusion of the audit was that, in most faculties, there was indeed a severe imbalance in favour of men.

The direct result was the establishment of a university-wide Affirmative Action Committee. The role of this body was to make recommendations to the vice-president, Academic (who was in charge of academic hirings) concerning how the university could make more strenuous efforts towards hiring women faculty members. By late 1989, the committee had formulated a three-phase proposal which, after some negotiation, was reluctantly approved by the vice-president, Academic and was ratified by the university senate and the president. The proposal contained the following provisions.

1. That each department formulate an affirmative action hiring plan that would outline:
   - how women candidates could be located and be encouraged to apply for forthcoming positions;
   - in the assessment of candidates, how the department will take into account that many women may not have had the same opportunities as men to complete doctorates or to publish as prolificly in academic journals, but should still be considered on a par with men who have;

- how, at the time when job offers are being made, women candidates with acceptable qualifications would be offered the position prior to any men.
2. Each department's plan would then be submitted to the Affirmative Action Committee for approval. No hirings would take place until an acceptable plan had been worked out between the department and the committee.
3. No men candidates for faculty positions would be submitted to the vice-president, Academic for hiring unless the Affirmative Action Committee and the department agreed that no acceptable woman candidate could be found.

The vice-president (male) had felt that the plan was too rigid, and that it might result in "the best candidates" not being considered. Even in cases where the lack of qualified women finally resulted in approval to hire a man, the vice-president suggested that the best candidates would have taken positions elsewhere by the time the process worked through to the stage where an offer could be made to a man. The Affirmative Action Committee, comprised in the majority of women faculty members and librarians, countered that the systems of graduate studies, academic faculties, and scholarly publishing in Canada were so dominated by men that there was an implicit set of values that effectively excluded women. Only by increasing the number of women in academic positions in a direct and forceful manner, the committee stated, would this male-dominated environment be altered.

By mid-1990, almost all university departments had successfully negotiated a plan with the Affirmative Action Committee. An exception was the department of Business Studies. Its plan had been rejected once in January 1990 as woefully inadequate, and the department had not so far attempted to re-open negotiations with the committee. In university circles, it was widely known that many Business Studies' faculty members, 85% of whom were men, had nothing but disdain for the committee and its work and openly stated it.

Then, in November 1990, an alumnus bequest gave Business Studies sufficient funding to hire a new faculty member in the finance area. Rather than actively pursue approval of their affirmative action plan, however, the department's efforts were put towards attracting and interviewing candidates. As it happened, the best candidate to emerge was a woman. This person's credentials were so strong, that unless action was taken quickly, she would certainly take a position elsewhere. The department, believing that it would face no impediments, forwarded its recommendation to the vice-president, Academic. However, once the Affirmative Action Committee found out, they immediately moved to block the appointment as no affirmative action hiring plan had been approved.

The department, with the concurrence of the vice-president, appealed directly to the president. They put the case forward that the objection of the committee was a politically motivated disruptive tactic. The Affirmative Action Committee replied that it was not this appointment that was important, but rather it was having an appropriate procedure in place that would guarantee better access for faculty jobs for women. Every department in the university had to follow the same rules. They also stated that the woman candidate was an exceptional case and would find a position regardless. But without strict policies, many other deserving women candidates would be out of luck. Catering to the wishes of the Business department now would make it appear that the committee was "selling out."

With seemingly no possibility of a resolution between the parties, the vice-president, Academic and the Affirmative Action Committee appealed to the president of the university for a final decision.

QUESTIONS

1. Discuss the affirmative action policy of the University of Selkirk. Is it practical? Is it fair?
2. In the case of the preferred candidate for the department of Business Studies, does the end justify the means?
3. How would you advise the president to resolve the problem in respect of this hiring and any wider issues?

Automation in the Book Store

My name is Lisa and I am a fourth year student in honours Biology at the University of Southern Ontario. Last summer I took a part-time job three evenings a week in a book store. My regular summer job provided me with good work experience, but it didn't pay too well. This story is about my experience in the book store.

I worked for a medium-sized book store, part of a chain which had two outlets in different malls in our city. The manager was glad to hire me because I had retail experience with Eaton's and Zeller's, and I was glad to work for them because I like to read and didn't want a part-time job that included weekend hours. I like to go camping with my friends.

The store was not very large. There were only three full-time employees: the manager, her assistant, and another woman. There were five part-time employees. One woman worked days, and the rest of us worked evenings and weekends. Only one other employee was a student, he worked the opposite shift to me. The rest were older women.

I liked the sales work. Employees were expected to serve a customer from our first contact with them through to the end of the sale, so it meant that I would approach a customer and offer assistance and stay with them until I had rung up any purchase the customer made. This made the work varied and interesting. It was a lot more personal than just standing at a cash register ringing up sales.

Shortly after I arrived the manager announced that the store was going to join the company computer system. We had been managing with a simple system using a till and written record of sales. The computer system would record cash sales, credit card sales, and inventory as well as maintain other records which were not explained to us. It was supposed to make our work go faster because it included a scanning device to read the product code on the books and other items in the store. We also assumed that the switch-over had something to do with the imposition of the new Goods and Services Tax which was expected in the new year. Books had not previously been taxed, and this would greatly ease the registering of this new sales tax.

The older staff were quite apprehensive about this new system. None of them had any previous experience with computers. I had worked with this kind of system at Eaton's, so I was curious to see how this one would work. The other student was experienced with computers but had never worked with this kind of machine.

There was a great deal of discussion about what the computers could actually do. We were all assigned an ID number to use when recording our sales, and the people realized that it meant their work could be watched by the computer. Nobody liked that although we really didn't know what could or could not be monitored.

The training was pretty skimpy. Head office sent the manager to the other store in the city to learn on their system. When she got back, our system was installed and our training began. There were two parts to the training. First we watched training tapes; there were two of them, each half an hour long. I found them to be boring and insulting. A man in the tape taught a dumb woman how to run the system. It was very patronizing.

The second part was better. We were given a training manual containing a series of exercises to do. The technician who installed the machine told us the system was in the training mode for the next week, and we could go ahead and do the exercises in the book. Later the machine would go "on line."

For two days we made progress. Even the most hesitant employees relaxed a bit as they rang up thousands of dollars in fictitious sales. We read how the main computer would keep track of these sales and maintain a record of our store inventory and decide when we needed more supplies and so on. The scanner used to read the bar code worked pretty well. People were worried about having to read those long numbers and punch them into the register. The credit card system was terrific. It automatically made up the slip and phoned to get authorization for the card sale.

On the third day things fell apart. It turned out that our register was not in the training mode at all. It was on line and loaded with fictitious sales. This unfortunate incident confirmed the worst fears of those who had doubts about the change in the first place. There was lots of talk. The best comment was "If you really want to make a mess, use a computer." The manager was dismayed and head office wanted to assign blame. The technician said it was our fault since the system says when it is in the training mode and we should have noticed that it was not. I told him he had it backwards. We had never seen the training mode and what we saw looked exactly like it showed in the manual.

By the next week this mess was cleaned up, and we got down to regular use of the new system. There were three lingering problems. The first was an omission in the training. It did not include instructions on how to close up at the end of the day. Somehow nobody noticed this until the first day. The manager had to come in and prepare a hand-written set of instructions about this routine.

The other two problems were related. The employees continued to be concerned about work monitoring. I had experienced this at Eaton's where my supervisor had told me that if my sales were much higher than the others in my area, they would take it to mean that I was not helping out on the floor but rather was just standing there ringing up the cash register. Our manager at the book store would not confirm or deny any of these concerns.

The other problem had to do with signing in and out. We were supposed to sign in with our ID number when making a sale and sign out after. We found this was time consuming. The actual registering of a sale was fast and this additional step was unwelcome. The procedure seemed to be at odds with the previous standard of providing individual service to customers and might have encouraged a system of having one person on cash while the others dealt with customer enquiries. We opted to ignore the individual sign in/out step. This also had the effect of scuttling any worker monitoring that the system might have done.

It took about a month for everything to settle down. I don't think the change to the new system was handled very well.

QUESTIONS

1. Conduct an analysis of this change.
    (a) Identify the forces supporting the change, the forces opposing the change, and the currently neutral forces that might be tipped one way or another once the change process has begun.
    (b) Develop a better change strategy which is based on strengthening the forces in favour of change, weakening the forces opposing change, and which covers the contingencies arising from the tipping of currently neutral forces.
    (c) Develop a strategy for "unfreezing" the status quo to begin the change process.
2. Why did the change, as it was carried out, create motivational dysfunctions for Lisa and the other particicpants?

Bank of Connecticut in Canada

The Bank of Connecticut in Canada (BCC), located in the financial district of Toronto, is the head office of that bank's Foreign Currency Services. With a total of more than 20 offices over the world, this office operates as a foreign currency wholesale centre as well as a retail bank for local accounts. The elite foreign exchange operating section of BCC is on the 33d floor of a highrise tower. Each of its 7 departments is headed by its own manager. Under these managers are 13 supervisors who report to them. Three vice-presidents also have their offices on the 33d floor. They have responsibilities for this operating section and accountability to the senior vice-president who is in charge of the Canadian operations as a whole.

The 33d floor acts as the money maker of BCC. In the past, it was a very busy, efficient, and cooperative place. People there were very friendly and polite. Employees who were assigned to the 33d floor were always regarded as providing good performance and having better qualifications to merit their placement. However, things changed a lot in the last few years. Fewer and fewer greetings were heard and more and more complaints were being raised. People talked more loudly than before. Somehow, this office made people feel as if there was no other way to accomplish things without shouting or getting upset. A lot of the employees who in the past had dressed up to come to work did not seem to care any more about their appearances. Some employees dressed so casually, no one would believe that they worked in a downtown financial office. In 1990, two managers had resigned. Both of them had been working on the 33d floor for over 6 years. Thirty percent of the senior employees had left for other companies. People even talked openly about changing jobs or applying to other firms. It became a matter

---

Adapted by Randy Hoffman from a paper by Ying Sa. Copyright © 1991, 1994 by Randy Hoffman.

of common sense for competent employees to contemplate quitting. Within this work environment, the operating performance also showed a marked tendency to decline. More and more expenses were incurred for compensation of inefficient and incompetent transactions. Everybody knew this was mostly caused by carelessness, and the large group of new employees were believed (if not accused outrightly) to be chiefly at fault.

The Bank of Connecticut in Canada had been growing at a very rapid pace recently. Its size had doubled in three years. A lot of new positions had opened, constantly requiring new employees from outside. Aside from the foreign exchange operations, however, the office carried on a complete spectrum of commercial banking operations. Everyone who worked for BCC was expected to have a very broad banking knowledge in order to be able to play different roles and to take on diverse responsibilities. However, 70% of the newly hired employees were recent immigrants who had educational qualifications but no prior Canadian experience. Many of these employees spoke English poorly. BCC was paying them $3,000–$4,000 less per annum than the "going rate." They started to learn and to do their jobs in a very slow and inefficient way. Because of the language barrier, it took a long time for their supervisors to make them understand what they were to do.

Rather than provide the new staff with formal training, the employees were forced to learn their jobs by trial and error. As turnover began to increase, the only people who trained the new staff were the employees who were leaving the company. Some of the other employees just refused to do so because they had never been trained by anyone. They too had learned their job with a struggle. The new employees were not the only ones who were lacking in professional training, however. Quite a few of the supervisors had obtained their jobs as a result of a family connection with the firm and managed with whatever knowledge they had. Everyone who worked in BCC had become aware that the hiring and promotion policies were based on personal relationships rather than on technical qualifications. Although the rules stated that the yearly raise varied from 7% to 15%, one lower-level employee received a 30% increase soon after a relative of his started working in BCC as a vice-president.

In the Verification and Accounting departments, 50% of the employees (including one manager who subsequently left and two supervisors) were from Hong Kong and were all previously acquainted prior to immigrating to Canada. Other departments started calling these two departments the "Hong Kong Branch." The Hong Kong people always had lunch together on the 15th floor lunch room. Nobody else would join them because they felt excluded from this ethnically homogeneous group. In addition, Chinese was spoken even in the office. Many of the other staff members were intimidated because they did not understand the language, and their attention would be aroused when their name was heard but they could not understand the context.

An example used by the non-Chinese staff in their often-voiced grievances was Norman (from Hong Kong). He worked in the Accounting department as a credit clerk. He often had conflicts with other people from other departments and would complain about others not cooperating with him and being mean to him. But other people felt that his speech was too rude to be acceptable. Canadian-born employees were afraid to deal with him because of his constant arguing with them in his broken English and his defensive and stubborn personality.

Throughout the organization a very authoritarian style of leadership was employed. The person on the top is the only decision maker. Top management set up rules to restrict the subordinate's scope for action. For example, employees were not allowed to report to their manager or to the vice-presidential level without notifying their immediate supervisors and giving them at least three opportunities to respond. This rule limited the chances for an employee to relieve feelings of oppression from direct supervision. If a staff member could not get along with his or her respective supervisor, it would mean a hard time; and for this organization it would mean another piece of dead wood.

Communication within BCC matched this style of leadership. Management made all decisions, typically sent them out by memo, and never asked for employee input. The only role that the majority of the employees would play in the decision-making process would be to carry out orders. There were quite a few memos issued everyday. Employees complained that it was just too much work to read them all. Some memos were even passed to the wrong department. As a result, they were thrown into the wastebasket without a look. Employees never had the opportunity to question these directives, and they never tried to improve the company by contributing new ideas.

Because BCC paid employees less money in comparison to other banks, the complaint heard most often was, "I have been underpaid." This comment was made frequently despite the fact that the benefit system was excellent. Even the new employees, who many thought were lucky to have a job considering that they had no Canadian experience, felt underpaid after a certain length of time. Some of them became outstanding performers in bank operation until frustration set in. Everybody knew that there were almost no opportunities for people to be promoted on merit from the bottom levels into middle or senior management. The only way to obtain a better position and develop self-esteem was to find another job or know a "higher-up" very well.

One supposed example of many of the organizational abuses prevalent in BCC was the promotion of Susan, the new manager of the Verification Department. She was promoted by someone who ignored the fact that her formal education consisted only of a Canadian high school diploma and five years of related experience. Being regarded with suspicion by her subordinates, many of whom she could only understand with difficulty, she constantly checked to make sure that everyone was working by the rules. Susan did not seem to trust anyone. The staff became even more defensive towards this new manager, even though she worked very hard herself — coming in early and leaving late. They interpreted her actions as making sure that no one was cheating on company time. She frequently used phrases such as, "listen, I said..." or "you have to...." This demonstrated her power, but it did not improve the overall performance of the department. On the contrary, more and more people called in sick and most seemed reluctant to cooperate on the job.

The physical environment was also a problem. As the bank grew, the number of employees increased on the 33d floor, but the office space still remained the same and became extremely crowded. The aged transaction reports, documents, and boxes were piled up to the ceiling and were spread everywhere. Employees were saying that they felt that they were "white collar factory workers." There was a rumour that the bank was searching for larger premises, but no official word had been given.

QUESTIONS

1. In what ways does BCC follow or not follow the bureaucratic model?
2. Identify all the factors that contributed to the high rate of employee turnover, poor motivation, and the increasing instances of unsatisfactory performance.
3. Evaluate management policies with respect to hiring, promotion, compensation, and supervision. Is it wrong for the firm to hire large numbers of immigrants?
4. Suggest measures for BCC management to take that will alleviate the problems you have identified.
5. How can these measures be implemented? Suggest a plan for organizational change.

Barry Wilson

Barry Wilson is Executive Director of the Communications Division of the Ontario Ministry of Transportation and Communications. The communications division has a staff of about 120 people divided into four offices: Policy Development, Cable/Broadcast Research Office, Engineering, and Regulatory Affairs. The division also has an Administrative Services unit which supports the work of these four offices. Each office, including the unit, is headed by a manager. Wilson is the senior ranking officer in the division and is responsible for the efficient and effective operation of the division including the cooperative efforts and team work of all managers.

On one occasion, Wilson was called into the deputy minister's office and was directed to start preparing a briefing manual for the minister for an important upcoming federal-provincial conference on communications. Since the federal government would be represented by the minister of communications, the minister wanted to use this opportunity to press the federal government for further control over cable television within Ontario's boundaries. The minister's briefing manual for this conference had to be completed in one week. It had to include background on the issue, where the other provinces stand, possible tactics and strategies to gain support for the objective, possible consequences for Ontario if the federal government accepts Ontario's demands, and the consequences if it does not. In short, the briefing manual was quite detailed and comprehensive. A special meeting had been scheduled for the following week to review the briefing manual with the minister.

As Wilson leaves the deputy minister's office, he is wondering how to allocate this obviously sensitive and important project among his managers in order to produce a quality briefing manual within the limited timeframe he has to work with. He knows that the staff members have not always successfully collaborated on major projects in the past. He is also aware of the uneven quality and talents of his management team. The best manager is Ms. Edwards who is in charge of the Policy Development Office. He often thought that Edwards could be his successor when he moves on. But Wilson is aware of how jealous and resentful the other managers can be if Edwards, yet again, gets the choice project. Wilson must decide on how best to delegate responsibility for this project. He is also aware that by successfully completing this project he could be in a better position for possible promotion to assistant deputy minister or deputy minister status.

QUESTIONS

1. What leadership issues arise in this case?
2. Is it always best to choose the most competent person to work on an important project, regardless of the consequences?
3. What should Barry Wilson do about allocating responsibility for this project?

Case 8

Brewmaster Limited

Brewmaster Limited is a broadly based food and beverage company with major participation in the brewing, consumer foods, and agricultural products industries. Its head office is located in Alberta. It employs 12,500 people and had gross sales in the last five years averaging 800 million dollars.

Employee alcohol abuse is not unique to Brewmaster itself but is experienced in most if not all industries. The case will deal with a situation concerning approximately 300 employees at the Brewmaster brewing plant in Calgary.

ALCOHOL ABUSE IN INDUSTRY, CANADA WIDE[1]

The "alcohol abuser" or "problem drinker" presents problems to his employer, fellow workers, friends, and family. The cost of maintaining the "alcohol abuser" on the payroll is estimated to cost Canadian industry $1 million a day in sick benefits, job-related absenteeism, property damage, and low production. The average rate of absenteeism for those not regularly indulging is six to ten days, but for the "problem drinker," it is twenty-four to thirty-six days a year, a four-fold increase. Not only is the cost to industry enormous, but there is also the question of safety for the worker and fellow employees. With the industry being highly mechanized, the accident rate has risen sharply due to intoxicated personnel operating machines.

It has been estimated that approximately three to ten percent of the working population are classified as being either alcohol abusers or problem drinkers. The many problems associated with these employees have prompted many industries to initiate their own programs. Management wants to identify these people and reduce costs to the company. Statistics repeatedly point out the savings in dollars after successful programs have been inaugurated.

Copyright © 1991, 1994 by Randy Hoffman.

[1] "Alcoholism Programs Needed," *Labour Gazette*, Vol. 8, August 1975, p. 485.

HISTORY OF PROBLEMS AT BREWMASTER BREWERY, CALGARY

At Brewmaster's, the worker was in constant contact with the very product whose consumption management was trying to restrict. This situation alone created problems that most other companies do not have to deal with.

The company had been plagued with an alcohol abuse problem since its early days of operation in 1970. Because the workers were producing beer, management initially decided it would institute a policy whereby no alcohol consumption was allowed at any time on the premises. By outlawing it completely, management hoped that employee drinking would drop for fear of breaking company rules and of having their positions terminated. Unfortunately, this approach of restriction had the same effect on the workers as happens when many desired things become restricted; the demand for it became more intense. Management found that production per worker was dropping, absenteeism related to alcohol abuse was increasing, and the morale of the workers was hitting a new low. The temptation to obtain a beer overcame many employees. During working hours when production was low, it was noticed that breaks became longer, as did lunch time. The frequency of a worker leaving a machine to go to the men's room was also increasing.

It was soon clear to management that the prohibition currently in force was not working as well as had been hoped. It became necessary to develop a new approach. This new policy would allow the employees to indulge for 35 minutes after their shift had been completed. An area off the cafeteria was provided as a "bar" or "pub." The beer was kept (Brewmaster brands only) in a huge cooler, and consumption was not restricted as it was a self-serve bar. Each man was also given a 12-pack each month or a case of 24 beers for production rates that approached plant capacity. These measures were implemented with the hope that the employees would restrict their consumption until after work and that time lost during the day and accidents would decrease.

If it was determined by the supervisor that an employee's absenteeism and efficiency were deteriorating, he would be referred to the medical department for tests and a checkup to determine the reasons. Should it be discovered that the problem was alcohol abuse, the worker would then be offered assistance. In cases where the employee refused the assistance, the union was informed of the refusal, and the employee was warned and given one more chance. If the employee was caught in a less than sober state or in the act of consuming alcohol on the job again and refused treatment, it led to job termination. In cases where the workers accepted help, they were usually referred to the Western Institute for alcohol abuse for approximately three to four weeks. The employee paid half the fee ($600–$700) and management paid the remaining 50%. During this time all employment benefits were paid, including 70% of the employee's salary. If after treatment, male workers still had a recurring alcohol abuse problem, they were again referred to the Institute or to Alpha House (rehabilitation centre for hard-core male alcoholics), and the treatment steps were repeated. A third recurrence led to management terminating employment. (See Exhibit 5.) It should also be mentioned that all privileges with respect to indulging after work were lost by the offending worker for anywhere up to one year. As management proceeded with each step, the union was notified of each recurrence. Once management attempted to terminate employment, the union required that the case go to arbitration for the final decision.

BACKGROUND

The reasons for an alcohol abuse problem are many and are of varying degrees of importance. Management and the union have tried to determine some of these factors. Both tended to shift the blame to the other side. Some of the reasons both groups have given are: the age of the employee; the relationship between union and management; the nature of the work itself (whether it is shift work or not, and what type of work it is, e.g., specialized, physical, non-skilled, and interesting); the availability of alcohol; the policy currently in effect; and the social situations which the company has little or no control over.

It appeared to management that, as they hired younger employees (20–29 yrs.), there had been an increase in the alcohol abuse reports related to this age group. This seemed to be the result of the general lack of education regarding the "problem drinker" as well as the temptation of the novelty of free beer. At first the younger employee attempted to "keep up" with his older, more experienced counterparts. This led to drinking while working (usually done when the supervisor was known to be in another part of the plant) as well as indulging after work. Unfortunately, as the novelty wears off, the dependence on alcohol does not.

Union and management were in a rather difficult position. Management's main concern was the increased productivity of the worker and reduction of lost time. Both these results would have increased profits for the company. The union would have liked to get its hands on the extra profits in the form of increased wages, or extra benefits. However, they had to protect the employee, even if it meant that the company took the extra profits and put it into an alcohol abuse program. This reduced the amount of money available to increase wages, etc.; but the alcoholic worker was entitled to representation by the union. Supervisory personnel were also in a very unfortunate position. Management was relying on the supervisor to identify the alcohol abuser or problem drinker. Otherwise, the policy would break down at the very start. The union, on the other hand, questioned the qualifications of the supervisor when he had to determine whom he felt was a problem drinker or alcohol abuser. To keep the supervisor from reaching a too hasty decision, some union members would bring a grievance against the supervisor or would instigate a slight slowdown in production. Both these methods caused management to re-evaluate the supervisor, bringing more pressure to bear on him. This type of situation usually resulted in the supervisor being concerned only with the most blatant violations.

The nature and type of work has been shown to be a factor in the alcohol abuse problem. The brewery is a very highly mechanized plant employing the latest computerized and high-speed equipment. Except for three or four stations on the "assembly line," all other work took the form of visual inspection and ensuring that conveyors moved along smoothly. Any problems that resulted in "down time" were delegated out to mechanics or electricians. The men on the line were not allowed to deal with the problem or to attempt to correct the situation. The work was neither physically demanding nor interesting. There was no reward for working at an increased rate or contributing more to the production of a line's output. Each worker was paid the same wage as well as benefits and each had to do shift work. This routine work and lack of incentives seemed to encourage the employee to leave a station for a drink (usually hiding behind a full pallet of beer). Or, if they remained at the machine, they would hide beside it and quickly consume as much as they could. They were not missed unless a problem developed at that checkpoint. To try to reduce the monotony, management started a rotation system whereby the worker rotated from one position to another down the line each hour. It seemed to work well for a period of time, but eventually the rotation system itself began to become tedious and boring to the employee. He knew each hour exactly which task he would be performing and how monotonous it would become. When asked how a worker can tolerate the monotony, John Smith replied, "After a few beers, things seem to pick up, and you don't really think about what you're doing."

The availability of the alcohol presented a unique problem to management. It was impossible to keep the line running and not have the workers come in contact with the beer. The ease of obtaining a beer created situations that most other industries or organizations do not face. How could a supervisor determine that the person had been drinking, just because he happened to be holding a beer bottle in his hand? The handling of the product was a necessary part of producing it. Arriving at a hasty decision would have repercussions for the supervisor. The person must have literally been showing signs of intoxication before action could be taken. By this time though, the problem had already developed into a serious concern.

A NEW POLICY

The policy that was in effect has now been slightly altered to come to better grips with the abuse problem. Management had tried in vain to deal with the problem by allowing the workers access to all the beer they could consume after hours. As could be expected, the company could not revert back to the original policy of prohibition; first, because that particular policy did not work; and second, now that workers were given the privilege of indulging after work, they were not about to let management take it away from them. Management's next move was to remove the self-serve cooler and build an enclosed "bar," serviced by a bartender (union worker) who was allowed to serve beer 15 minutes **after** the shift was over for 35 minutes. It was hoped that by not allowing the employees easy access to the beer until shifts had changed, they would be restricted from indulging before work and having too much afterward. The bartender was also to refuse beer to anyone whom he felt might be overindulging. This measure has not proved to be effective. The workers now began hiding cases of beer in the various refrigerated storage rooms, which ensured themselves of relatively easy access to a cold beer. Those men who could not leave their station would signal a fork lift driver by wiping their brows or stroking their throats. This indicated a thirst, and the appropriate relief would be brought from the storage rooms.

THE JOHN GROOVER CASE

John Groover had been working at Brewmaster Breweries for the past eight years. He was 35 years old, married with three children. John was working on the docks loading and unloading trucks as well as stacking full pallets of beer as they came off the line.

John was proud of his status on the loading docks. He was known by his fellow workers as a "rough neck," who didn't really care about the work at hand. He would not rush his job to accommodate extra production. John felt that if they wanted him to move faster, they could either pay him more or hire more help to get his job done. Along with his independent state of mind, John had a flagrant attitude towards company rules when he reported for work. One day John had one of his frequent disagreements with his wife regarding the time spent at work. His wife felt he was spending too much time at work and not enough at home. John would leave about an hour and a half before his shift (although it was only a 15 minute drive from his home to the plant) and arrive home two hours after his shift ended, usually with the smell of beer on his breath.

As usual, the argument ended with John storming out the door and rushing off to work. He arrived an hour before his shift and headed straight for the cafeteria and the bar for a quick beer to calm himself. He had little trouble gaining access to the bar even though it was to be locked until the shift previous to John's was over. A quick-witted remark and a plea for a thirst-quenching brew was enough to convince the bartender to open up. Besides, George (the bartender) was a good friend of John's, so that made it all the easier. John sat down and began indulging. At the same time he started to discuss his domestic argument with a couple of truck drivers who had just finished their delivery run.

As John began drinking more and more, the problems being discussed included not only his wife, but work, supervisors hassling him, and general discontent with his lifestyle. By the time John's shift was due to start, John had consumed enough beer to make walking difficult. As John was leaving the bar, he stumbled into a chair which he grabbed and tossed aside. It crossed four tables and crashed noisily against the wall. John then barged through the door narrowly missing his supervisor, Dave, who was on his way up to the cafeteria for a cup of coffee. Upon seeing John in an apparently inebriated state, Dave called him over to the side, and asked if he felt well enough to carry on with his job. To this, John answered with an obscene remark in the affirmative. Dave, relying on his better judgement, asked John to go down to the staging office and wait for him, saying that he would be about 10 minutes. While John went down to the office, Dave headed for the supervisors' lounge to get the help of Todd, a senior supervisor. This was common practice whenever a supervisor was anticipating a problem with an employee. It was used for documented protection so that the employee report could be written up. While Dave was speaking with Todd, John found the waiting a bit aggravating, so he went to the cold storage for another beer. Dave, Todd, and John walked into the staging office at about the same time. Todd immediately saw that John had had too many beers, so he recommended that John lie down and rest until he felt he was able to continue his job. To this, John retorted with his customary phrase, pushed both Todd and Dave aside, and headed for his fork lift. Todd and Dave realized the danger if John were allowed to continue on with his job. They again approached John and this time recommended that he go home and take the rest of the shift off. This seemed to aggravate John even more, and he took a wild swing at Dave. He missed Dave, lost his balance, and ended up falling against a pallet of beer. John picked himself up and screamed that he wasn't drunk, and that they had no right to classify him as being so. The commotion brought other workers running. Eventually, a heated exchange of words erupted, with the workers vowing to walk out, and the two supervisors vowing to recommend termination for John.

CONFLICTS

The company's chief medical officer and the personnel manager feel that the current alcohol abuse policy is an effective, comprehensive attempt at dealing with the problem. There seems to be conflicting opinions though from supervisory staff and the medical department at the Calgary plant. Supervisors feel that the policy is too general and leaves too much room for misinterpretation by supervisory staff as well as the union. The medical department feels the policy is adequate but that it is not being implemented properly or consistently enough by the supervisors. They view this hesitancy as a lack of personal conviction. They feel that the supervisors and upper managers are too concerned with moving up the corporate ladder. They believe that the less disturbance they create, the easier and quicker the climb will be. Supervisors feel that they need more support from upper management. They are damned if they attempt to implement the policy to the letter and damned if they allow the employees to function at a level that reduces production and increases costs to Brewmaster.

QUESTIONS

1. Should Brewmaster provide for the consumption of beer after work? If so, under what circumstances?
2. Evaluate the company's alcohol abuse program. Is it likely to be effective?
3. What went wrong in the John Groover incident? Who or what is (are) to blame?
4. What other measures can the company take to reduce alcohol abuse.
5. Is Brewmaster morally responsible for a worker's alcohol abuse to any extent? Give reasons for your answer.

EXHIBIT 1
BREWMASTER POLICY

Management believes that alcohol or drug abuse is an illness requiring treatment. It is the policy of the company to provide such treatment through its medical and personnel departments.

Guidelines

1. It is essential for the general well-being of the Company and its employees that high standards of job performance be established and achieved. An employee with an alcohol or drug problem will be unable, over time, to live up to his responsibilities at work.
2. Where unsatisfactory performance is suspected to be due to alcoholism or drug abuse, the supervisor should encourage the employee to consult the Company doctor to obtain treatment.
3. When unacceptable performance is clearly due to drinking or to drug abuse and medical or professional treatment is required, such treatment is mandatory.
4. An employee who is absent from work while undergoing medical treatment for an alcohol or drug problem will receive normal benefits through the Company's Weekly Indemnity, Sick Leave, and Salary Continuation programs with the concurrence of the Medical department.
5. The Company will make every reasonable effort to help the employee back to normal health and job performance. Only when it has been established that medical treatment and other measures have failed should dismissal be considered.
6. The Company will encourage the involvement of the union in its Alcohol and Drug Abuse Program.
7. Through contacts with governmental and other agencies, the Company through its Medical and Personnel departments will make available to supervisors and other interested employees training and information on the control of alcoholism and drug abuse.

EXHIBIT 2

Signs of Job Performance Decline That
May Be Noted by Supervisors & Managers

1. Excessive lateness
2. Excessive absenteeism
3. Excessive sick leave
4. Morale problem (difficulty with other employees or supervisors)
5. Accident prone
6. Work output or quality decline
7. Abuse of lunch and break periods
8. Leaving the job without permission
9. Excessive overstaying on company property
10. Inability to cope with unexpected change in routine
11. Unexplained memory lapses
12. Inconsistent or drastic change in performance of job

EXHIBIT 3

Some Helpful Hints for Supervisors and Managers

DO
- remember alcoholism is a progressive illness
- help is available through the Medical department
- make it clear that the company is concerned only with job performance
- emphasize that all aspects of the program are confidential
- remember the importance of documentation

DON'T
- cover up for a friend or fellow employee
- be misled by manipulation and sympathy-evoking tactics — the alcoholic is an expert
- accept substandard job performance from anyone
- moralize — restrict discussion to job performance
- discuss drinking unless it occurs on the job
- try to diagnose the problem
- try to counsel an employee

EXHIBIT 4

Some Responsibilities of Union Representatives

1. To be familiar with the policy and procedures of the alcohol and drug abuse program.
2. To provide information on the program and encourage employees who may have an alcohol or drug problem to seek assistance voluntarily before job performance is affected.
3. To ensure that the rights of bargaining unit employees are explained to them.
4. To advise employees of their options should they refuse the help offered through the program.
5. To participate in ensuring support and follow-up on the job to facilitate the employee's rehabilitation.

EXHIBIT 5

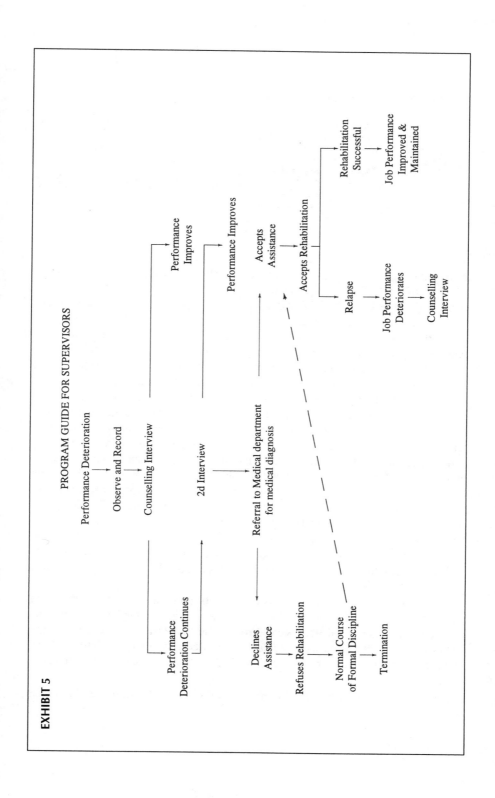

PROGRAM GUIDE FOR SUPERVISORS

Performance Deterioration

Observe and Record

Counselling Interview → Performance Improves

Performance Deterioration Continues

2d Interview → Performance Improves

Referral to Medical department for medical diagnosis

Declines Assistance

Refuses Rehabilitation

Normal Course of Formal Discipline

Termination

Accepts Assistance

Accepts Rehabilitation

Rehabilitation Successful → Job Performance Improved & Maintained

Relapse → Job Performance Deteriorates → Counselling Interview

Canada Post AdMail

Mary hung up the phone and turned to Tom and said, "Well it's happened again. I've just told my Admail helpers that there wasn't a delivery this week, and now there will be one after all. Why can't the managers plan far enough ahead so that we don't have to go through this confusion? That's the third time this quarter."

Tom replied, "I've had two at my stations, it really is discouraging to the Admail helpers. They can't count on regular work or even regular time off."

Mary returned to the phone to attempt to recall her Admail helpers at the Oakville station in the hopes of tracking down enough of them to be able to get the advertising fliers for the grocery stores delivered before the specials they advertised had expired. She found this part of her job very stressful. She found it difficult to achieve what she saw as a good performance. The current situation was strictly damage control. If she put a lot of pressure on her Admail helpers to cancel their personal plans and deliver the mail, she would encounter resistance and resentment. Some might even quit. If she didn't get the mail delivered on time her manager would be critical of her performance. Neither prospect was pleasing and Mary was near the end of her patience with this job. She had been with Admail since its beginning in May of 1988 and was originally attracted by the prospect of being in on the ground floor of a new venture. She saw herself as an achievement-oriented person with good organizational and interpersonal skills as well as a flexible attitude. This new business venture by Canada Post seemed perfect for her.

Admail was a division of Canada Post Corporation which was created to accommodate the delivery of advertising mail. Prior to the creation of this division, advertising mail that went through Canada Post was delivered by the Letter Carrier sections on their regular routes. Recently, many of these sections were choosing to not carry this mail and Canada Post decided to explore an alternative strategy which might provide uniform service. Admail was in the planning stages for two years prior to being implemented across Canada.

Admail is a separate division of Canada Post and has a national director. The organization in Toronto is divided into Admail East and Admail West, reflecting the geographic territory that each covers. Each section is comprised of approximately 15 office workers and 400–500 Admail helpers who actually deliver the mail. A section has its own manager with a senior officer, junior officer, administrative clerks, and finally the Admail helpers. The Admail helpers are not full-time employees. The Admail helpers are further organized into stations which are smaller territories organized for delivery purposes.

From a structural point of view, Canada Post, Corporation as a whole is largely mechanistic, relying on formal routines, well-established procedures, and a hierarchy with highly institutionalized relations and a full-time work force. Admail itself is a much more organic structure. Flexibility and the ability to cope with change are essential qualities in the office workers and extremely desirable in the helpers. The organization faces a great deal of uncertainty each and every week in that the situation may change at any given moment. For example, it might be that a particular station (i.e., Oakville) won't be receiving any mail this particular week. Therefore, as helpers from that station phone in to see if they have mail to deliver that coming weekend, the clerk in charge of the Oakville station tells them that they will not be working that weekend because there is no mail to be delivered in that area. As a result, these helpers may or may not make other plans. The delivery timetable requires that the officers and clerks must have all the routes covered and the paper work ready by Friday afternoon when the drivers begin delivering the mail to the helpers. The household delivery begins the following day. A problem arises when the office staff is notified late Friday morning that there will be mail going to that station after all. The staff must quickly and efficiently choose among alternative courses of action with the prime objective being to get that mail delivered to the satisfaction of the client.

Because there are so many variables involved, it is difficult to establish too many rules and procedures. A sudden snow storm may leave the staff scrambling to have the mail picked up from helpers who refuse to deliver it and to either redirect it to other helpers who may be induced (through bonuses, etc.) to deliver it, or to establish truck routes to deliver it at much greater expense to the organization. It may be discovered midway through the week that an Admail helper has dumped his/her mail in a heap somewhere rather than delivering it door to door as she/he was supposed to do. Again, the staff must find some way of honouring Canada Post's commitment to its clients.

There are two major patterns of communication at work in this subgroup of Canada Post. The communication that exists in the office itself can be described as "downward communication." Information and instructions flow from the manager through the junior officer, finally arriving at the administrative staff. The manager is the first to know what stations will be receiving the mail and in what quantities. This information is vital to the administrative staff in assessing what courses of action are necessary to ensure that the mail is delivered on time. If mail is to be delivered in stations that are not fully staffed, then extra effort must go into finding helpers to fill those vacant routes and ensuring that they have the proper maps, crown keys, and any necessary special instructions. A delay in receiving this information often leaves the clerk scrambling to meet the deadline and prone to mistakes which will cost the organization time and money. For example, placing the wrong route numbers beside a helper's name and address on the pay sheet will result in that helper getting someone else's mail. If it is discovered before the helper delivers it, the best that will happen is that a special trip costing in the neighbourhood of $35 will have to be made to pick up the mail and then to deliver it to the helper who is supposed to have it. If it is not discovered in time, that mail will be delivered door to door on the wrong route. In this case Canada Post will have violated its agreement with the client and will have to pay damages. What's more, it could lose that client's business. Loblaws may not want its flyers delivered to houses and apartments in Rexdale when its store is in Mississauga. The flyers being delivered are time sensitive because they usually advertise weekly sales. Thus, timely communication is of the utmost importance. However, all too often the information sits with the senior officer causing problems like the one discussed above.

Any communication that does exist between the manager and the administrative staff is basically one-way communication. He speaks only in terms of the results that he expects and allows little room for discussion on what circumstances may keep the large organization from reaching its goals. Often times there are large discrepancies between the number of flyers that are supposed to be delivered and the actual amounts received from the printers. When approached with this problem, the manager's response is, "Well, do the best you can to get the job done." This in fact is not much of a response at all. What he's really saying is, "You figure it out." Once again, this in neither efficient nor productive.

The other pattern of communication which exists is that between the administrative clerk and the Admail helper. The clerk is the office's liaison with the helper who, in the end, must get the mail to where it is going. The nature of this relationship is such that two-way communication is essential. The clerks release information and instructions over the phone and are available to answer any questions or problems that the helper may have. The clerk must not only listen but also respond. For example, if a helper calls in to say that he is short a certain number of flyers to complete his route and that he can't get into a particular apartment building because his key doesn't work, the clerk must find a way of helping to solve the problem or the job simply won't get done. In this case, it would be the clerk's responsibility to find out which key the helper needs to get into that particular apartment building and to get that key and the necessary mail to the helper in a hurry so that the helper can meet his deadline. This type of communication is much more reciprocal in nature and is crucial to accomplishing the immediate goal of the organization; getting the mail delivered on time.

Admail helpers make $6 per hour for the specified time value of their route (which is usually four to six hours) plus a $3 flat bonus for any route which has more than three flyers to be delivered on any particular week. They receive their mail on Saturday morning and are expected to have it delivered by Tuesday night. Delays in getting the mail to them occur frequently, giving them even less time to meet their Tuesday deadline. When the weather is bad, Admail helpers usually feel that it is not even worth their while to complete or even start their routes. This usually means alternate and sometimes more expensive delivery means must be found, such as using the regular letter carriers on an overtime basis.

For the most part, the Admail helper is motivated by the opportunity to make some extra money. Often the degree of effort they put into delivering their mail (i.e., delivering it on time, putting it in the mail boxes and not throwing it on the front lawn, delivering even when it is cold and snowing, etc.) is directly related to how badly they want to keep their route; that is, how badly they value the reward. The amount of money to be earned by delivering Admail is small, and helpers have no guarantee that there will be mail for their routes on any given week. The value of the reward in this sense is quite low. However, there are those who value the exercise they get while out on their routes; they can get their exercise, talk to people, and make a little money while they're at it. For these people, the value of the reward is considerably higher and the rewards tend to be intrinsic rather than extrinsic. They do the job because they actually enjoy the job itself. It is interesting to note that this latter group of people are usually the more dependable workers. Unfortunately for Admail, there are too few of these helpers. For the most part, people take the job in an attempt to earn extra money. On average, an Admail helper makes between $25 and $40 per week when there is mail to deliver on their route. This serves as little incentive to keep the job or to do it well; as a result, there is a high rate of turnover in Admail helpers.

If Admail is to succeed rather than just survive, the rate of job turnover must decrease. The best way to do this is to increase the reward for an Admail helper. An increased cost of labour would be largely offset by the decreased costs of bringing new workers on board only to have them quit a month later. Every time a helper is hired, the organization expends resources to train him/her, put him/her on the payroll, set up a "new employee record," etc., not to mention the costs of picking up mail that has been dumped and compensating the client for not rendering the service promised to them. Motivation is a key factor in increasing productivity and efficiency.

Admail helpers rely on administrative clerks for guidance and instruction during times of uncertainty; however, the clerks are often poorly informed and not trained to handle these situations. The weekly deadlines for getting the mail out combined with a basic uncertainty about the strategy for achieving the goals of the organization often leaves the administrative staff frustrated and unmotivated.

Last month Mary left her job as an administrative clerk at Admail. She decided that the job could not be done as presently organized. Her manager was not interested in her suggestions for improvement. He is hopeful of getting a mangement posting back into the main part of Canada Post.

QUESTIONS

1. Analyze the sources of job stress for the administrative clerks. What could be done to reduce this stress?
2. Write a revised job description for the administrative clerk position.
3. Identify the problems with the reward system for the Admail helpers. Propose improvements aimed at reducing employee turnover and at improving motivational levels generally.
4. Propose changes to the organizational structure aimed at resolving the communication problems identified in the case.

Chemplus Inc. (A)

Chemplus Inc. was a Canadian firm that provided sophisticated instrumentation and applications engineering assistance to research laboratories, chiefly in analytical chemistry and biology. The company, with annual sales of about $12 million in 1990, had its head office in Montreal and branch offices in Halifax, Ottawa-Hull, Toronto, Winnipeg, Edmonton, and Vancouver.

AN OVERVIEW OF CHEMPLUS (See Figure 1)

The head office took care of promotion, sales fulfilment, general administrative functions, and Montreal-region sales. The president, a sales force of two sales engineers, a repair department with a service manager and two technicians, and an administrative and warehouse staff of seven were located in a 600 square metre facility in a suburban industrial area. Except in Halifax, each branch office had two sales engineers (one of whom served as regional manager) and a secretarial staff of one. Toronto and Vancouver offices also had small repair departments, each staffed by one technician. The President, Harry Barlow, spent more than one-half of his time in direct sales activities with certain key accounts, which he alone served, and in supervising the two Montreal-based sales engineers.

The instrumentation that Chemplus sold was, for the most part, imported from foreign suppliers with which the firm had exclusive distribution arrangements for Canada. Most of the time, the equipment was simply shipped to the customer and set up in a researcher's laboratory by the responsible sales engineer. Occasionally, the technicians in the Montreal office would preassemble various pieces of equipment and perhaps add some part that they had fabricated in order to meet the customer's needs for instrumentation that was not available "off the shelf."

Virtually all the sales engineering staff had an educational background in science — usually in chemistry, physics, or in engineering itself. It was Harry

FIGURE 1 ORGANIZATIONAL CHART OF CHEMPLUS

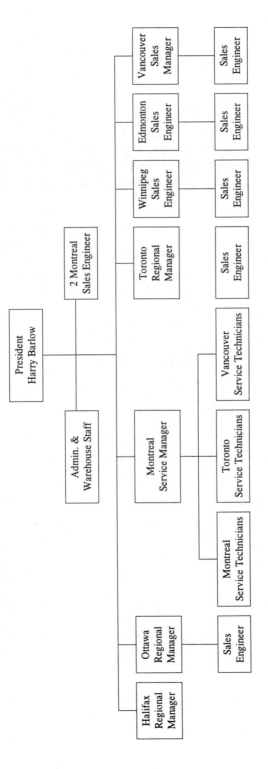

Barlow's opinion that sales training could be learned, but that the technical education required to sell effectively in their market had to be of a level that would enable the sales engineer to converse intelligently with researchers about their work. In fact, two of the 13 sales engineers actually had doctorates. Service technicians, on the other hand were usually selected purely on their ability to repair diverse types of electronic equipment, and they had mixed formal qualifications — from a university degree to only completing high school and being self-taught beyond that. Although technicians and sales engineers were "laterally" related with no formal reporting relationship from one to the other, the sales engineers enjoyed greater respect, better compensation, and more pleasant working conditions.

When Harry Barlow began Chemplus in 1973, he had just left a laboratory where he had been a junior researcher. He began his entrepreneurial life as a sales engineer and hired the services of repair people as needed. He fondly remembered his days of travelling across Canada by car while his wife back in Montreal provided all the administrative support. Since the couple owned all the shares, profits had an immediate impact on their material well-being. Harry sometimes forgot that the incentive for his employees was not as strong. He paid salaries that were just within the top third of the industry and was reluctant to pay much higher, regardless of performance. Commission or bonuses for good sales performance was being talked about but was not yet implemented. Often, he was annoyed when he called a branch office at six PM and found that everyone had already left. He routinely put in 12-hour days and six and one-half-day weeks. If he had a philosophy of success, it was that hard work could make up for any minor lack of ability and work would always pay off. The existence of three other firms in Canada with similar product lines all competing for the same market strengthened his belief in these contentions. Although a pleasant person in personal relationships, it was often difficult to get him off the topic of business; and about business, he was always serious.

THE OTTAWA-HULL OFFICE

Located in Hull, because Harry Barlow thought that the rents would be cheaper there, this office was managed by Marie Benoit. She had a master's degree in Analytical Chemistry and had previously served as a sales engineer in the Montreal head office for two and one-half years. There, she had impressed the president with her dedication and very satisfactory sales levels. When a resignation opened up the regional manager's job in Ottawa-Hull, she was an easy choice. Her appointment raised eyebrows and some resentment among more experienced staff in other offices who would have liked the promotion. She was the first woman hired for a sales engineering position, and it was clear that some of her peers felt that just being hired in the first place was "good for a woman."

While Marie herself had no doubts about deserving the promotion, she did wonder about her ability to manage an office, even though the staff complement was only one other sales engineer and a secretary. It was just that she had no managerial experience or training. She voiced these fears to her friends who reassured her, but not within the company where it might comfort those who envied her.

THE ALEX CLINTON SITUATION

Only days after her arrival in the Ottawa area, she was confronted by the resignation of the other sales engineer in the office, Carl St. Pierre, whom she was to supervise. He stated, as reasons for leaving, an excellent offer from a competitor and the prospect of working in their Vancouver office. In order to discuss the situation and the plans for hiring a replacement, she drove down to Montreal on a Saturday morning to meet with the president. On her arrival, she found out that he thought he had already solved the problem.

"This may surprise you, Marie, but I'm sending you Alex Clinton."

"For the sales job? He's a technician. I mean he is a great technician — probably our best. But a sales engineer...?"

"Well frankly, Marie, he's been bugging me for about 6 months now. He wants to get into sales. I'm afraid if I don't try him this time, he'll leave. And with his abilities, I know the competition would love to get their hands on him."

"Gee, I don't know, Harry," she said, "He's not even really fluent in French."

"I've already thought of that, you can give him only English speaking accounts. Anyway, in your territory there's many more of them. Look, its just something that we have to try. I'm only sorry that, with Carl quitting, there's no time to give him any sales training here at head office. You'll have to give him guidance on that. I know you can do it," Harry said, flashing a smile.

"Okay, I guess I'll have to make the best of it. But I'm going to be honest with you. I don't think its a good idea. Alex is not really suitable. I've been with him on repair visits. The customers just love him because he can fix anything, and he just laps up the praise. It's not the same in sales. You've got to be tactful and empathetic. And you don't always get such a great reception when you arrive at the customer's office."

"Work on it with him, Marie. If anyone can turn him into a sales engineer, you can. By the way, he's arriving in ten days."

Marie drove back to Ottawa in a sombre mood. She understood Alex Clinton's desire to get out of the service shop. The service manager was a strict and humourless individual who felt superior to those he supervised because he had a university degree. Among repair personnel, only the technician in Vancouver shared that qualification. Alex himself actually had little formal postsecondary education, but had easily taught himself the repair of mechanical and electronic equipment. He had the reputation of being able to fix anything, an attribute that did not endear him to the service manager who preferred to take credit personally. And although repair competence did endear him to the sales staff, it would never earn him equal status.

Marie was also somewhat discomfited by the prospect of a supervisory relationship with someone who had kept calling her "dear" and had often winked at her conspiratorially when she had worked in Montreal. Well, she thought to herself, that would be the first thing to get squared away between them.

As it happened, that issue never arose. Alex was obviously as surprised as Marie had been that he had actually succeeded in getting the position. During the first two weeks, when Marie introduced him around to the customers and during their discussions in the office, he was the model of attentiveness and obviously had a serious intention not to blow this opportunity. Marie was almost beginning to feel relieved. It was during the third week that misgivings began to surface once more. It was Marie's plan to now let Alex do the sales presentations. She would observe and go over his performance with him later. Alex was obviously ill at ease in that role. In the past, customers had always been delighted to see him, because he was there to repair some equipment that they badly needed. Now they appeared impatient as he haltingly went through a sales presentation for products that they had no present intention to purchase. It seemed to Alex, that the customers were looking down upon him. Often, he would turn to Marie with a look of mild panic, and she would be forced to take over from him. Marie asked Alex in the office about these incidents. Away from the sales situation, however, he seemed more poised and confident. He would quickly brush aside her comments and questions with a statement that suggested that Marie's impressions were totally wrong. She decided to inform Harry Barlow of this problem by telephone.

"Harry, I'm worried about Alex. He's not doing well talking to customers. He's stumbling over his words, and I keep having to help him out. He doesn't know how to get the customer interested. I try to give him some pointers, and he does okay in the office. But when we get out there, he seems like a different person."

"How long has he been with you now, Marie, a few weeks? You know, you've been doing this for a few years and its a lot easier for you. He's probably nervous about you being there watching him. Maybe its time to let him out on his own a bit. I'd like to come down and help, but I'm not sure I could do anything that you're not doing. Anyway, Mike (the Halifax Sales Engineer) is in the hospital for a couple weeks and I've got to get down there and fill in for him. The best advice you can give Alex is to work hard at it. He's sure to improve. I gather he's bought a house now in Kanata (a suburb of Ottawa). If he doesn't work out in your office, we'll definitely lose him. And with what he knows about the technical problems with some of our products... I don't want to think about the consequences. Give him some room to breathe, Marie. Take some of your lower priority accounts and work up a week's schedule for him. He'll solve his problem."

"I don't think he believes that he's got a problem, Harry. But I'll try what you suggested."

After a week of letting Alex go out on his own, it seemed that Harry Barlow's suggestion might be succeeding. Every evening, Marie discussed the day's sales activities with Alex and then went over his sales reports of visits with prospective customers. The initial discussions provided Marie with little useful information, but by the end of the week, the reports were showing that Alex was getting into more substantive product discussions. She decided to try another two weeks and gratefully began to concentrate more on her own sales responsibilities. During the second week, the reports continued to show evidence of improved sales presentations, and by the third week, definite expressions of interest in purchasing instrumentation began to appear. Alex's demeanor around the office seemed almost overly cheerful, but he still avoided any detailed discussion of his activities. Marie felt that it might take more time to develop a rapport between them and decided to let him plan the next couple weeks for her approval.

At this time, a quarterly sales forecast was due, and it was Marie's responsibility to submit it for her region. Alex was asked to provide an estimate for the customers he had visited so far, which he completed. Due to his inexperience, however, Marie felt that she should corroborate his data by checking with some of his key customers for whom he reported good sales prospects. As she knew most of them herself, she began to make some phone calls. The first few, from sales reports dating back to the second week that Alex was on his own, drew a puzzled response. The prospective purchasers seemed not to recall expressing any purchasing intentions. A few indicated that Alex had only been to in to see them very briefly in order to drop off some sales literature. The next group of customers she called was from the next week of his sales reports and Marie received much more startling responses to her inquiries. Alex had not been in to see them at all!

QUESTIONS

1. Why had Alex Clinton been falsifying call reports?
2. What communication, motivation, and leadership factors have contributed to this situation? Who is (are) responsible?
3. What should Marie do now?
4. (a) What steps should Harry Barlow take immediately?
   (b) What should he do so that this situation will not occur again? Include revised personnel selection procedures.
5. Is the organizational structure of Chemplus Inc. appropriate? Why or why not? Suggest any alterations that you feel would be beneficial.

Chemplus Inc. (B)

About six months after the events described in the (A) case, Harry Barlow was once again facing the possible defection of a senior sales representative to the competition. This time it was Gary Hill, the manager of the Vancouver office. Only after numerous telephone calls and finally a quick trip to the remote office was Harry able to negotiate an improved salary that convinced Gary to remain with Chemplus. While Gary got a nice raise, Harry Barlow reflected that it was very expensive to get into a bidding war with the competition. He also worried that a precedent would be set with the others.

"We're becoming a training school for sales engineers," Harry mused on the plane back to Montreal. Certainly, there was some truth in the statement. Although sales training was sporadic, Chemplus' technical training program was better than any similar firm in the industry. Extensive training sessions took place in Montreal periodically. Each sales engineer also attended several one- or two-week sessions per year in the United States at the offices of manufacturers represented by Chemplus. After three years of employment, the investment in each sales engineer was substantial — and so was the value put on Chemplus' personnel by competitive firms. Although the training was specific to the particular product line represented, most of the competitors handled equipment that was, on the whole, very similar. The technical aspects of the training were totally relevant for any of the firms, and a sales engineer acquired from Chemplus with detailed product knowledge would be very effective in then selling against his or her former employer. Some competitors seemed to have developed a strategy of hiring only experienced and knowledgable sales engineers from competitors rather than hiring and training novices. The money they saved on training would help cover salaries that were just high enough to tempt valued personnel away from the firm that trained them. Harry could cut back on training and only hire more experienced people as well, but that wasn't his style. He liked the idea of fielding a competent sales force trained in the way he preferred.

A forthcoming general sales meeting gave Harry Barlow an opportunity to take action against "sales engineer piracy." The solution, he thought, was an employment contract. Its main provisions were to stipulate a salary (initially, the one already being received) and to prevent any sales engineer who voluntarily left the firm from accepting a job with a competitor for two years. The plan had its obvious attractions, but Harry Barlow was also a little worried. No other company in the market had such a contract. He wondered whether it might cause a general revolt if presented at the meeting without warning. To ease into it gradually, he sent a memo to all concerned across Canada that a discussion of an employment contract would be on the agenda of the meeting. He offered no information concerning its contents, but he stated that a benefits package, tied to the contract, would be introduced later.

This immediately provoked a frantic round of telephone calls among all the sales engineers. Since Harry had used one of the Montreal people as a sounding board, the details of the contract eventually leaked out. By the time everyone gathered for the meeting, it seemed that a consensus had formed to oppose it. Bob Elliott, manager of the Toronto office, was chosen to act as spokesman.

The meeting began with a brief discussion of the agenda. Then the firm's accountant, Denise Lacroix, who was unknown to all present except Harry, started to discuss the need for a contract. Her pitch basically covered two points. The sales engineers would have their employment terms guaranteed (as long as performance was satisfactory) and the company would feel more secure in making a substantial investment in training. In the future, this might also lead to a company-supported pension plan and improved health benefits.

Denise read a simple two-page draft contract to the meeting and then paused for questions. Bob Elliott cleared his throat and stood up. "I guess I was picked to speak for the group. I'm afraid we're not interested. There's really nothing in it for us."

"Wait a minute, the intention is really to improve employment conditions in the near future," countered Denise. "You've got to..."

"I SAID WE ARE NOT INTERESTED," Bob interrupted loudly.

"HEY, CAN YOU LET ME...," Denise began with equal volume.

Harry Barlow, looking dismayed, stood up abruptly. "Okay, calm down everyone. Denise, I think we'd better delay this discussion of the contract. I'll speak with you later."

Exhaling noisily, Denise packed up her papers and left.

Harry sat down and announced that they would now take up the second item on the agenda, sales targets. For the remainder of that day's discussions, he stared grimly at his papers and generally avoided eye contact with the sales engineers. The next day, he seemed to be in a better frame of mind, but the contract was not mentioned again.

QUESTIONS

1. What are the positive and negative aspects of an employment contract for:
    (a)   The sales engineers?
    (b)   The company?

2. Was the employment contract an appropriate response to "sales engineer piracy?"

3. Critically assess the way in which it was communicated to the sales engineers.

4. What should Harry Barlow do as of the end of the case about the issues raised here?

The Cigarette Company

This case concerns a major cigarette manufacturer in Canada, CIG Inc. In the summer of 1988, the Federal Government introduced the "Tobacco Products Control Act", Bill C-51, which was specifically designed to prohibit the advertising and promotion of tobacco products.

The Government believed that to protect the health of Canadians — it must stop tobacco advertising since it led to an increase in smoking and high health care costs. The company believed that it had been proved innumerable times by such reputable authorities as the World Health Organization, that advertising does not produce an increase in tobacco consumption. What advertising really does is to give an option to smokers regarding the various brands available. It is similar to other consumer product advertising in the market place.

As a result of this new legislation and other municipal by-laws regarding smoking, the tobacco industry and those dependent on it for a livelihood were faced with a real challenge. However, while CIG Inc. was convinced that elimination of tobacco advertising is inconsistent with the tradition of free speech guaranteed by the Constitution — the firm decided that it would fully comply with the requirements of the tobacco Products Control Act.

Within CIG, the message of the Federal Government through its legislation was received with a certain amount of trepidation and uncertainty by employees who believed that an advertising ban would lead to a faster decline of the industry. As a result, they thought, CIG probably would not be able to afford to maintain a large sales force and marketing team. There was a lot of speculation, but nobody really knew the truth. The fear of losing their jobs and livelihood frightened people who had been with the Company for a long time (CIG looks after its people very

Adapted by Randy Hoffman from a paper by Subhendu Sanyal. Copyright © 1994 by Randy Hoffman.

well) and would have to start all over again in another organization or industry, as well as those who were relatively new and would lose an opportunity to work for a fine organization. I was scared too. I belonged to the latter group in a middle management position. To start sending resumes all over again really bothered me.

The major task confronting senior managers was not so much the legislation itself, but how it would affect the internal organization — the morale and motivation of its employees. In other words, how could they create the conditions necessary to evoke superior performance and motivation for excellence and productivity in spite of the legislation. They initially came to our sales office for a meeting with all of us. They explained the legislation and how it would affect us and answered all our questions. I believe they were extremely straight forward and honest. At the end of the day we received reassurances and most of us went home satisfied.

CIG and its senior managers recognized that what was of paramount importance was **jobs**. To effectively deal with this situation, CIG took clear steps to reassure the marketing staff. For example, they:

- did not reduce sales staff and in fact on a timely basis hired sales representatives to fill in vacant positions;
- improved benefit packages;
- gave sales representatives new vehicles;
- launched brand extensions and new products.

In addition, Human Resources and the Sales Planning department together developed new job redesign and enrichment programs as follows:

- They increased the responsibility and accountability of individual sales representatives over their own territory with regard to clients, frequency of visits, budgets and merchandising contracts. This autonomy created a greater sense of responsibility and satisfaction.
- At the beginning of every month, a sales meeting was held when brand shares and activities taking place in the market place were discussed. This gave all of us a feeling of "relatedness" to the organizational goals.
- At this meeting, sales objectives and budgets were set after individual discussions with the sales staff. This became a basis for the monthly performance appraisal system. CIG believes that a monthly performance appraisal system leaves no surprises on each person's anniversary. It is fair because it allows individual achievements to be highlighted and any shortfalls to be corrected during the year.
- In an attempt to satisfy the "affiliation" and "social" needs of individuals, the organization has begun monthly "rendezvous nights" at our head office. During this time employees, irrespective of title or responsibility, meet in a social gathering to enhance the people relationship outside the business context.
- Because of competition, good jobs involve lifelong learning, constant training, and skills updating. For CIG, training means a competitive edge and a satisfied

and motivated work force. In the Canadian market place, products will only be as good as the people CIG has, and the sales staff will only be as good as the training and motivation they get. Having said that, I must emphasize that CIG provides the sales staff constant training through their District Sales Managers and special training managers.

- Job rotation has been another approach to stimulating and satisfying high achievers. We have a program specifically designed to help employees who have future potential to receive "quality movement" through various departments. Furthermore, several times during the year staff from various departments go out with the sales representatives to learn a little more about the market place and the sales job. This also helps reduce conflict between functional areas.

With the introduction of Bill C-51, managers realized that they would have to modify the way they do business and to create "a new way of life". To make that happen, they had to foster change and take risks. In these turbulent times, employees felt the need for leadership. The feelings of uncertainty and insecurity which accompanied this legislation caused people to seek reassurances and a sense of direction from those who knew where they were going while inspiring confidence and trust.

CIG was changing from an over-managed organization where managers excelled in handling the daily routine to one where managers could not only do things right but selectively seek our right things to do. They had to emphasize the creative side of both managers and subordinates — stimulating and generating original ideas for new products, and new ways of solving problems. It was this change in leadership thinking that created several new products in the "roll your own" tobacco segment leading to higher market shares and employee morale. A vision by product development and research translated into reality and catapulted CIG from a minor player to the leader in the fine cut segment in Canada.

CIG clearly emphasizes that all managers treat their staff fairly both in terms of time spent, work input, and budget allocations. While I agree with this concept, I still believe that managers must be able to discriminate. Discrimination is implicit in the concept of leadership. In other words, people do not want to be treated the same as others. They want to be treated fairly and according to merit. Failure to discriminate creates instant mediocrity.

When it comes to motivating employees, altruism is good business. In CIG, people are not propelled by a single-minded desire to make more money. They are propelled by a need to fulfil their vision and to make a difference to people. CIG and its employees have been supporting many charitable causes. In fact, we have a program in place whereby if an employee contributes to any charitable organization, CIG will match it dollar for dollar. To employees it means a chance to make a difference, and to CIG it means greater loyalty and higher productivity.

QUESTIONS

1. What are the threats posed by Bill C-51 to company's performance?
2. Identify the actions taken by CIG to counter these threats.
3. How will the steps taken by management affect "corporate culture"? Why is a strong "corporate culture" particularly important in this case?
4. Will these actions be effective, in your view? Why or Why not?

Case 13

Computer Shared Services (A)

BACKGROUND

Computer Shared Services (CSS) is the data processing division of a large Canadian telecommunications firm comprised of several business units serving communication markets. The division is staffed by 125 people and is located in a self-contained data centre remote from the major business units it serves.

CSS's mandate is to provide mainframe computing and network facilities to the other business units in the same firm. It works hard to achieve this through an Operations group, a Mainframe Technical Support group and a Network group consisting of 60, 30 and 25 people respectively. Many of the client businesses, however, think that the services provided by CSS are overpriced and substandard. In fact, most business units have studied the implications of downsizing to what they call "...more accessible, more responsive and less costly..." computer environments. Several of the business units are starting up pilot projects to explore the implications of downsizing in greater detail.

One large business unit has already announced its intention to have all of its data processing pulled off the mainframe in three to five years. It cited competitive pressures to improve service levels to the public as a primary motive. That business unit is convinced that building customer care systems using Graphical User Interfaces, distributed databases, intelligent workstations and Local Area Networks as a technology base to integrate the functionally provided by the new data, voice, and video technologies is the way to achieve enhanced customer service levels. These technologies either aren't available in, or suited to, a mainframe environment. The other motive is cost. It is expected that significant

Adapted by Randy Hoffman from a paper by Eric Adams. Copyright © 1994 by Randy Hoffman.

ORGANIZATIONAL CHART FOR COMPUTER SHARED SERVICES

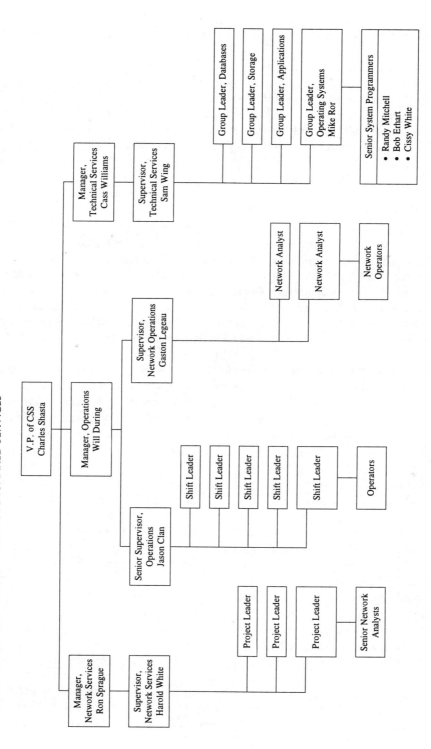

savings will be realized in both acquisition and operational costs by moving away from the mainframe.

Despite all the indications in the computer industry at large that technology advances had reached a point where cost effective, technically feasible alternatives to the traditional data centre were not only available but necessary from a competitive perspective, this shift of focus on the part of their internal customers has caught CSS by surprise. A major upgrade costing about $8,000,000 was done to the mainframe system less than a year ago and another significant upgrade has been in the works for several months. This newest upgrade is being delayed while CSS reviews all its options.

THE DETAILS

Most of the options being considered exploit new computer technologies that enable CSS to decentralize computer facilities to the department or workgroup level, thus reducing the role of the mainframe. This represents a radical change in philosophy and technology within the organization; one that has left many people concerned about their future. And while the study of the options shows clear cost and functionally benefits to downsizing, most CSS management and staff cannot understand why any of the client businesses would want to abandon a stable, mature mainframe environment for one that they consider to be no better than a Personal Computer environment.

Indeed, Will During, Manager of Operations, points proudly to the volumes of processing and printing that his department does and asks derisively. "Can your oversized PC's do that?" Will's group prepares monthly reports and he has lately been very aggressive about emphasizing what he considers successes in the monthly management meetings. The operations group oversees the processing and printing of nearly three million invoices per month. It provides support and runs reporting for a common financial system that processes close to one hundred million dollars in revenues per month. "All this", says Will, "while maintaining daily on-line system availability that exceeds our published service commitments to our users."

Last month, after Will finished delivering his report, Sarah Rushawa, Financial Manager for the Mobile Communications division, asked him why, if things were so rosy in the Operations Department, it had taken them close to four months to implement a critical new report. Will replied that the report had first to be developed and then put into a procedure so that the Ops group could fit it into the existing schedule. Sara then showed Will a study that concluded that if the report had been ready only one month earlier, the Mobile Communications group could have saved $50,000 by cancelling two projects that were clearly going nowhere. Will was unmoved by the study and stated that the success of any Operations group depended on the observance of procedures written to enrure the efficient functioning of the data centre. It was obvious that Sarah was angered by Will's total lack of appreciation of the situation. She contented herself with the muttered comment, "Your stupid procedures will put all of us out of business!"

All the clients complain about the interminable procedures that must be followed before even the smallest change can be implemented. The broadcasting division remembers a simple request for access to their own information residing on the mainframe that took three months, five meetings, and the involvement of ten CSS personnel to satisfy. Each of the CSS personnel had a specific area of expertise, had to be consulted, and their various approvals had to be obtained through their managers. In the end, of the ten CSS staffers, only two were involved in actually doing the work.

Traditionally, the organization is procedure driven. Everything is done by the book and employees who fail to follow the published procedures could face a range of disciplinary measures up to and including termination. There are six people who spend all their time maintaining the procedure manuals and reviewing system and problem logs for any actions or decisions that violate procedures. These include a strictly enforced provision to escalate all production problems to management if no solution is found within a fifteen minute time limit. This results in management involvement in most production problems, with the result that many support people have developed a healthy dislike for those they call the "non-producers". In one instance, Bob Erhart, a Senior Systems Programmer in the operating system support group, estimated that constant demands for status checks and explanations by his manager, Cass Williams, extended a system outage by a full hour. Cass's report of the incident credits her early involvement in the situation with its rapid resolution although the report is sketchy on the details of her contribution.

Cass, whose official title is Manager of Technical Services, recently called the Tech Services group together for a meeting to announce a new procedure for handling production problems on the mainframe. Will During also attended. Cass and Will had analyzed the trouble logs for a six month period and had discovered that most of the problems had been resolved by rebooting the computer. Tech involvement had merely extended the downtime associated with the problem. Since the objective was to minimize downtime, the Tech group would now have only ten minutes to respond to a call, diagnose and fix the problem. If the problem was still unresolved after ten minutes, the duty Operations Shift Leader, with "his finger on the trigger", would initiate a reboot of the computer. This new procedure was not at all well received by the Tech group. Randy Mitchell, a Senior Systems Programmer, questioned the analysis of the trouble logs and asked to review it. Cass responded by saying that his time could be better spent on working with Operations to promote the new procedure into production as quickly as possible. Randy persisted and tried to explain that the time Technical Services spends in diagnosing a problem is time well spent, especially in those cases where the immediate problem is really only a symptom of a more serious problem such as impending equipment failure. Will pointed out that while Tech may find the time useful, it was the Operations group that was responsible for system availability and he could no longer tolerate system outages that made his group look bad. Cass agreed and brought the meeting to a close by assigning the implementation of the new procedure to Randy.

The management team keeps a tight rein on the organization in other ways, as well. All change requests are approved by management personnel only. This is in spite of the fact that most of the managers are either no longer technically up-to-date or involved to accurately assess the impact of a proposed change. They constantly confer with and act on the advice of the technical support or production personnel. Recently, a manager asked the appropriate support person if a change should be approved and was, in turn, requested by the support person to withhold approval pending his review of the change request. Instead, the manager rejected the change request and was embarrassed when he was unable to explain his reasons to the client who was annoyed enough to escalate the issue to senior levels within CSS. An angry exchange of E-mail messages passed between the manager and the employee involved. A new procedure was implemented requiring employees to pre-approve all change requests in writing, thus eliminating all confusion in the official process performed by the managers.

The pressures created by the need to meet client demands are generating friction within the organization itself. Not only are the new technical skills required to implement satisfactory solutions lacking, but the business skills needed to work more closely with the various client businesses are also in extremely short supply. In addition, demands by the businesses for more streamlined, responsive work processes have so far caused only confusion. Management is reluctant to relinquish any authority or control and employees appear unable to work effectively in the absence of procedures, concerned as they are with avoiding disciplinary action. A user request for an account on one of the new mini-computers was delayed for four days while the technical support person assigned responsibility for the machine consulted his manager for advice on the proper course of action. Since this was a new type of machine, it was unclear exactly what procedure was appropriate and the subordinate refused to act without clarification. In the end, due largely to the howls of anger from the user, it was decided that accounts could be added if an authorization form, signed by the requesting manager, was presented to the Technical Services manager. The employee was later criticized by his manager for allowing the situation to drag on without making an effort.

In another incident, Jim Andrews, a Director of Information Technology in a department of the mobile communications division, left a voicemail for Charles Shasta, VP of Operations at CSS, complaining about a long outstanding request for a network connection for his PC. Charles called the supervisor concerned and told him to "fix the problem today or don't show up for work tomorrow". Gaston, the supervisor, an excitable person at the best of times, rushed to provide the network connection and ended up having a heated exchange with Jim Andrews. It turned out that Jim had neglected to mention to Charles that his group had been relocated several times and was now in a new area of the building not yet serviced by the network. Jim had had a network connection in each of his other locations. To make matters worse, a formal reprimand had been entered into Gaston's personnel records, even though all admitted that it was much ado about nothing. Gaston was having a difficult time in getting the reprimand removed. It seems that

Charles feels it is justified based on Gaston's angry words to Jim Andrews who is, after all, the "customer".

Senior management seems to recognize the problems faced by the organization and attempts are being made to change. Recently, Will During, supported by Charles Shasta, held information seminars to present the plan for a major mainframe automation initiative to the employees in the hope that fears concerning continued employment would be offset by the many new job opportunities created by automation. The theme of the seminars was "Automation... the key to our success!". Will's presentation emphasized the fact that automation would eliminate the mundane, repetitive aspects of Operational tasks thus creating challenging positions with more fulfilling activities. This information was well received until a question from the floor concerning how individual employees could become involved in new opportunities of interest to them was asked. Will responded by saying that new opportunities would be matched to employees by management based on performance and demonstrated ability to deal with new technologies. Most attending employees interpreted this as a continuation of the current policy dealing with promotion which, summarized by them, is based on the criterion "It's not what you know, but who you know." It was also noticed that the people actually doing the automation work were not listed as team members, that privilege being reserved for managers and supervisors. Many people came away feeling unenthused by the initiative and convinced that, despite the half-day long dog-and pony show, it was business as usual.

CSS Senior Management also invited the employees to participate in the "Mission and Values" initiative kicked off six months ago and worked on by the management team at various retreats since then. The employee involvement consisted of half a day working in a team of about ten people sponsored by two or more "host" managers. None of the managers were to have any formal reporting relationship with any employee in their group. The goal was to give the employees an opportunity to review and critique the mission statement and organizational goals arrived at by the managers.

The process very quickly came to be called "Missing Values". Randy Mitchell found that one of the managers assigned to his group, Will During, was very defensive about the mission statement and met every suggestion for a change or addition with reasons why the mission statement should remain as it is. Will spent much of the short time allotted to the team relating stories about how hard the management team had worked in preparing the material. Randy broke in several times, to Will's great annoyance, in an effort to get the other employees involved in discussing the issues at hand. He was successful and the employee team worked hard to put together their thoughts in the final half hour of the session. Will didn't agree with some of the points raised by the employees, but Randy reminded him that his agreement was not required. All Will had to do now was to present the team's comments to the management team.

Most of the employee teams, however, allowed the host managers to guide them through the half day exercise without much participation beyond showing the approval and acceptance of the Mission and Values document that appeared to be expected of them. Indeed, the process was handled more as a step in a controlled procedure than as a sincere effort to encourage employee participation. Management had committed itself to publishing the employee comments but has not yet done so.

It is apparent that the new technological and customer service demands placed on the organization have found it unprepared. The gulf that exists between management and employees was made even more obvious in the last several weeks by a new policy that requires managers to have an office. Since all the offices are located in one part of the building, many managers' offices are removed from the area in which their people sit. Ron Sprague, the network manager, for example, sits in an entirely different part of the building from the rest of his department. No-one is overly concerned about this since most communications take place via voice or E-mail anyway.

QUESTIONS

1. What are the underlying causes of conflict between the CSS and their users?
2. What structural and communication issues are raised by this case?
3. How would you revise the structure and communication policies?
4. How does the company's and CSS' leadership contribute to the problem?

Computer Shared Services (B)

The ability of the organization to adjust to the new emphasis on quality customer service will have a direct on its performance. It seems that this fact is appreciated more by the employees than by management staff. Recently, Randy Mitchell requested a meeting of the senior members of the Technical Support group in order to raise this issue with his peers and management. The following people were in attendance:

Manager Technical Services — Cass Williams   Cass has ten plus years experience with IBM mainframes and has been employed for five years at CSS. She has been manager for less than a year and in that time has shown a marked preference for the administrative aspects of her job.

Supervisor of Technical Services — Sam Wing   Sam has ten plus years mainframe experience and has been employed at CSS for three years. It is rumoured that at one time Sam was a top technical person. Like Cass, however, Sam now appears to be more comfortable dealing with shift schedules and holiday authorization forms than the many technical issues that crop up on a daily basis.

Group Leader, Operating System Support — Mike Ror   Mike has seventeen years mainframe experience and has been employed at CSS for three years. Mike has no peer when it comes to resolving technical problems within the mainframe environment. Unfortunately, he has an ego to match his technical skills and most people, his co-workers included, dislike working with him.

Senior System Programmer — Randy Mitchell   Randy has thirteen years experience supporting minicomputers, PC's and networks. He has been employed

---

Adapted by Randy Hoffman from a paper by Eric Adams. Copyright © 1994 by Randy Hoffman.

by CSS for two years. Randy is very customer-focused and brimming with ideas that he thinks will help achieve customer satisfaction. He is full of energy and shows it whenever he gets an opportunity to expound on any of his ideas. He is well liked by everyone.

Senior System Programmer — Bob Erhart Bob has ten years mainframe experience and has been employed by CSS for three years. Bob does the work that is required in the allotted time but makes little effort to do more. Bob defines a good day as a day on which he has little work to do and on which he doesn't have to speak to Cass, Sam or, Mike.

Senior System Programmer — Cissy White Cissy has five years mainframe experience and has been employed by CSS for one year. She is considered to be a highly talented professional who continually strives to do more, better. She is known for her impatience with what she considers to be an overly bureaucratic department and for her willingness to talk about it.

Cass opened the meeting.

Cass: Well, Randy, you asked for this meeting...

Randy: Thanks, Cass. All of you know that we have been asked to provide support for some of the new equipment that is being introduced into our area. I thought it was time that we talked about how, exactly, we should be working with this equipment. I submitted a proposal to Cass several weeks ago and I passed it out to everyone yesterday.

Mike: I read it and I don't agree with all the organizational and equipment changes that you recommended. A computer is a computer is a computer. We can support this so-called new technology set just like we do the mainframe.

Sam: Well, I'm not sure of that. Randy has pointed out that the new technology environments are made up of many components from the workstation up to and including the mainframe. For example, it sounds like we will have to have a good understanding of networking in order to understand how the user accesses their host even though we won't be responsible for the network.

Randy: That's right, Sam. In the mainframe world everyone has his specific job and is not expected to know much beyond that. Now everyone is going to be expected to develop skills in all technology areas like PC's, networking and various operating systems like DOS and UNIX.

Bob: (startled and concerned) Wait a minute! That sounds like a lot of work! How are we supposed to develop an acceptable level of proficiency in all these areas? Are there training plans in place? Does everybody realize that we can't just take these responsibilities on overnight?

Randy: (laughing) Relax, Bob. That's why I wanted to raise the issue now. We still have time to put training plans in place and ease people into the new environments. Keep in mind that we have only begun to introduce the new technologies.

Mike: It won't work. It sounds like everyone will be responsible, and that means no one is responsible. Responsibility has to be fixed to the person or no work will get done.

Cass: I would like to focus on the recommendation that Randy made regarding equipment upgrades. The organizational issues will be decided by the Steering Committee.

Cissy: I hope the Steering Committee will consider our opinions. I think we should continue discussing the new skills required so that we can better understand how our jobs will be affected. We can then have some meaningful input into whatever decision the Steering Committee makes.

Cass: (sternly) The Committee will make those decisions. Lets move on. Randy, I didn't understand why you feel it's necessary to upgrade our existing equipment. What will an equipment upgrade achieve for us?

Randy: (animated) It will position us to provide "knock your socks off service" to our customers, Cass. Right now our customers are better equipped than we are; its obvious that our customers are leading the drive to new technologies. But they are introducing and applying these new technologies without any solid technical understanding and continually turn to us for help. And when they come to us for help we scramble to understand and fix the problems. If we can't help them, we pass them off to some other department which, as often as not, passes it right back to us. The poor customer may make several rounds before the problem is resolved.

So far we have been doing okay. With equipment and software like our customers have, though, we would develop an understanding of their whole environment from the workstation, across the network, to whatever host machine they use. We could help them implement applications in such a way that many of the problems could be dealt with up front. When problems do occur, we could follow the problem right through to resolution. If the problem is a network problem, for example, we could ensure, on behalf of the customer, that the Network group resolves it rather than passing it off as somebody else's problem. We would be reducing customer frustration by easing application implementation and problem resolution. It will mean greater customer satisfaction and more credibility for us. The customer will keep coming back for our support.

Mike: Right! That's **all** we need... more users calling us more often!

Cass: You said that so far we have been doing okay. I haven't heard any complaints about what we are doing in support of the new stuff.

Randy: That's because I have been able to handle what demand there is by myself so far. That's going to change within three months. By then we will have six new mini-computers and about sixty new PC's in the shop.

Cass, we should create a situation in which the customers choose to come to us. That way we will be invited to get involved in their development efforts as these efforts begin, as opposed to just before they want to implement a new application. We should provide a level of service that makes our customers sit up and take notice.

Cass: Well, our users, or customers as you call them, haven't asked us for that level of service. And besides, I don't have the budget for all these upgrades anyway.

Randy: They may never ask you for better service, Cass. They'll just go elsewhere.

Cissy: I agree with Randy. Everybody here knows that our mainframe users complain about everything we do. Sometimes I think that they hate us. I think that this may be an opportunity for us to start again. We have to do something differently and Randy's comments make a lot of sense.

Mike: (aggressively)   Wait a minute, there, Missy. We provide good service on the mainframe and most users complain for no reason. It's like cafeteria food; people feel obliged to complain but they eat the stuff just the same.

Sam: (quietly)   Maybe that's because they have no choice.

Bob: (loudly)   Mike's right. The users have no idea how difficult our job is. They just demand, demand, demand.

Randy: I think you folks are missing the point. One of the reasons our users are moving off the mainframe is that they feel they are not in control. They are at the mercy of uninterested, overbearing techies.

It's my opinion that, if we want to avoid a similar situation with the new technology environments, we have top rethink what we do and how we do it, and ultimately retool so that we participate in and contribute to our customers' business interests.

And yes, Cass, that will probably mean a budget review. It all comes down to our commitment to our customers.

Cass: Well, as I said... there is no push to enhance our service levels except for Randy's opinions and I can't initiate budget reviews every time someone has a bright idea.

Cissy: Randy makes a lot of sense, Cass. We get so many complaints on the mainframe side that maybe we just don't pay attention any more. Maybe we should consider those complaints as requests for a service level enhancement.

Mike: (annoyed)   What is it with you, Cissy? We do good work on the mainframe and our users are happy! The complaints you're talking about come from untrained users who don't know any better. No matter how good our service level is, there is just no way to make those people happy. So let's forget them.

Cissy: (innocently)   Like Paul Randall?

Mike: (angrily)   That was an honest mistake!

Cissy: (calmly)   I'm not talking about the mistake, Mike. I'm talking about the four days it took you to correct it!

Cass: (stridently)   OK! Settle down. I've made my decision and we all know what it is so let's get back to work.

   (annoyed) Randy, the next time you ask for a meeting I want to see an agenda first.

Senior management seems to know that changes must take place. The mainframe automation seminars and the "Mission and Values" sessions, as poorly handled as they are, are proof of this. The changes will obviously affect the technology provided and supported by CSS. Downsizing efforts, fuelled by customer needs, will continue and some senior staff even have a good idea of what the future holds from a technological perspective. What the organization will look like, however, is somewhat less clear. Some seniors see little change and expect to continue on, with modified procedures, very much as they do now. Other seniors see radical changes in the organization taking place. They feel that the only way to enhance service levels and to make effective use of the new technologies is to make the organization less structured, complete with a trimmed down management team and staff, mature and experienced enough to work in largely self-managed teams.

QUESTION

You are a consultant called in to help this group settle its interpersonal and professional differences and develop new policies to further CSS' and the parent organization's performance. How would you do it? Answer in detail.

Conavia "H"

At the end of 1987, Stanley Jackson, an experienced aviation consultant, had risen to become Senior Vice-President, Economics and Finance, of Conavia Canada Ltd., a Vancouver-based consulting firm specializing in avionics. He reported directly to George Markov, the President and surviving founder of the firm. Although there was a parallel Vice-President, Projects and Facilities, the position had remained unfilled for more than two years since the untimely death of its incumbent, Ron Gilbert. Stanley was, in fact, the number two executive with the company which had 9 employees.

Since 1981, when control of the company was restructured following the death of George Markov's founding partner Samuel Kahn, the firm's equity was distributed as follows:

	Shares	**Percent**
George Markov	3,100	52
Stanley Jackson	1,500	25
Paul Frees	750	12
Other employees	650	11

Share transfer was restricted by a shareholder's agreement requiring all shareholders to be employees of the company. In the event of termination of employment for whatever reason, outstanding shares were to be repurchased by the other shareholders, if they wished, or otherwise by the company on a fixed formula basis related to the previous year's financial statement. At the end of 1987, the formula value of the shares was determined to be equal to $27.22. This valued the entire company at $163,000, which was not unusual considering that it rarely did more than break even financially.

The three-person board of directors was composed of Markov, his wife Eleanor, and Marvin Kaplansky, the company's attorney. The full board met rarely, with most activity taking place within the fiction of the company's books.

Although Stanley was excluded from the board, he was not disturbed by it and believed that, as Conavia was effectively Markov's creation, he had the right to operate it as he saw fit. As most of Stanley's remuneration was in the form of salary, he did not believe that his elevation to the board would change his remuneration potential.

In early 1988, while at an airline operator's conference in San Juan, Puerto Rico, George Markov took Stanley aside, and, to his surprise, told him that he would be stepping down, at least temporarily.

"As you know," he said, "Jet BC have been losing a lot of good people during this latest ownership scramble, and they need help badly. To make a long story short, they've made me an offer I can't refuse, and it looks as if I'm going to take it." Jet BC was Canada's largest (and only) manufacturer of light business jets, producing a product line competitive with the Cessna Citation series. They were based on Vancouver Island and had recently been divested by the federal government after a five year stint as a Crown Corporation. An equity issue had been floated successfully.

Stanley, who had received no advance warning of the situation, was aghast: "I don't know what to say."

"You don't have to say anything, continued George, "because nothing is going to change. I'd like you to take over the leadership of Conavia, at least on a temporary basis, as Executive Vice-President. I'm certain that you'll do a fine job. While the company can't afford an immediate raise, I can promise you a substantially revised compensation package when you come up for review next year."

"Who do you have in mind for a new president," asked Stanley?

"At the moment, nobody," replied George. "I'm certain that you can handle the responsibilities yourself. Meanwhile, I'll always be at the other end of a phone, or a fax machine, or even the ferry. In fact," he continued, "from what I've seen, Jet BC could use a lot of sales engineering assistance. Who better to help out than Conavia?"

"Isn't that an obvious conflict of interest," Stanley suggested?

"It's been discussed," George answered. "My Conavia shares will be placed in a trust to be voted by Marvin. Meanwhile, I'll continue to serve as an outside director. And as long as Conavia can provide consulting services on a competitive basis, why should they be discriminated against?" He smiled enigmatically.

For the first time in several years, Stanley was forced to reexamine his relationship to the company. He had always worked in the shadow of George Markov, who, in addition to a demonstrated record of success, was also an extremely strong personality. Stanley had always deferred to George in matters of corporate strategy and had generally consulted him prior to proceeding with his own projects. The new organizational structure would clearly require more responsibility from Stanley, and he was uncertain how he would respond to it. Nonetheless, after considerable reflection, Stanley decided to accept the challenge. "Hell," he thought, "I've been more or less running my half of the business for five years anyway. There's no reason why I can't pick up the other half as well."

For the first six months, events proceeded smoothly. Although George moved to Sidney, BC, he was generally in Vancouver once a week and always stopped in to discuss business with Stanley. Stanley considered his advice useful and generally accepted George's suggestions.

The composition of Conavia's business, however, began to change. With 30 years of senior experience in the Canadian aerospace environment, George was welcome in the highest echelons of both Victoria and Ottawa. Conavia had received a substantial volume of sole source work in the strategic consulting area, including a major, two-year study with DIST (the federal Department of Industry, Science and Technology) regarding the future direction of Canada's aerospace industry. Stanley soon found, however, that while deputy ministers might respond to George, they rarely returned his calls, and the company's backlog of projects began to shrink. To compensate, Stanley began to develop business in areas where he was stronger, namely, the more technical (or at least project-specific) aspects of aviation which did not require as much input at the political level.

One immediate side-effect was lower rates. Whereas DIST showed no qualms about rates in the region of $1,200 per day ("Hell," said George, "that's dirt cheap compared to what Booz Allen or SRI would charge"), both Transport Canada and CIDA (Canadian International Development Agency), Conavia's next largest clients, balked at rates which were much in excess of $700. In fact, CIDA tried to adhere to a $500 maximum limitation.

"We can't make money at $500," said George, during one of his periodic visits. "You've got to get the rates up, Stanley."

"Actually we can," countered Stanley. "We're running a much lower overhead shop. No offense, but your costs in particular were always high, what with you charging off to Ottawa every second week, lunches at the Rideau Club, entertainment, and all that jazz. Don't get me wrong, it worked well for you, because you were always able to get the high-rated business to cover it, but I can't do it that way. If you check the six month P&L, you'll find that our net is about the same as always."

In fact, Stanley was very proud of the way he had managed to control expenses. He believed that if the company was to remain profitable under his stewardship, costs would have to drop, because he was not certain he could maintain Markov's level of revenue generation.

"Sure the net is the same," replied George, "for two basic reasons. One, is that we're still charging against the last of the old DIST contracts. Two, is that I've brought you a quarter of a million dollar's worth of business from Jet BC. That's what's keeping the company alive."

Although revenues and costs both dropped under Stanley's stewardship, the volume of business, as measured by chargeable man-hours, remained high. Stanley had particular success in obtaining business from CIDA, including a half-million dollar aerospace industrial offset project in Southeast Asia. Stanley was personally involved with it from mid-1988 until well into the spring of 1989, and much of his time was spent overseas. Conavia was staffed with seasoned veterans, however, and little direct administration was required.

In fact, this was a source of great pride to Stanley. Although gross revenues had dropped, he had managed to maintain the company's business volume at stable levels with no drop in the company's profits. He was also pleased with his success in moving the company into new business areas. The contracts Conavia had succeeded in obtaining were now strictly the results of Stanley's efforts, so he believed, rather than of George's.

The weekly meetings with George became less frequent because Stanley was out of the country more and more. However, this did not stop George from visiting Conavia and talking to Paul Frees, the next senior man, or his former secretary. Following some of these visits, Stanley would occasionally receive a fax from George the next day. Most dwelt on the rate situation.

"We can't continue like this," read one, in September, 1988. "Business at $500 is killing us, and you're not able to make the rounds in Ottawa and Victoria while you're sitting in a hotel room in Manila. Our backlog is down, and our revenues are down. You're going to have to spend more time getting higher quality business." Stanley was furious, and counted to 10 before replying that one paragraph faxes sent halfway around the world were not the proper medium in which to develop a sound business strategy.

Stanley returned home for a month in early October and immediately phoned George. "When do you want to meet?" he asked.

"It's a busy month," answered George. "Jet BC's agreement for federal funding is up for renewal, and I'll be east most of the month."

"What about the fax? Do you want a formal reply? George, we're making good money here, and it's not being done with mirrors. Under CIDA rules, I can charge for seven-day weeks while our staff is on overseas assignment. The time budget allows for it, and CIDA condones it. That's an effective 40% surcharge off the top. Check the project budget sheets: we're making money."

"I wouldn't worry about it, Stanley. It's not necessary to waste any more time on this. Just try and do your best."

While Stanley was upset by George's attitude, he chalked it up to personal idiosyncrasies and continued to manage the company as he saw fit, knowing full well that in the event of a confrontation with George, he would be supported by very positive financial results.

Stanley was correct. The profit and loss statements, although unaudited, were available from the computerized accounting system in early January and indicated that profit levels in 1988 were the highest in five years. The comparative results were as follows:

	Net Profit
1984	$ 90,000
1985	(123,000)
1986	17,000
1987	2,000
1988	39,000

In relation to 1987, revenues had dropped by $110,000, but costs had been reduced by $147,000.

Although Stanley knew approximately how the year would look, he did not see the figures immediately because he was in Kuala Lumpur at the time presiding over the completion of the CIDA job. When he returned in late January, 1989, he discovered that Conavia had a new president.

"You could have told me," he said to George, as soon as they could meet. "I don't object to a new president, that's your prerogative anyway, but you could have at least let me know in advance. Who the hell is Dennis Wilson, anyway?"

"You said you didn't like faxes in remote places," replied George, "and the whole thing came up suddenly, anyway. Dennis is an experienced executive with close ties to the federal Tories. He's responsible, among other things, for fund-raising in the lower mainland, and he's very close to the highest levels in Ottawa. He's exactly the man we need. He'll complement your skills. I still expect you to continue with the day-to-day running of the company: Dennis can't possibly do that, anyway. What he can do is get us some badly needed high-rated business in Ottawa."

"At what price? We're successful now due as much to cost control as to revenues."

"It'll be pay-as-you-go. No fixed salary. Is that OK by you?"

"I guess so," said Stanley.

If Stanley maintained his composure with George, he was fuming internally. In the course of his year's stewardship, he had succeeded in restructuring the company so that it could operate profitably in George's absence. He had maintained the company's size and profitability in the face of reduced revenues by stringent cost control. Now that the transition year had passed, he was looking forward to the firm growing, both in terms of size and profitability. Yet, he thought to himself, George had rewarded his outstanding performance by saddling him with a "politician" who had no experience in either aviation or, for that matter, business. In Stanley's vocabulary, "politician" was not a complement.

In the event, Dennis turned out to be a personable, if not brilliant, president. He was rarely in the office, and Stanley maintained effective control over Conavia. It was not until March that Stanley received his first surprise, an invoice from Dennis' holding company for an advance against commissions of $12,000.

"But we don't pay advances against commissions," said Stanley the following week, when he finally managed to meet with Dennis. "We don't even pay commissions themselves. We work on the basis of chargeable time: if you charge time to a project, you get paid for it. I can't authorize this."

"Presidents don't come cheap," explained Dennis. "I've given up a lot to take this job, at no salary whatever. I have to spend time in Ottawa, prepare proposals, meet people. This is just a bridge to cover expenses until the jobs start to come in."

"I didn't realize you were writing proposals," said Stanley. "I haven't seen anything cross my desk."

"Oh, nothing written. You can take care of the details after the fact. But I can tell you that I had some very promising discussions with a certain minister when he was in town last week. I'll let you know as soon as I need some back-up."

"I still can't authorize payment on this," said Stanley, stubbornly, waving the invoice. "Not without some indication that remunerative work has been done, somehow, somewhere."

"Then I'll have to get it authorized elsewhere," said Dennis, softly. "We'll talk about it later, Stanley."

If Stanley was upset when Dennis had been appointed, he was now starting to become frightened as well. The key to Conavia's success, he believed, had been his tight cost controls. Now, he was faced with a new president who apparently wanted to develop business in George's old style but without any demonstrated ability to bring in the compensating high-yield contracts. If costs were to increase without a new source of revenues, he was suddenly worried that he might be blamed for the overall results.

Following this latest conversation with Dennis, Stanley immediately tried to reach George, but discovered he was out of town and unavailable. He left messages at several locations, but his call was not returned. Six days later, he received an information copy of a director's resolution stating that, with immediate effect, Stanley's check-signing authority was to be transferred to Dennis Wilson.

Stanley's first urge was to dash off a letter of resignation in protest; in fact, he drafted one. A few hours of reflection after work, however, led him to the conclusion that, other than these recent management developments at Conavia, he really enjoyed his job. It was unlikely that the same degree of personal autonomy and the fascinating array of challenging projects in exotic locations would be available in another firm. Still he could not ignore a problem that was causing frequent, severe headaches and chronic fatigue due to many sleepless nights.

QUESTIONS

1. Critically assess George Markov's leadership. What are his strong and weak points?

2. What mistakes were made by Stanley Jackson in dealing with George Markov?

3. (a) From a motivational point of view, why did Stanley Jackson react so strongly to the new president and his practices?

   (b) Answer the same question with respect to George Markov's reaction to Stanley's activities.

4. How should George Markov have introduced Dennis Wilson to Stanley Jackson?

5. Recommend, in detail, a course of action for Stanley Jackson.

Easy-Money Department (A)

The organization involved in this Case is a revenue-producing department of a government ministry. Its head office is located in Ottawa which provides staff support to the field offices of its production section. The department has 500 employees throughout Ontario, and the payroll accounts for 30 percent of the department's expenditures.

The organizational structure of the Easy-Money department is divided into various functions. Recently, management has attempted to geographically decentralize. However, this attempt was restricted to the Production section, where the degree of decentralization is apparent in the organization chart (See "B" case). However, all decision making is still centralized at head office. The reorganization has resulted in confusion as to who has the responsibility for decisions: the territory managers, or the production head office managers?

The department is proactive in its environmental relations: various programs are designed to initiate contact with the private sector concerning the Taxation Statutes. These programs are designed to increase the department's visibility and act as an incentive for taxpayers to comply with the Statutes.

The department uses a three-pronged approach to achieve its objectives:

1. Liaising with the public — to inform and educate the general public, businesses, and professional associations;
2. Collections — to collect outstanding accounts receivable;
3. Audits — to administer and encourage compliance with the statutes.

The three functions are the responsibility of the Production section which spends 75% of the department's budget. The field offices of the section report to territorial managers who in turn report to the production head. Each office performs the three functions to obtain revenue.

In the operations of the Easy-Money department, the Administration, Legislation, and Systems and Planning sections are used in a consultative capacity. These sections, although operating independently, must ensure that the needs of the Production section are met, since Production is the revenue-producing area. There is always a substantial percentage of businesses and taxpayers complying with the Statutes. As a result, there is a general complacency that permeates throughout the organization — "All you need to do to maintain the system is to oil it now and again." New program initiatives are designed to give the department high visibility to senior ministry officials — "Emphasis on giving back money instead of hard-nose tactics like audits and collections." Such programs are usually very diluted in effect by the time they reach the field office level.

THE MAIDSTONE FIELD OFFICE (Production Section)

The Maidstone Field Office is one of the larger offices of Easy-Money department. There are approximately 70 employees who are evenly distributed among the four functions:

1. **Administration**
    Responsible for typing, petty cash, equipment, etc.
2. **Collections**
    Responsible for collecting outstanding accounts receivable.
3. **Public Relations**
    Providing services to the public — answering interpretation calls, conducting seminars, liaising with professional organizations.
4. **Audit**
    Responsible for examining books of accounts and levying assessments where non-compliance of the taxing statute is uncovered.

Decision-making is centralized at head office. Policies are sent to the field offices as directives through the chain of command.

Mr. Fred Jones was promoted to the position of Field Office Manager three years ago. His prior position was at head office where he conducted research on developments of audit techniques and approaches. Mr. Jones is aware that the audit area is encountering problems: staff turnover is very high — approximately 60% of the audit staff has less than one year experience; absenteeism is high — the average is eight days per year per employee.

The audit area is directly supervised by Mr. John Smith and indirectly by Mr. Fred Jones. Both of the supervisors are middle-aged, and qualified accountants. Mr. Jones is aware that the quality of work from the audit area is well below average, because he personally reviews all of the completed audits. Mr. Jones knows the audit supervisors fairly well because they were all working in the same section at head office. He also heard through the "grapevine" that Mr. John Smith was the latest "Hot Shot" and was sent by head office to keep an eye on Mr. Jones because the Maidstone office was performing poorly.

Because of the high turnover, Mr. Jones was frequently forced to recruit from universities and colleges to fill the vacancies. A year ago Mr. Ray Bourke applied for the audit trainee position and was successful. Ray was a recent business graduate from a rural college and was happy that he had won the position. Ray was given an intensive training course which lasted four weeks and covered the audit program, audit techniques, interviewing skills, the Taxing Statutes, and administrative matters (how to complete forms, etc.). On the first day, Mr. Jones addressed the new group of audit trainees — "I want you all to know that this group should do well in the Easy-Money department and will significantly contribute to my efforts in making the Maidstone Field Office the no. 1 office in the department. I have an open-door policy and welcome you to discuss anything on your mind. However, please make an appointment with my secretary when you wish to see me."

After the training period was over, Ray felt that his knowledge of the Statutes was inadequate, and he conveyed his concern to the training supervisor. This person said that the Act is complex and Ray should not worry about the inadequacy of his legislative knowledge because it takes time to develop close familiarity with its many provisions.

Ray was assigned to a regular audit group supervised by Mr. Smith. A few days before his assignment began, he spoke to one of the auditors in Mr. Smith's group.

Ray: How do you like working for Mr. Smith?

Auditor: Well Ray, there are a couple of things that you should know about Mr. Smith. He is a former member of the military, and he has a tendency to extend his military habits to the work environment. Smith is performance oriented; he is very conscious of the number of completed audits, revenue per audit, and especially the number of audits with no assessments.

Ray: I don't think there will be a problem with performance. But is he helpful? Is he easy to get along with?

Auditor: If you have a problem with the Statute, forget it. Smith does not know the Act, so it is no use asking him to solve your problem. He does not trust his auditors — he always questions nil assessments. Occasionally, he phones the auditor at the taxpayer's place of business just before quitting time to find out if he left. One more thing, you have to be careful when Mr. Jones (Field Office Manager) is around, he has a habit of listening to your conversations while pretending that he is looking for a file in the cabinets.

After the conversation with the auditor, Ray was apprehensive about being assigned to Mr. Smith's group. Ray also gathered from the conversation that the auditors did not have a good rapport with Mr. Smith because of his suspicious and unsupportive nature. Ray could not believe the auditor's comment on Mr. Jones because it seemed to be a sneaky way of gathering information on auditors.

Mr. Smith requested a meeting with Ray to familiarize him with the rules that must be followed in his section.

Mr. Smith: Welcome to my section, Ray. There are a couple of things that you should be aware of when working here:

(1)   time reports must be submitted on time and each hour worked must be recorded on the time sheet, and

(2)   Any problems that you have must be channelled through me.

Ray: Sure thing. The training section taught me to complete the time sheets. Do I have to contact you on interpretation problems?

Mr. Smith: Yes Ray, all problems. I should also remind you that you are still on probation and an employee appraisal will be prepared within the next three months. The level of performance indicated on the appraisal will form the basis for increments, and also your being classified as permanent staff.

After the meeting, Ray realized that the high staff turnover could be attributed to the management/staff relationship. Managers like Mr. Smith are traditional — performance oriented, employing close supervision, and suspicious. Ray felt that his relationship with Mr. Smith would not be too smooth.

Ray's first audit was of a manufacturer of canned food products. Ray was comfortable with the audit procedures because the audit program was specific and easy to follow. However, after examining a piece of manufacturing equipment, Ray was unsure whether the item was taxable or not. He consulted his interpretation guide and was unable to resolve the problem. Finally, he decided to call Mr. Smith for assistance:

Ray: Mr. Smith, I am having some difficulty in establishing whether an item attracts tax or not.

Mr. Smith: Did you check your guide for assistance?

Ray: Yes, and I am inclined to believe that it is not taxable.

Mr. Smith: You have to be careful when classifying an item as exempt of tax. However, you are in the field and would be in the best position to determine the status of the item. You should try to make your own decisions and use the knowledge gained during training sessions.

The next time Ray encountered an interpretation problem, he spoke to one of the auditors in Mr. Smith's section. Unfortunately, Mr. Jones was conducting one of his eavesdropping sessions and overheard Ray's conversation. Mr. Jones decided to speak to Mr. Smith regarding the matter.

Mr. Jones: I heard one of your auditors discussing an interpretation matter with another auditor.

Mr. Smith: Oh, which one of the auditors?

Mr. Jones: One of the new auditors, Ray Bourke.

Mr. Smith: I told that guy when he joined the section about the protocol to be followed if a problem is encountered.

Mr. Jones: I would suggest that you remind him of the procedures. You know I don't understand these auditors, they should feel lucky to have a secure job when there are millions of unemployed out in the market place.

Mr. Smith: I will speak to Ray about his procedures.

Mr. Smith felt that Mr. Jones was criticizing his section too much; this was the third incident of a similar nature that Mr. Jones brought to his attention. All Mr. Jones was concerned about was making the Maidstone Office no. 1 so that he would look good. However, Mr. Smith knew he had to reprimand Ray in any event.

Mr. Smith: I was advised that you were consulting someone on an interpretation problem.

Ray: I was, because I was unsure of the status of the item. Who advised you of my conversation?

Mr. Smith: Mr. Jones. You should be reminded that all problems have to be channelled through me. In addition, you have been spending too much time on your audits which has resulted in a low revenue per hour.

After the meeting Ray was upset and concerned. He wondered what effect the incident would have on his employee appraisal and increment.

QUESTIONS

1. In the Maidstone office, how do the interpersonal relations and attitudes of Mr. Jones and Smith affect the task and work environment for new auditors like Ray Bourke? What is likely to be the motivational effect?
2. Comment on the leadership styles and modes of communication of the two supervisors.
3. Present a more appropriate set of policies and procedures to better serve the needs of new auditors.

Easy-Money Department (B)

SYSTEM AND PLANNING SECTION

The Systems and Planning section within the department contains a section head, two managers, and a mixture of junior and senior planning specialists. The structure of the section resembles a matrix where planning specialists report to a specific manager depending upon the type of project.

The previous department head had emphasized the importance of the section because he viewed planning as the most important ingredientfor operating a successful organization. However, the current department head feels that production alone is crucial. This has resulted in the reduction of the Systems and Planning section's staff by 50%, the majority of whom were transferred to the Production section.

Mr. Karl Darmody is a junior planning specialist who began his career in one of the department's field offices (Production section) and was promoted to his current position four years ago. Karl's job responsibilities include research projects and development of computer-based manual systems. He has developed a good rapport with his fellow workers and is satisfied with his salary. The job is structured and there are manuals that stipulate the methods of conducting projects. However, objectives and user requirements are difficult to define. Karl's current manager is Mr. Wallace, who has a pleasant personality and is easy to deal with. However, it is difficult to obtain decisions from Mr. Wallace, and he does not follow up on assignments given to his staff. In addition, there is no feedback from Mr. Wallace regarding completed projects. Therefore, the staff is unaware whether their performance is satisfactory or not. Decisions and policies are made by the managers, and in many cases the impact of their decisions on the employee

FIGURE 1 ORGANIZATION CHART OF THE EASY-MONEY DEPARTMENT

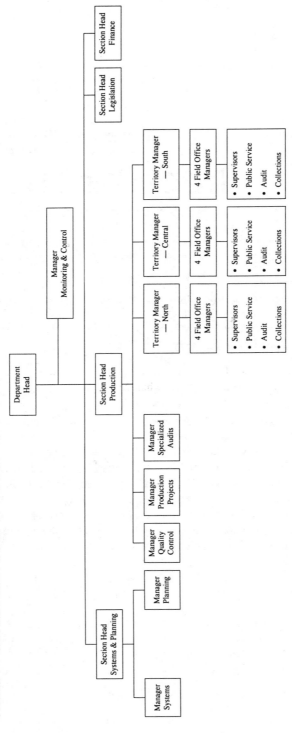

is never considered. A month ago, Karl was summoned to a meeting with all the managers:

Mr. Cameron (Systems and Planning):   Karl, we (the managers) have decided that you will be taken off your current project — you know, the project that will develop tools to aid managers with their planning process.
Karl: Why? The project team has the right mix of skills to complete the project successfully, we have a good team spirit, and why change the team after only six months?
Mr. Wallace (Manager):   This change will be good for you Karl. Consider it to be a career-development change. You will be exposed to other projects.

After the meeting Karl was furious and frustrated. The Planning Project was the first major project in Corporate Planning, and he had enjoyed working on it. The others are "fire fighting" projects — "fix this, fix that" — which were boring and repetitive. Karl thought that the phrase "career development" was a joke because the Systems and Planning section was small and promotional opportunities were low. He did not want to go back to the Production section because management there is dictatorial, employees are treated poorly, and the environment is unstable — "One day you could be working at head office and the next day you are in a field office in Thunder Bay." Karl remembered Mr. Persaud who was switched from office to office — six field offices in two years. Mr. Persaud's social life suffered and his marriage almost ended in a divorce. Karl was always a little nervous when Mr. O'Keefe (Production Head) spoke to Mr. Cameron (Systems & Planning Head) because Karl was afraid that he might be asked to go back to the Production section. Mr. O'Keefe has a habit of raiding the section for good employees.

Once such a request was made, Karl would be able to do nothing. If he did not go, he would be labelled as an employee with a "negative attitude." The Systems and Planning management is powerless in dealing with the Production section management, since the department head always emphasizes the importance of the latter. Work done in the Systems and Planning section is either unknown to the other areas of the branch or regarded as having little importance.

Within the last 18 months, Karl has observed an additional decline in the status of his section. Two recent committees were formed to foster horizontal communication among the various sections in the Easy-Money department and to resolve policy issues that operating units encounter in performing their tasks. However, the Systems and Planning section was excluded from these committees. Karl felt that this omission truly reflected the lack of regard for Systems and Planning in the department.

One of the objectives of the section is "to monitor and adapt to the changing technological environment." The staff feels that the objective is facetious because one of the recent technological developments — microcomputers — is absent from the section. Other departments are using microcomputers regularly, but budgetary requests for this equipment from Systems and Planning have so far been denied.

During the last section's staff meeting, the relationship between Systems and Planning and the Production section was discussed.

Mr. Rose (Senior Specialist):   And why is it so difficult and frustrating when dealing with the Production section staff?

Karl: I worked in Production before. Those guys take a dim view of us and basically have no respect for our section. They always complain that we are too slow and cautious.

Mr. Rose: I get the same feeling too. The Production managers feel that their request should be treated as top priority.

Mr. Bond (Junior Planning Specialist):   Those guys in Production never communicate with each other, and when there is a foul-up, we get the blame. Remember the request that Production made to change Report 40. Well, Mr. Wallace and I had a meeting with the manager in Production to discuss the changes that he wanted. We went ahead and made the change. However, after the new Report 40 was printed, one of the manager's local supervisors came running to me and asked "who authorized you to change Report 40?" I told him to see his boss. I never heard from them again.

Mr. Wallace: From now on, when they want a change, they have to put it in writing; no more verbal agreements.

There is hardly any socializing among the various sections, and staff members tend to think in terms of their area of specialization and not from a departmental perspective. Each section isolates itself from the others because they are comfortable within their own sphere of influence. Even within sections this problem often occurs. This low level of communication has resulted in a lack of coordination among the sections and a suspicious atmosphere within The Easy-Money department. The situation is illustrated by the following examples:

1.   One section purchased three expensive word processing machines because the central word-processing service was accused of being slow. In reality, the extra equipment was unnecessary.
2.   A taxpayer phoned four different field offices for an interpretation of the Act and got four different answers.

Office politics is an accepted norm within the Easy-Money department. Each section views each other suspiciously, and memoranda are filtered for hidden motives and innuendoes which cause the information contained in the memo to be distorted. Recently, a production staff member was caught searching and reading letters on a planning officer's desk.

The Systems and Planning managers feel that their staff are treated fairly, are well paid, and their basic needs are met. The managers feel that their ability to change procedures, work environment, etc., is restricted because of the high degree of bureaucratization of the organization. Too much of their time is devoted to fighting their counterparts in the Production section, which prevents them from dealing with their own internal problems. The Systems and Planning managers recently conducted a survey to determine job attitudes experienced by their employees. The results indicated that there is a need for employee recognition, incentive to work is low, and feedback is almost non-existent.

SURVEY

From a scale of 1 (low) to 10 (high) rate the following dimensions in your current job.

			Average Score
1.	Variety of skill	degree of use of different skills, abilities, and talents?	7
2.	Identity of tasks	do you do a job from beginning to end with a visible outcome?	3
3.	Significance of the task	does your job have a significant impact on others internal and external to the section?	2
4.	Autonomy	do you have freedom, independence, and discretion in determining how to do your job?	4
5.	Feedback	are you provided with clear and direct information about job outcomes and performance?	1

QUESTIONS

1. Why are the coordination and communication problems within the branch felt more acutely in the Systems and Planning section, than in Production?
2. Evaluate the motivational state of Karl Darmody and specify how the bureaucratic structure and the style of leadership influenced it.
3. What changes in the department generally, and in the Systems and Planning section specifically, would improve the latter's operation and benefit the productivity of its employees?

Expansion at Dimitri's Baked Goods Inc.

BACKGROUND

Dimitri's Baked Goods is a Windsor-based bakery specializing in Macedonian pastries, "zelnik" and "vielnik," sweet and regular bread, and traditional Christmas and Easter cakes. The company employs four sales representatives, two secretaries, and a production staff that varies between 24 and 32 people. The firm also employs a small sales staff of three at its only retail outlet. The pastry, bread, and cakes are distributed all over Ontario and Western Canada. Distribution channels in Eastern Canada are in the process of being established.

Dimitri Leakos started this business in a small shop over 30 years ago. Leakos was not self-employed when he first settled in Canada from the Macedonian region of Greece. Macedonians are proud of their heritage although they are not well-recognized as a distinct ethnic group. The Canadian census did not even list Macedonians or the Macedonian language until 1981. This neglect is the result of the fact that historic Macedonia falls today within three Balkan countries: Bulgaria, Greece, and Yugoslavia. Throughout its recent history, Macedonia has been subjected to external and sometimes divisive control. The first significant immigration to Canada probably came as a result of uprisings against the Ottoman Empire in the early years of the 20th century. Both world wars led to further waves of immigration. Most Macedonians live in the Toronto-Hamilton area, but a group from one Macedonian village settled in Windsor.

It was important to Leakos that he became established in a Macedonian community, and Windsor provided that for him. At first he was an employee in a bakery owned by others in order to learn the business and to learn to read and write English. But he always had the need to control his own environment and was motivated more by this need than by any ideas of greater wealth.

Dimitri's Baked Goods began as a small bakery near the tunnel to Detroit. It was close to the downtown area of Windsor and in the heart of the local Macedonian area. He still maintains this original location as a retail sales outlet, although he has had to move his production and distribution to a suburban area where larger quarters were available. Leakos expanded his business to a 3,000 square metre facility on Dougall Avenue.

Dimitri's growth was based on two factors. The first was the growing demand from the Macedonian community for commercially produced versions of ethnic food which were originally produced at home. While many first generation Macedonians still do their own baking, the next generation is more inclined to buy it. The second factor was his success in broadening his market beyond its original Macedonian base. This is by far the most important cause of his growth. His enthusiastic marketing to non-Macedonians has been enormously successful.

Leakos is the stereotypical workaholic small businessperson. He is the owner, plant manager, production manager, sales supervisor, marketing manager, product development supervisor, and also one of the line workers at Dimitri. These duties force him to work between 12 and 17 hours a day, 7 days a week, but he allows himself to take three-week long vacations spread throughout the year. He is a moderate risk taker who does not undertake new ventures without a great deal of research to prove to himself it will be successful. Once he starts a task, he remains committed to it until it is accomplished. He prefers tasks that provide immediate feedback to those with only long-term prospects. For example, when any of his sophisticated machinery breaks down and engineers are flown in from the manufacturers in Europe. he will spend as much time as possible with them in order to learn how to perform the repairs.

STRUCTURE

Decision making is extremely centralized at Dimitri's Baked Goods. Leakos has total control over his business. He has been running it this way for three decades with great success and, until recently, he has seen no reason to change. He feels centralization makes his business more flexible because he can act without delay when problems arise.

The structure at Dimitri's is quite informal. Leakos deals with all of his employees on an individual basis. The production roles in the bakery vary at different times. Workers are not forced to specialize in one skill. Their work might rotate among packaging, shipping, and maintenance. Only the bakers are somewhat specialized, but they too "help to get the goods delivered." The hierarchy is extremely flat and has very little horizontal differentiation. There is a production department, a sales department, two office workers, plus the retail outlet. Leakos handles all the staff functions of personnel, planning, and budgeting. Every employee at Dimitri reports to Leakos. Dimitri has followed this functional structure since the business was first developed.

LEADERSHIP STYLE

Because Leakos is the only supervisor at Dimitri's, his practices have defined the supervisory style. He seems to practise an employee-oriented leadership. He helps his people with personal problems, treats them as equals, and avoids punitive actions. Leakos seldom refuses to compromise nor does he insist things be done his way. His style is unobtrusive, leading by example rather than by threats. Everyone admires his personal effort on the production floor every day. He is more concerned with results than methods.

Leakos's supervisory methods have developed very high employee morale. As a result of this, there are few grievances and a low turnover rate. Many employees have been with the company for 10–15 years. His main problem comes during peak seasons such as Christmas and Easter, when production cannot keep up with demand. At those times, Leakos is forced to hire seasonal staff and many employees have to work overtime and weekends. Then, Leakos becomes more authoritarian and grievances increase. These holiday work schedules conflict with family and social festivities. Because of his excellent personal relationships with his employees, he is able to keep turnover low even though these problems arise.

Motivation is often a problem in assembly line work, and may result in high absenteeism and employee turnover. Leakos uses a strategy of job rotation and job enlargement. This strategy grew naturally from the expansion of the business over the years rather than from any deliberate policy on his part. He has avoided job specialization, only because it was not natural for him to have it. Leakos also understands the need for rewarding desirable behaviour. At Christmas and Easter, when he needs employees to come in on weekends, he rewards them with praise, free coffee and doughnuts, packages of pastry, and legs of lamb to take home to their families. He also has a Christmas bonus program which he uses to reward those who are willing to work overtime. He schedules a one-week vacation period after the peak Christmas and Easter seasons and again during the first week in August. Leakos is fairly generous with pay and benefits. The production employees are paid about twice the legal minimum wage and get time-and-a-half for overtime. They have all statutory holidays off or are paid overtime for working them. There are three weeks of paid vacation. He provides personal time off with pay for family emergencies and illnesses and is also understanding of the needs of his workers to fulfil family duties. Leakos is very generous when his employees have a wedding or Christening in the family.

Almost all of the workers at Dimitri's are from the Macedonian community in Windsor and speak Macedonian. Most of them are housewives earning a second income. They are unskilled and have little formal education. At Dimitri's, employees find themselves in a comfortable environment where they can speak their own language and affiliate with others with similar cultural background and interests. Since the Macedonian community in Windsor is well organized, the employees know each other from outside and see each other on their own time. They all know about upcoming weddings and planned outings to the Boufsko

Cello, the Macedonian community park on Lake Erie. Whenever a new position becomes available, the employees are encouraged to spread the word to others in their circle who might be interested.

EXPANSION PRESSURES

Sales are now escalating so quickly that production facilities are unable to keep up with demand. Leakos has had to delay his plans to expand into the US market even though he knows his products are popular in Detroit. The customs officers at the Windsor/Detroit Tunnel tell him they see his cakes and pastry every day (bought in Windsor and carried over the border). Some of his pastries are served in the Greek restaurants in downtown Detroit. The recent Free Trade Agreement with the US has led him to think that now is the time for a major marketing move into the US.

Another development is that his two children will be graduating this spring, and he hopes that they will join the business on a full-time basis. They have always worked at Dimitri's during vacations and when needed during the busy seasons. His son is graduating with a diploma in business administration from St. Clair College. His daughter is graduating from the dietician program at the University of Windsor. Both of his children have talked about finding work elsewhere, but Leakos believes that if he can come up with the right incentives, he can convince them to join the family business. He particularly thinks that they would be interested in his ideas for expansion. His plan is to get them together this Sunday afternoon to discuss the expansion and their roles in the future of Dimitri's Baked Goods Inc. If all goes well, Leakos can look forward to a very bright future and maybe even think about retirement.

QUESTIONS

1. (a) Draw the existing organization chart for Dimitri's Baked Goods Inc.
   (b) Develop an alternate organizational design complete with job descriptions and reporting relationships for Leakos and his two children. Describe any required changes in the functionally-oriented structure. Since the plan is to expand, include contingency measures to accomodate growth.

2. Major expansion would probably mean that many non-Macedonians would have to be recruited into the plant. Discuss the implications of altering the monocultural work environment.

3. Describe the current employee benefits and discuss whether they need to be formalized.

4. Is the company ready to undertake geographical expansion?

Federal Airlines

Federal Airlines, founded prior to World War II, employed just over 15,000 persons in the early 1990s and operated a large modern fleet of aircraft.

Although the 19th largest airline in the world, the company recently found itself in a highly competitive situation. Routes once monopolized by the company now had several other airlines competing for a market share. However, the company was confident that it could retain and improve its market share as long as it undertook an aggressive $4 billion program to upgrade facilities and equipment over the next 10 years.

One of the programs that management planned to undertake was a new Work Improvement Program (WIP) for employees working at the airport maintenance hanger. A highly respected industrial psychologist, Jack Miller, was hired to help implement the program. During previous contracts with the numerous firms, he had often been able to increase labour productivity and morale and decrease absenteeism and employee turnover. After six months of work with senior management staff and the union, the program was implemented with excellent results.

During Miller's WIP implementation at the airport Maintenance base, other unions carefully watched and weighed the results. They quickly noticed the benefits in terms of employee morale that were surfacing from the program. One union in particular saw an immediate need for his services. The Canadian Airline Employee's Association (CALEA), which represents 3,000 reservation and passenger service agents, was in contract negotiations with the company. One of the concessions won by CALEA was that the next department to implement WIP would be the Reservations department.

Word of the agreement reached by the company and the union spread swiftly throughout the union ranks. The company took advantage of this mood by proclaiming that this program would be the greatest example yet of "the quality

By Anwar Rashid. Copyright © 1991, 1994 by L & S Management Publications.

FIGURE 1 ORGANIZATION CHART OF RESERVATIONS DEPARTMENT OF
FEDERAL AIRLINES DURING WIP IMPLEMENTATION

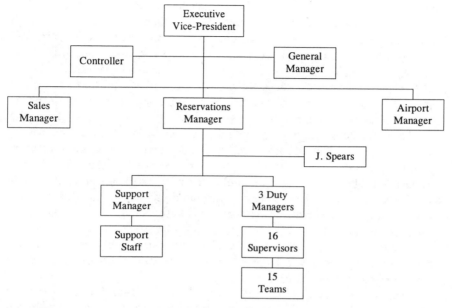

Microscopic View of a Team During Work Improvement Program

Total 20 Agents
- 1 Supervisory Replacement   1 Back-up
- Fare Expert   1 Back-up
- Equipment Export   1 Back-up
- Tours Expert   1 Back-up
- Committee Representative

* Prior to WIP, each team had 20 agents answering the phones.

of work philosophy." The program would strip away the daily drudgery and routine associated with the job. Agents were to become human beings once more and not mindless attachments to computers.

Newspaper reporters and TV crews suddenly appeared on the reservation floor, shooting thousands of feet of film, snapping pictures, and interviewing managers, supervisors, and agents. This wave of interest swept over everyone involved and only reinforced what the company had said and what the agents wanted to feel. However, no one had bothered to ask the question: "How will WIP actually change my daily job?"

THE PROBLEM

The reservations department employed over 300 agents along with 16 supervisors, 3 duty managers, 1 support manager and staff, and the reservations manager.

Results of a behavioural test written earlier in the year by every employee of CALEA indicated that morale was at an extremely low level. The results also indicated that only those individuals working in the Group, Charter and Tour sections of the Reservations department enjoyed their work. This was mainly because the section had little supervision, individuals were able to prioritize their work, no time clock was used, and if an individual wanted to be transferred to the section, he or she had to be recognized as a high potential candidate.

Jack Miller felt that the results indicated that work should start immediately with the reservation teams and that Group, Charter, and Tour should be the last rather than the first section to introduce WIP.

The mandate of the reservations manager was to achieve a Promptness of Service (POS) factor of 80% at the end of a month. This factor would be achieved by answering 80% of all calls within 20 seconds of the first ring. Agents were responsible for keeping plugged-in for calls for at least 80% of their total working day. The average team had 20 agents, with an agent taking approximately 115 calls per shift. Over a period of two months, the Reservations department received over 1.25 million calls.

Miller faced a department with generally low morale, high absenteeism, and poor productivity and in which the POS mandate of 80% was underachieved and performance was stalled at 65%.

The first step taken by the WIP committee (Miller; Elford, a senior training instructor; and Smith, a supervisor with a BA in Philosophy) was to take the job performed by the agent, break it down into its many different aspects, and then organize the agents into teams of "experts." Normally an agent worked with a VDT, answered calls through a headset, booked flights, cars and hotels, and quoted fares. Miller felt that each team should be a self-reliant entity; therefore, each team would have (a) a VDT and headphone expert responsible for answering questions regarding equipment; (b) a tours expert; (c) a rates expert who could sort out the complicated and often confusing tariffs; (d) an individual who would take over the team in the absence of the supervisor; and (e) the right to elect a member to represent the team when new policies and procedures were being studied.

However, once WIP was introduced, problems soon started to be noticed. Teams were carrying WIP one step further by electing backups to the experts. Experts were being pulled out of line for long periods of time to help fellow agents, and if the expert on the team was busy, agents would go to the backup agent and pull that agent out of line. Every expert on the team belonged to a committee which met at least once a month. The Promptness of Service factor dropped dramatically to below 50%. Supervisors had been assigned the role of observers with little authority to eradicate abuses by agents. Prior to WIP it was unusual to see three or four agents standing or walking through the office unless they were on a break. During WIP, it was the exception to see just four agents out of line. Everyone seemed to be standing and talking to each other or walking through the office.

Eight months after the official start of WIP, a corporate directive was sent to CALEA headquarters notifying the union of the termination of the project.

Within weeks, the team experts were once again telephone agents, and supervisors were given carte blanche to discipline any individual not meeting the office standards. New information systems were purchased to compile reservation statistics on every agent as they worked. The system kept track of the number of calls taken, agent in time, agent out of time, fatigue factor, and duration of the average call. This information was accumulated per agent, team, and office for a timeframe of an hour, day, month, and year.

Federal Airlines, or rather its management, intended to make sure that the performance of its agents, supervisors, and managers was once again monitored by computers. It looked as if no vague concepts such as job enrichment, job enlargement, or quality of work life would ever be seriously considered again.

Finally, six months after the termination of WIP, the office Promptness of Service had risen to a satisfactory 83 %

QUESTIONS

1. Identify and discuss the key reasons why WIP was a failure with the Reservations department. Refer to issues in:
   (a) motivation
   (b) status and role
   (c) communication
   (d) informal group behaviour

2. Do you feel that job enrichment is still appropriate for the Reservations department? Give your rationale.

3. What are the general prospects for job enrichment in the Reservations department?

4. If you were executive vice-president of the company, would you continue to keep Miller as a consultant? Answer with particular reference to the role of a consultant in organizational development programs.

The Georgian Rescue Squad

During the mid 1970's a rescue squad emerged in Georgian County. This development was partly in response to a few dramatic highway accidents which featured media stories of victims trapped in vehicles for prolonged periods of time. A multi-vehicle accident on the major divided highway in the county, during a winter storm, resulting in several deaths and provided a particular stimulus.

A secondary stimulus for the squad came from the development by fire equipment manufacturers of rescue tools such as the Jaws of Life which use hydraulic power to open crushed vehicles. This development replaced the previous reliance on acetylene cutting torches, axes, pry bars, etc. which had been the tools of choice.

Georgian County is a large (population 500,000) rural (urban proportion less than 20%) county located north of Toronto. It consists of eight townships, two of them quite large, and a small city. The city does not participate in the county government structure. The county is in the heart of a four season vacation region and straddles the major highway arteries connecting Southern Ontario with Northern Ontario and Western Canada. In the southern parts of the county there are major bedroom communities for Toronto workers. Various studies have estimated that approximately 20% of county breadwinners are daily commuters. The highway traffic in the county is extremely heavy.

Basically the squad was a group of volunteers who maintained a truck loaded with rescue equipment. Most of their time was actually spent training which was done at car wrecking yards. The truck did not have a permanent home and was moved amongst the members on a rotating basis. When called by police, fire, tow trucks, ambulance, witnesses, or others, they would rush to the accident scene to help out. They also monitored emergency radio frequencies. When the need arose, a call would go out to the volunteers to respond. The member with the truck would proceed directly to the accident and the others would arrive when possible. Telephones and radio pagers were used for this call-up. The squad was not paid for the service they rendered nor were the squad members compensated financially, although they were all strongly motivated by the other rewards of the service.

Money was a problem. The trucks and especially the equipment were very expensive. The squad began with one vehicle for the whole county and later added another to provide separate northern and southern squads. Plans were under way for another expansion in the more heavily developed area in the southern part of the county. There were fund raising campaigns at each stage of the expansion. At first the money was raised by private donations from individuals and service clubs. When the equipment bills increased, the squad approached various townships in the county for grants for the purchase of particular pieces of equipment. The squad began presenting itself as a new county service even though its existence had never been approved by the county or any township.

Small townships in the county had little use for the service. Residents simply did not expect much from their municipality and would never expect it to provide a sophisticated service such as this. Two larger townships gained some benefit. They both had major highways running through them and their fire departments were regularly called upon to render what service they could in highway accidents. Supporting the Georgian Rescue Squad was cheaper than equipping their own fire departments and training their staff. Furthermore many of the Rescue Squad members were volunteers in their own fire departments. They had made grants in the past and could be expected to contribute in the future. The city did not participate. Their own fire department was fully equipped for rescue work. Calls for the Georgian Rescue Squad from the city were rare and only initiated by private citizens.

The Georgian Rescue Squad was a media favourite. The aftermath of a highway traffic accident was always a good photo opportunity. The "uncrushing" of a vehicle and the rescue of a victim made good TV coverage. Technical descriptions of the rescue were readily available by the volunteers. Media crews were rarely far behind the Rescue Squad when the call for help went out.

In Georgian County the related emergency services were organized as follows:

1. **Police:** The provincial police patrolled the major highways and policed most townships. The two larger townships and the city had their own police departments.

2. **Fire Fighting:** Each township and the city provided their own fire fighting services. Only the city had a large full-time fire fighting department. The others were part-time "paid" volunteers headed up by a municipal employee who had other duties such as building inspector, etc. A mutual aid agreement existed in Georgian County whereby townships could call on the

fire fighting resources of their neighbours. An annual reckoning balanced out costs and benefits. The hourly rates were high enough to discourage frivolous calls.

3. **Ambulance Service:** Ambulance services were provided by the provincial Ministry of Health and were centralized in Georgian County at the regional hospital in the city.

4. **Tow Trucks:** Emergency towing was under the control of the police and the different forces followed their own policy as to who to call. The Provincial police used a rotating list system to spread out the work. The city police used a selected contractor. The township police called local businesses as available.

5. **Road Maintenance:** Roads were maintained by the province, the townships and the city. The county coordinated road projects.

6. **Medical Services:** All emergency medical services in Georgian County were organized through the hospital in the city. Municipal governments played only a small role in this function.

RE-ORGANIZING THE RESCUE SQUAD

Last January the County council elected its new Warden. Sheila Woodley was well prepared for the job. She was reeve of the smallest township in the county but had managed to impress her county colleagues with her political skills. She had been particularly adept at implementing new programs and services in her township. She viewed the Georgian Rescue Squad with less enthusiasm. The squad was now keen to expand again and was beginning to push forward suggestions that it ought to become a formal service of the county. The head of the squad would dearly love to make it a full-time job and be able to divert his energy from fund raising to rescue work.

Woodley wanted none of it. As far as she was concerned the squad should have a fire fighting function, and should not be a county-wide service. She also had a problem with the image of the squad. Many county politicians shared her view that this group seemed to have developed an inflated opinion of itself. Another politician had applied the old epithet "the bigger the boys, the more expensive the toys" at the last budget request by the squad.

As she saw it, all she had to do was organize the political forces needed to dismantle the "volunteer" county squad, transfer the function and the squad equipment to the townships and leave the county unburdened by this uninvited and unwelcome new service.

QUESTIONS

Conduct a Lewin Force Field analysis of this proposed change.

1. Identify the forces supporting the change, the forces opposing the change, and the currently neutral forces that might be tipped one way or another once the change process has begun.

LEWIN FORCE FIELD ANALYSIS OF THE GEORGIAN RESCUE SQUAD

A Forces supporting a change to the Georgian Rescue Squad.

1. _____
2. _____
3. _____
4. _____
5. _____
6. _____
7. _____
8. _____

B Forces opposing a change to the Georgian Rescue Squad.

1. _____
2. _____
3. _____
4. _____
5. _____
6. _____
7. _____
8. _____

C Forces neutral to a change to the Georgian Rescue Squad but might be tipped once the change process has begun.

1. _____
2. _____
3. _____
4. _____
5. _____
6. _____
7. _____
8. _____

D Strategy for "unfreezing" the status quo to begin the change process.

1. _____
2. _____
3. _____
4. _____
5. _____
6. _____
7. _____
8. _____

Continued…

LEWIN FORCE FIELD ANALYSIS OF THE GEORGIAN RESCUE SQUAD (Continued)

E Change strategy including contingency planning.

1. _____
2. _____
3. _____
4. _____
5. _____
6. _____
7. _____
8. _____

F Strategy for "refreezing" the new status quo at the end of the change process.

1. _____
2. _____
3. _____
4. _____
5. _____
6. _____
7. _____
8. _____

2. Develop a change strategy which is based on strengthening the forces in favour of change, weakening the forces opposing change, and covers the contingencies arising from the tipping of currently neutral forces.

3. Develop a strategy for "unfreezing" the status quo so as to begin the change process.

Greig's Supermarket

This supermarket, located in an urban area, has been in operation for over 25 years. The store employs approximately 150 employees, of whom about 40 percent work on a part-time basis. Employee turnover is quite high, particularly among the part-time workers. Many of these are students who quit because of school graduation pressures.

The hierarchical structure of the organization is quite simple, being of a purely "line" nature. The store manager, who is changed every two or three years, is the pinnacle of authority in the store. Under the store manager is an assistant manager (changed slightly less often, about every 4–5 years), followed by six managers of equal authority: the head cashier, grocery manager, meat manager, produce manager, general merchandise and snack bar manager, and the bakery manager.

The head cashier is responsible for approximately 40 cashiers (20 part-time students working nights and 10 part-time and full-time older women working the day shifts). She is also responsible for two full-time and 10 part-time "packers" who run the parcel pick-up and assist cashiers and patrons at the checkouts.

The organization generally follows the "authoritarian" model, where orders come down from the store manager or the department managers and employees comply without questioning. Socializing is strongly discouraged. Few suggestions, if any, to improve the operation are made by employees, mainly because there are no rewards offered in return.

For some time, there have been rumours among the cashiers that the store was going to switch over to computerized cash registers that automatically updated inventories. Suddenly, near the end of August, employees were formally informed of the imminent change. Cashiers were approached individually by the head cashier, and told that a schedule for training on the new cash registers was being set up. The training would take place at another Greig's store some miles away.

By Anwar Rashid. Copyright © 1991, 1994 by L & S Management Publications.

Each cashier was required to attend training at this store for a period of 16 hours, spread over four sessions, each of four hours. The cashiers would be paid their regular hourly wages for the time spent in training. However, no transportation would be provided or paid for, nor would the time spent in travel to and from the training site (well over half an hour in each direction) be compensated for by the company.

One week after the training of all the cashiers was completed, the new cash registers were installed. This was accomplished outside of store hours in only one weekend. As of the following Monday morning, all cashiers were required to operate the new registers in actual, real transactions. No further training was allowed for anyone. The complete change-over, including training and installation, took place in a period of only three to four weeks.

Fourteen new registers were installed. All were hooked up to a main computer located in the office that overlooked the store. Cashiers would ring in groceries using a coding system that would identify the various products (e.g., a cashier punches in #728, and the register tape shows one bag, 2% milk, and the price). Initially, a set of 300 codes was put into use through this system. One year later, however, the old codes were abandoned and a new set, consisting of over 700 codes, was implemented. This set is still in use today.

A booklet containing all the codes and the procedure for ringing in transactions is attached to each register. However, it is impossible for a cashier to maintain any type of speed and efficiency without memorizing approximately 80% of the codes. Also, the design of the new, accompanying checkout counter is such that the cashier is now required to ring groceries in with one hand while simultaneously packing the groceries with the other. Previously, this was a two-step process, whereby the cashier rang groceries in first before packing the bags with both hands. The old method also provided for the assistance of a packer who packed the groceries into bags while the cashier rang the items in. The new system was specifically designed to eliminate this assistance.

The new registers were also capable of recording the level of performance achieved by each operator. Several aspects of individual performance, in fact, were analyzed and recorded by management, and a comparison of cashiers constantly took place. This had not been possible before the introduction of the new registers. Supervision, then, became much stricter. Standards of performance were arbitrarily set by management (employees were given no say in the matter) and feedback was provided to individual cashiers. While direct threats were not imposed, employees were urged to "try harder."

Curiosity and excitement were the first reactions to the rumours of the impending change. However, when faced with the actuality of training and adjustment, the cashiers were in general both fearful and angry. They resented the fact that the training schedule had been arranged without first consulting them. They also resented the fact that the training took place at only one strange and very distant location which had to be reached by their own means. The older women resented being trained by strangers who were younger than themselves.

In addition, some cashiers felt that the training time was insufficient, whereas others complained it was too long and repetitive.

Once the system was implemented, the cashiers were eager to receive feedback on their performances, both individual and relative to the others. The assessment of performance revealed that the older cashiers who worked the day shift performed at a much lower rate than did the younger cashiers. Many of former groups had been employed at the store for over 10 years, and it was generally felt that, due to their resentment at being required to change after such a long period of time, they intentionally kept their speed down. They appeared to be very set in their ways and determined to hold things up. They spoke of being confused about the necessity of the change and voiced annoyance at having to memorize all the new codes and procedures.

The younger cashiers, on the other hand, seemed to enjoy the challenge and often spoke of the new registers initially as being similar to computer games.

All the cashiers felt, however, that they could not pack the bags as well with only one hand as they used to do with two. It was harder to grasp and manipulate products and more difficult to arrange things so that more goods would fit into one bag and fit snugly. They also missed the opportunity of socializing with the packers. This form of socialization was considered very important to many cashiers, who claimed it helped to reduce the boredom often experienced on the job.

As the new registers led to increased efficiency and time saving, both the cashiers and the packers (who were now given odd jobs) feared both reduced hours of work and layoffs. As it turned out, their fears, at least in part, were justified. The hours per cashier and packer were reduced by 15 to 20 percent, and, for a few months, former packers who quit were not replaced.

QUESTIONS

1. Why did each group (experienced cashiers and younger students) react to the introduction of the new equipment in the way they did? Answer from the point of view of (a) motivation, (b) communication, (c) leadership, and (d) quality of work life issues.

2. Identify ways in which this organizational change was badly designed and implemented.

3. Suggest how this change could have been brought about with better results and a greater degree of employee satisfaction.

Harassment in the Ministry

Rebecca Cheung, a female supervisor of a team of cleaners with a federal ministry, was sexually harassed by her foreman, Alphonse Legault, on several occasions. There were numerous conversations of a sexual nature and several physical encounters including attempted sexual intercourse. All of these incidents, except the last, took place while Rebecca was on probation for her job. Rebecca testified that she was afraid and intimidated. She continually told Alphonse to stop and that his advances were unwelcome.

Alphonse made comments to Rebecca such as "If you don't have my support you'll fall flat on your face" and "I am your boss and I'll charge you with disobedience." He used this authority to persuade her to agree to acts to which she would not otherwise have agreed.

The Canadian Human Rights Tribunal that first heard the case identified three characteristics of sexual harassment:

- the encounters must be unsolicited by the complainant, unwelcome to the complainant and expressly or implicitly known by the respondent to be unwelcome;
- the conduct must either continue despite the complainant's protests or, if the conduct stops, the complainant's protests must have led to negative employment consequences; and
- the complainant's cooperation must be due to employment-related threats or promises.

The Ministry was held responsible for Alphonse's acts. When it appealed, the Supreme Court of Canada stated in its decision that an employer has a responsibility to provide a work environment free of harassment. It added that "only an employer can remedy undesirable effects (of discrimination); only an employer can provide the most important remedy — a healthy work environment." Holding employers responsible for all acts of their employees that are "in some way related or associated with employment" places "responsibility for an organization on those who control it and are in a position to take effective remedial action to remove undesirable conditions."

Rebecca and the Ministry agreed to an "out of court" settlement. However, the settlement did not make any provision for an apology to Rebecca from the Ministry, or any compensation for hurt feelings. A review tribunal found that the remedies provided for in the Canadian Human Rights Act were designed for two purposes — to compensate for private, personal harm, and to serve the public interest by acting as a deterrent to future harassers and/or as a means of education. Compensation for pain and suffering and an apology are in the public interest. Since they were not provided for in the settlement, the review tribunal ordered that they be provided in addition. The Ministry was therefore ordered to pay Rebecca $5,000 for pain and suffering, the maximum amount available for this purpose under the Act. The Ministry was also ordered to formally apologize and post the written apology in all its facilities.

QUESTIONS

1. Comment on the appropriateness of the 3 identified characteristics of sexual harassment.
2. Describe other characteristics which might generally define sexual harassment.
3. Is it appropriate that an employer be held responsible for all employment-related acts of its people?
4. Were the penalties imposed sufficient? Would you prescribe different penalties?

The Hiring Process

There was a requirement to fill a vacant Clerical/Financial Services Officer position with a federal government department in Ottawa. Jennifer Logan-Smith, an executive-level manager, requested the advisory services of a Staffing Officer from the Personnel Department to assist her in filling this position. It had historically been staffed by open competition.

In accordance with Federal Government regulations, the Public Service Commission referred the candidates for the competition and the Staffing Officer sent the candidates' resumes to Logan-Smith. She in turn was required to convene a Screening Board. However, despite the requirement for a board, Logan Smith, with one other Board member, proceeded to interview only three of the seven candidates. They assessed the third candidate, a Mr. John Groats, as entirely suitable for the position, told him that he had been successful, and informed the Staffing Officer of their decision. The remaining four candidates were not contacted and were not interviewed. Mr. Groats commenced his new position two days later.

The Staffing Officer advised Logan-Smith that the Public Service Employment Act had been contravened in that all seven candidates should have been assessed to determine that the successful candidate was in fact, the most qualified person. Logan-Smith thanked the Staffing Officer for his advice but insisted that "the Board was completely satisfied with its decision and intended to validate the appointment of Mr. Groats, and that should other vacancies occur, which regularly happened, the other candidates would then be assessed." She added that her supervisors supported the Board's decision, and insisted that the Staffing Officer complete the necessary paperwork confirming Groats' appointment as soon as possible.

This response troubled the Staffing Officer. His advice had been ignored and the fundamental "raisons d'etre" of a validated and reliable staffing system had been called into question. Although the Staffing Officer's involvement with the Screening Board was of an advisory nature, he also held, by delegation, the ultimate authority to make the staffing appointment on behalf of the Federal Government, in accordance with the Public Service Employment Act and its regulations, selection standards and orders.

The Staffing Officer felt uneasy about signing the appointment documents, knowing that the screening process was flawed and that any subsequent audit or review of this process would impact negatively on his reputation. On the other hand, it is his duty to assist Logan-Smith to achieve her staffing objectives and to ensure client satisfaction with the staffing outcome. Significantly, his supervisor encourages actions that lead to client satisfaction. That approach is preferred to the more procedurally controlled approach to staffing.

QUESTIONS

1. What issues in personnel selection are involved in this case?
2. Could proper procedures as well as Jennifer Logan-Smith's preferences be satisfied? If so, how?
3. As the Staffing Officer in this case, what action(s) would you take? Explain why.

The Honourable Head-Hunter

PART I

Bob Marshall finally knew it was wrong when George Baker bluntly told him, "Don't send me any black applicants." That forthright statement by his client rang the bell. The problem was what should he do about it?

Bob worked as a head-hunter for the Adanac Employment agency in the City of Winnipeg. He had been on the job for about a year. Before that he had worked in sales. But as the economy grew sluggish, he found it opportune to move into this new kind of sales career. For reasons he was only now understanding it was a growth industry when the rest of the economy was weakening.

The business was fairly straight forward. A local business would hire Adanac to refer candidates to them for jobs they had open. Small and medium sized businesses found this to be easier than maintaining their own personnel departments. The client would send over a job description with a list of the qualifications they were looking for. The head-hunter would look through Adanac's pool of applicants to find suitable matches and arrange interviews. A fair amount of time was spent with these job applicants, making sure the information about them was complete, accurate, and up to date.

Adanac earned a fee when a client selected one of its candidates. The head-hunter earned a commission on the same basis as if the match had been a sale. When Bob first joined Adanac he was assured it was a sales job like any other, "Just give the employer what he wants." Bob learned it was a different sales job in one important way...the money could be terrific. To a guy such as him, who was accustomed to the hustle of the sales world, it was like putting a fox in charge of the chicken coop. None of the other head-hunters at Adanac had a sales background. Mostly they had been office workers or in a few cases blue collar people. He quickly realized that he could climb to the top and that could mean salary and commission approaching $100,000 per year.

The problem was "giving the employer what he wants." As long as he stuck to the application form and the job qualifications it seemed easy enough. The reality was different. He would send over a perfect match only to have him or her rejected. Naturally Bob would follow up, eager to close the sale and wanting to know how to improve his product. The employer would just say, "The applicant had a bad attitude." When he would ask for particulars, none would be forthcoming.

Another common response from the employers when rejecting an applicant would be that, "The chemistry wasn't just right." "Chemistry" seemed to be as obscure a concept as "attitude." He asked one of the other consultants about this and one of them suggested that he was not looking at the right aspect of attitude or chemistry. Maybe he had better look at the offices of the clients and see if his candidates would fit in ethnically or racially. Bob checked it out. He made certain that the next candidate he forwarded to the employer was a suitably white anglosaxon even though her formal qualifications for the job were actually a poor fit.

She got the job. In a post hiring interview with the employer he was advised that the job as a receptionist was highly visible and looks mattered more than anything else.

Bob realized that to find the person the client wants including the right attitude and chemistry was going to mean a supplementary set of job qualifications. And even more importantly it meant a supplementary set of candidates' qualifications. The problem with both of these tasks was that it was frowned on by the Human Rights Commission. Modern "approved" application forms and job postings are remarkably sterile documents. All they tell you about the job is what skills, knowledge, experience etc. is required. The same with the candidate's resume. It tells what they can do and have done. Neither has a word to offer about "attitude" or "chemistry."

Bob learned to get around this problem by making his own shorthand notes on the forms about these off-the-record attributes and requirements. He even learned there was a sort of office code in use: "Mary" meant Jamaican, a paper clip identified an Oriental, an asterisk marked a handicapped applicant and a reference under working conditions stating that this job was "in public view" meant "Send over white applicants only." One unexpected observation he made was that these "marked" candidates seemed to be exceptionally well qualified. Whenever an employer did not refer to attitude or chemistry, they ended up with a very suitable employee.

The other thing he learned was how to justify all this subterfuge. The head-hunters had their conventional wisdom about the job. "Our business is to find the person the client wants. We get paid to find the right attitude." "If a client wants to discriminate in hiring, that's their look out. Me, I don't hire anyone." "Why should I waste everyone's time sending over a candidate I know isn't going to get the job." "The client doesn't hire me to teach him about the law. If he wants to know the law he'll hire a lawyer."

Over a period of months Bob came to realize that one of the reasons for the growth of the employment agency business even as the economy slowed was that the agencies had taken on a whole new role. They were serving as a route around the Human Rights Act. Employers were very leery of running afoul of the act especially after there had been a recent, high profile and costly settlement against an electronics retailer for overtly discriminating against non-white applicants. Smaller firms were prepared to pay experts to cover for them.

Despite these nagging concerns, Bob managed to convince himself that while what he was doing may not be righteous, at least it was OK. His rationalizations were in place. He knew that if he did not do the job, someone else would. And the money was becoming very wonderful.

George Baker rang the bell good and loud. By bluntly directing Bob to not send any black applicants, he had pushed things over the edge. Up until then his relationship with the employers had maintained the subterfuge of discrete even polite discrimination, if such was possible. The cover was now off and Bob could feel his helpful justifications falling away. If he undertook a direct contract to discriminate against blacks in the hiring process for George Baker then he was Baker's agent and he would clearly be breaking the law. He might even be implicating Adanac and its owner Harvey McGill in the offence since he was following the policy of "meeting their clients needs."

It was late enough on Friday afternoon for him to leave and take the weekend to decide what to do.

QUESTION

Help Bob with his weekend. Summarize the issues and concerns he faces. What are his options? What contingencies exist with the different options? Draw up a plan for him to follow to deal with the conflict he now feels.

PART II

Bob's strategy was simple. If he was going to break the law he was not going to do it alone and without his employer's knowledge and consent. In other words he wanted Harvey McGill on board and backing him all the way. His major concern was being isolated on this problem.

He had every reason to expect Harvey's support with this problem. Harvey had singled him out for praise and recognition several times and was quite interested in his sales skills in filling their clients needs. Their interpersonal relationship was also quite solid. Bob had even been invited to join Harvey and a couple of the old timers for an after work happy hour on a couple of occasions.

He arranged to see Harvey first thing Monday morning. At their meeting Bob laid it all out. If he was going to comply with George Baker's request then Bob expected Harvey to back him up. The back-up would consist of a written statement from Harvey that Anadac expected its head-hunters to comply with all of the clients requests.

Harvey was cagey. It was quickly apparent to Bob that he was not going to get a written directive. Harvey correctly pointed out that such a document would be damning evidence in any case that resulted. Furthermore, Harvey stated, he did not condone any subterfuge carried out by his employees aimed at circumventing the Human Rights Act. He did acknowledge that he was aware that a few isolated liberties were occasionally taken but that these were the exception not the rule.

Bob was stunned by all this. He challenged Harvey's plea of ignorance about the usual office practices and pointed out that Harvey had to be aware of this powerful drive behind the current growth of his business. Bob also pointed out that the whole structure of the business, with head-hunters heavily reliant on commissions to earn a decent living, clearly indicated management support for the practices they were following.

The meeting ended unsatisfactorily. Bob did not get his cover as he had hoped, and he was even more confused than ever by what was going on.

Later that afternoon Harvey stopped by Bob's office and invited him out for a friendly drink. Just the two of them. After they got settled into a quiet corner of a nearby lounge Harvey began by saying that this was just a friendly off-the-record chat. Harvey said he did not want Bob to be confused as a result of their official meeting this morning. He explained that he knew exactly how his business operated, and that he realized the nature of the requests his head-hunters were sometimes called upon to fill. He was aware of the dodges they used to hide their true work. But, he explained, it was important to maintain the formal cover of compliance with the law. That meant learning how to accommodate the George Bakers and their blunt requests. He went on to say that he saw all this as a transitional phase with some remaining old style business people who had not recognized the changing colour of the community and the work force. He commented that eventually everyone would realize that discrimination cut you off from too large of a pool of talent and that nobody would care if your image had a little variety in it. He added that he saw all this current scramble to circumvent the Human Rights Act as a backlash against employment equity programs espoused by governments.

He concluded his remarks by assuring Bob that he greatly valued his work and that Bob would be receiving a memo the next morning informing him that he would receive a raise in his commission rate. Bob felt he had little choice but to thank Harvey for this background information and for the raise. This off-the-record support was better than the deceit of the morning. He now knew exactly where each of them stood.

QUESTION

Exactly where do Bob and Harvey stand? What does Bob do now? Have his concerns been resolved enough to allow him to continue with his job? Do Harvey's rationalizations help smooth things over?

PART III

After mulling things over for the rest of the week, Bob realized that there was some truth in what Harvey had said about the changing nature of the community and about the workforce. He also agreed that this might be the last backlash of a fading majority, not yet ready to welcome the future. He also suspected that Harvey, like his clients, was one step behind the times.

He reviewed his files of applicants to confirm his earlier feeling about how well qualified these "marked" applicants were. His suspicions were correct. In almost any job category if you requested white only or some such restriction you invariably lowered what you could get for the other job related attributes. The pool of well qualified WASPs was getting dry.

He also checked out the employment equity programs and quickly realized the enormous pressure that recruiters for these programs were under. But he saw this as a trend that business would eventually have to follow. New government legislation ensured this trend. A few phone calls confirmed that this was indeed a significant market niche.

His business plan began to take shape. He would help companies meet their employment equity targets. Maybe he could set up a subsidiary to help prepare employment equity plans. There were many possibilities.

Bob decided to cut his association with Adanac and launch his new business with one stroke. He blew the whistle on Adanac and its illegal and unethical practices. He contacted a reporter for a major daily paper which he knew to have a progressive editorial policy and he told all.

The reporter covered the story with additional material from rights groups, a representative of an employment agencies association as well as the usual politicians. The big play was from the Human Rights Commission which announced an immediate investigation.

As a footnote the reporter announced Bob's plan for a new employment service of minority head-hunting.

QUESTION

Evaluate Bob's business plan and develop improvements.

PART IV

Bob's business got off to a roaring good start. He soon had a large pool of very well qualified job applicants. The jobs were a little harder to find but they were coming in. He has had a problem getting government agencies to use his services. They are not accustomed to using a head-hunter.

Bob is now worried that he has acted precipitously. He wonders if the whistle blowing strategy was injudicious. He certainly received a lot of negative feedback to the newspaper story.

Harvey sent him a very brief note. It said, "Nobody, but nobody, likes a Whistle Blower."

QUESTION

Discuss whistle blowing as employee behaviour. What are the ethical and practical considerations involved?

PART V

Six months later, the following story appeared in the same newspaper.

JOB AGENCY SHOWED BIAS, RIGHTS BODY CONCLUDES

The Human Rights Commission has concluded that some staff from Adanac, a metro area employment agency, did comply with employer requests to discriminate when sending them job candidates. But the commission did conclude that Harvey McGill, the owner of the company, did not create, ratify, authorize, sanction or condone a deliberate discriminatory policy. The commission did order the company to draw up a comprehensive employment equity program which the commission will oversee. The program will include better staff training. A commission official stated that this was an extremely stern step for it to take and set a new standard of employment practice.

QUESTION

Evaluate this solution by the Human Rights Commission.

The John Highfield Company

The John Highfield Company is a large department store that has been in existence for many years. The company's main store and head office are located in the downtown area of one of Canada's largest cities, but the company also operates a number of branch stores in the surrounding suburbs as well as in a number of other cities. The particular branch being discussed in this case is located in a suburban area and has been operating successfully for close to 10 years.

The store is divided into 20 different departments headed by three store managers who have joint responsibility for running the entire store. Figure 1 indicates the rough organizational structure of each department. As can be seen, the employees in each department report to their respective superiors in the hierarchy, but they may also receive instructions from any of the higher managerial levels. Consequently they may at times report directly to any one or more of the four higher levels of supervision. The employees have grown accustomed to this system or at least have not expressed much concern about the overlap. The section head reports to the assistant manager as well as to the department manager while the assistant manager reports only to the department manager. It has been established by tradition that the department manager is the only person from each department to report directly to the store managers. Basically, each department operates as a single unit competing with other departments for profitability and budget purposes.

The Furniture and Appliances department of this store had always maintained a good sales record and was generally regarded as a very profitable unit. The employees of this department were recognized as "high performers" and the department came to be regarded as the "ideal" department to work in. Mr. Guthrie, the previous department manager, was an amiable person and an

By Anwar Rashid. Copyright © 1991, 1994 by L & S Management Publications.

FIGURE 1   ORGANIZATION CHART OF BRANCH STORE,
THE JOHN HIGHFIELD COMPANY

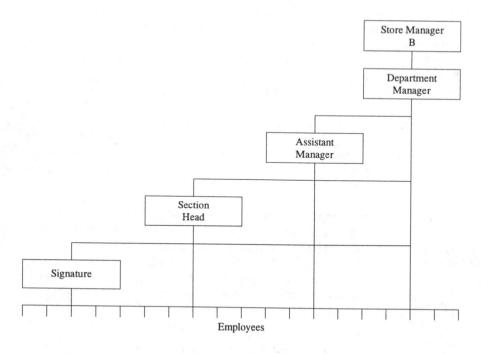

effective boss who was highly respected not only by his own employees but also by the other employees throughout the store. The employees enjoyed working for him and they seemed to derive a great deal of satisfaction from their work. Unfortunately, during the last few months, major changes have taken place in the management of this department. All the existing managers or superiors were either promoted or transferred to other newly established departments, and a whole new set of managerial staff have taken over the vacant positions. Mr. Guthrie was replaced by Mr. Broadbent as the department manager.

Mr. Broadbent is 30 years old. He has been with the company for seven years and has worked himself up from the position of salesman in the hardware department to the department manager of Furniture and Appliances. Before coming to work at John Highfield, Mr. Broadbent was studying for a degree in Psychology, which he did not complete. Originally, it was his ambition to become the personnel manager of this company. However, he relinquished this goal because of his failure to obtain his psychology degree which he believed, rightly or wrongly, was an essential prerequisite for the job.

The Furniture and Appliances department is no longer viewed by the employees as an "ideal" department to work in. They now refer to it as "the prison" with Mr. Broadbent as the "prison guard." In fact, his favourite position seems to resemble that of a prison guard — standing at the far end of the department with his arms folded, watching over his employees. As a result of his extremely close supervision, the employees in the department have become uptight and apprehensive, always wondering whether they are doing the right thing according to his expectations. Furthermore, Mr. Broadbent does not converse with any of his employees, and it is a rare privilege to get a "good morning" or "good night" out of him. If an employee greets him, it is very unlikely that he will get any response. The only persons that he treats in a normal way are the three supervisors below him in the department. However, he seems to be more than willing to "tell them off" if he is not pleased with their work. One of the company's policies is that employees must not talk to the store manager under any circumstances. They may speak if they are spoken to but they must not initiate the communication. If an employee violates this unwritten policy, he is severely reprimanded by his or her department manager.

Mr. Broadbent has an unusual way of running his department. He actually said to a newly hired employee, "Within three months I intend to have you all fully trained so that you people can run this department without any help from me." At the same time, however, he also said to him that he must not do any work without checking with him first. No employee is to do work on his own initiative except serving the customers and tidying the area. Furthermore, if any work is done for any of the other supervisors without Mr. Broadbent's prior approval, then the employee concerned will be penalized. An employee will also be penalized for receiving personal phone calls each day, but he considers that his position entitles him to this privilege.

Lately, the employees have been expressing more and more their dissatisfaction with the present state of affairs. Working simultaneously with the four levels of supervision, an employee may be instructed to perform several different tasks at the same time, each task assigned by a superior who has his own notion regarding the importance of the work he wants to get done. A problem of this nature arose three weeks ago when an employee by the name of Derek Matthews was told to do two different jobs by two different bosses. Mr. Broadbent had asked him to check the arrangement of some merchandise, which had in fact already been done that morning by another employee. However, the assistant manager approached Derek and asked him to do an important stock requisition that had to be sent out right away. This being a priority job, Derek dropped his merchandise-checking work and proceeded to compete the stock requisition. When Mr. Broadbent later saw Derek filling the requisition, he told him that he had no business undertaking the assignment given by the assistant manager when he had already been told to do something else by himself.

Occasionally, although very rarely, Mr. Broadbent will seek an employee's opinion on something related to departmental work. However, the employees have learned not to volunteer any opinion because Mr. Broadbent will criticize the idea from every possible angle simply to prove that he is always right. A general feeling of "worthlessness" now prevails among the employees of this department. They have developed the "couldn't care less" or "who cares" type of an attitude. Mr. Broadbent constantly gives them meaningless or unnecessary tasks just to keep them busy while he watches over them and cuts them down to size whenever a mistake is made. The employees believe that Mr. Broadbent has no feelings for his employees. Since all the other supervisory staff in the department are also relatively new, the employees do not really know how they stand in relation to these new bosses. A couple of weeks ago, Mr. Broadbent yelled at a female employee in front of customers and other employees, causing her to end up in tears in the stock room. The assistant manager went to comfort her and then approached Mr. Broadbent about the incident. Mr. Broadbent laughed it off by saying, "I really can't see why she was so upset. Don't worry, she'll get over it. And she probably won't make the same mistake again."

Another development worth mentioning is the high incidence of employees calling in sick ever since the change-over took place in the management of this department. The total number of persons employed is ten plus four members of the supervisory staff. On an average, three to four people report sick each week as opposed to an average of one every two weeks in the previous set-up under Mr. Guthrie. Several employees have said privately that they don't really care if they show up for work or not. They have neither the desire to help the company nor any sympathy with the department's management staff. In fact, they don't think twice now about calling in sick at the shortest possible notice. Even some of the students employed in the department began to stay home and study rather than go to work there, which shows how bad the situation was. As a result, when employees do show up for work, they generally do not do any more work than the bare minimum. They also tend to take longer breaks and lunches than are allowed. With Mr. Guthrie this was never as problem. Employees went to lunch on time and returned on time. However, it is now becoming a major issue in the department. People leave early and return late. This upsets the whole department's schedule. Because of this problem, Mr. Broadbent recently posted a sign reading "Break and Lunch: 15 minutes and one hour: Return on Time and Leave on Time." In response to this sign, employees now leave even earlier and arrive back even later, giving all manner of excuses when caught.

Unfortunately, many employees who previously enjoyed their job now dread it. One particular employee would really like to keep her job because she enjoys this type of work. However, she cannot tolerate the "prison" any longer. The only solution, other than quitting altogether, is to apply to head office for a transfer to Mr. Guthrie's new department. However, any such transfer would first have to be approved by Mr. Broadbent who has already stated that "if any employee seeks a transfer from this department, he will try to have him or her fired before he grants permission." Therefore, an employee who applies for a transfer really has only the choice of quitting the firm or staying in the same department with Mr. Broadbent and facing some retaliatory action.

The general employee dissatisfaction within the department and the dislike for Mr. Broadbent are becoming painfully apparent. It is so bad right now that four employees (four of the ten who have been there the longest and know the most about the department and its merchandise) have decided to quit. However, that is not all. They are all going to quit at the same time and plan on doing so the week before Christmas. As a result, the "prison" and Mr. Broadbent would be left high and dry in the busy season. Before they quit, the employees intend to go as a group to the store manager and have a discussion with him about the present circumstances. Although the pay and the discount privileges are good, they are not enough to compensate for the environment in which they work.

QUESTIONS

1. Identify and critically analyze Mr. Broadbent's leadership style.
2. Why have the employees become demotivated?
3. Have the organizational structure and policies contributed to the problem?
4. What should the store manager say when the group of quitting employees arrive for a discussion?

Kerwood General Hospital Case

The Kerwood General Hospital, (known as "The General"), was an 800 bed acute care community hospital in the suburbs of a large urban centre. It had recently opened a medical/retail office mall added to the front of the building.

Near the lobby were a gift shop, a pharmacy, a private lab, and a fast food restaurant, as well as hospital departments. Staff received a ten percent discount at the pharmacy. The newly renovated and decorated cafeteria on the second floor opened onto the atrium area above the lobby.

The quality of the physical plant had not been set aside in pursuit of a balanced budget. The atmosphere was friendly. If patients appeared lost, staff stopped and provided them with directions. It was part of the culture of the hospital and the nature of the staff it attracted.

The Executive Team consisted of Steve Hilman, President; Gail Jones Executive V.P. of two months standing; Lynda Wilson, V.P. of Facilities, Continuing Care and Rehabilitation of two months standing; Martin Corm, V.P. Finance; Jill Howard, V.P. Human Resources and finally Dr. Shirley Meyer, V.P. Medical Affairs.

In February 1992, the Ministry of Health in accordance with its plans to decentralize health care away from expensive, wasteful hospitals and back into the community, announced a budget increase of only one percent for 1992/93 for all hospitals. This would mean a projected budget deficit of nine million dollars for The General. There was a four month period to identify savings in supplies and drugs and to reduce jobs by 125 full and part time positions to bring the deficit down to zero. The policy of the Board of Directors was a balanced budget.

Adapted by Randy Hoffman from a paper by Cynthia Dudley. Copyright © 1994 by Randy Hoffman.

ORGANIZATIONAL CHART OF KERWOOD GENERAL HOSPITAL

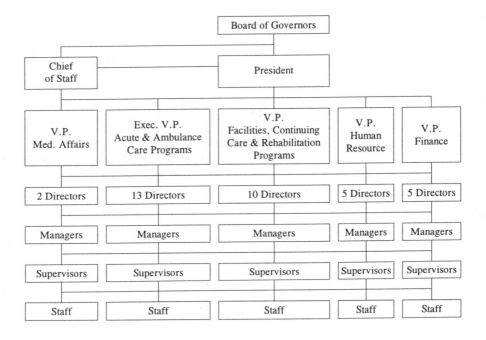

For the previous six months, jobs had been frozen in anticipation of reduced funding. Over the next four months all those already involved with the budget process worked extremely hard. In June of 1992 the Executive knew that the budget deficit could be addressed completely. This balance could be accomplished by: eliminating a vice presidential position; freezing management salaries; closing a nursing unit and dispersing those nurses to other units (not without nurses in the receiving unit complaining to the administration that the transferred nurses were less qualified than necessary); reducing part time and casual nursing hours (not without a letter to the press and the President objecting that several of them had many years service and cuts should take tenure into account); reducing the number of nurse managers and nurse coordinators, (not without noticeable stress on the nursing Directors and the remaining Nurse Managers); employing attrition, early retirement, and anticipating renegotiations downward of previous wage settlements with the unions to reduce (but not eliminate) the number of full and part time staff to be laid off.

President Steve Hilman, kept the staff well informed through meetings with the Board, the Executive, the unions, the management, and through the use of the "President's Update" information sessions for general staff. In the Kerwood weekly newsletter, he provided words of appreciation of staff efforts, encouragement in the process of downsizing, and a touch of humour. He described the direction of the Ministry for the future. Although it meant funding cuts for the hospital, he portrayed the future in a positive light. He set high expectations for everyone in the organization to re-examine their departmental functions. When he talked about cutting out waste in departments, he spoke in the same breath of increased quality of service to patients. Hilman created high expectations for his Executive team, and patient care was the bottom line. These measures would help them prepare proactively for the future. They knew well that their institution was a step ahead of the other area hospitals.

At the end of the budget process, staff were much relieved that their jobs were secure for the moment, even though Steve Hilman had warned them that the Ministry had just begun their budget cuts, and that the next year would likely be similar. A degree of guarded optimism among staff and trust from the unions was accomplished.

Gail Jones had been promoted to Executive Vice President Acute and Ambulatory Care Programmes, as the previous incumbent had left two months previously to become President at another facility. With Gail's title came five departments to add to her previous responsibilities for a total of thirteen departments, as another V.P. would not be hired. After her promotion, she was controlling almost half of the hospital's one hundred million dollar budget. She had a good rapport with the President, but there was a certain reserve with the rest of the executive team. Because of her schedule, booking a meeting with her was more difficult than meeting with the President.

Lynda Wilson had been promoted from Director of Marketing and Strategic Planning to Vice President, Facilities, Continuing Care, and Rehabilitation. She was now responsible for eleven departments, one of which was Protection (Security and Parking) and Communications. Lynda, like the other vice presidents, held monthly divisional meetings with directors. She had good rapport with the President and Executive Team and was considered a team player.

A "hot" issue arose for Lynda Wilson with the completion of negotiations for an automated parking system that could be installed within six weeks. It would operate using a ticket issued by machine at the gate which would be paid for at another machine in the building on exit. The ticket would be stamped as paid allowing exit from the lot. Staff and physicians would continue to use their identity cards for entry and exit at the gate. (Payment was deducted from payroll for staff and physicians paid by cheque). The automated system would save the hospital half a million dollars in the 1992/93 budget. Unfortunately, the price tag included the layoffs of twelve security/parking guards who staffed the kiosks. This was necessary to accommodate the capital expenditure for the system and to complete the current budget cuts to eliminate the deficit.

The automated parking system was to be installed by June 1st. As of June 8th, Wilson had given the matter a great deal of thought. She had reservations about the possible negative impact of the parking system on the culture of the organization. Anything automated brought negative reactions from people.

The President wanted the budget position improved, but at the same time he was worried about the negative effects on staff, physicians, and patient relations that the automated system could have. He wanted Lynda to present arguments at the weekly Executive Committee meeting and come up with a quick solution.

Gail Jones would certainly have input from the nursing side of things. Morale was not great in her area, and the threat of an attack on nursing staff in the parking lot late at night with no security present was a real concern. The lots would be observed with video cameras monitored by security staff in the building.

The V.P., Finance said that Kerwood would not have a balanced budget if the system were not introduced immediately. He also understood some of the repercussions, but those did not contribute to figures in the budget. If it were up to Martin Lam, he would go ahead with the new system and deal with staff unrest later.

The V.P. of Human Resources, had worked four very long months with two committees to identify and reduce the jobs which afforded a balanced budget resulting in only five layoffs of permanent staff. He was not happy about any disturbance of the delicate balance in the organizational culture at the moment, particularly with the unions. He was thinking of the future, and the impact that distrust could have on union negotiations as well as staff motivation.

Dr. Shirley Meyer remembered the sensitivity of physicians to any parking fee increase. If a physician were delayed at the guard rail of a kiosk due to mechanical failure of the automated system, it could have patient care impact, as well as costs for gate replacement should the physician drive through it. Parking had always been a sore spot at the hospital. There was always much discussion before Board approval of fee increases was given, and the public regularly complained directly to Board members about the costs.

The automated system would save money and remove any possible human difficulty or error such as scheduling of personnel, absenteeism, negative attitude with the public, errors in collecting parking fees, and theft. The video cameras installed to monitor the lots would allow one person to monitor all parking lots and grounds from a central (interior) location.

The Executive Team would have to work together to come up with a solution at the next meeting. Lynda made certain they were informed of all the issues. It was a matter that the Administrative Manual of policies and procedures could not help them to address.

Lynda wanted the new parking system approved. It was an initiative from her division that would save five hundred thousand dollars in this year's budget. It would communicate her leadership and gain respect from her division, and would help to cement an informal communication link with the Martin Lam V.P. of Finance, due to her assistance in maintaining the budget. It would likely cause a conflict in relations with the nursing side, some of whom report to her in the Continuing Care area. Certainly Gail Jones would not wish this option to go through because of threats to the nurses' safety. She also wondered how the Ministry of Health of an NDP provincial government would view the loss of twelve jobs, should a laid off security/parking guard contact them.

The Human Resources division would certainly be disappointed that their monumental efforts over four months to save jobs succeeded, only to have the

Executive Team ignore their attempts to save jobs and maintain motivation by going ahead with the layoff of twelve people in six weeks.

The union of the security/parking guards would certainly raise an alarm — especially in view of the number of hospitals in the city with similar jobs at stake. Pickets outside the hospital would be likely, unless the union saw that the move was absolutely justified, or that the staff would be retained in another capacity.

Alternatives for Lynda Wilson to suggest include:

1. Go ahead with the installation of the automated parking system and lay off the twelve parking guards to reduce the deficit to zero.
2. Delay the installation of the system for a few months until there would be time to properly prepare a plan of action that would limit the negative effects of the layoffs of twelve people.
3. Proceed with the six week process of installation, while at the same time preparing the union and the staff to accept management's decision. Then, lay off only nine parking guards. Retain two security guards for a one year contract to staff one kiosk on a rotating basis to allow time for the automated system to be installed and iron out any "bugs". The third guard would be the symbol of management's sincerity in their attempt to limit layoffs. He or she would take part in a new job initiative. This employee would have a one year contract to inspect, identify and make recommendations on the security of each department in the building. He or she would report to the Manger of Security. The cost of the three employees would be approximately one hundred thousand dollars for one year.

QUESTIONS

1. Option 3 is a compromise that would make no one completely happy. What are its benefits and drawbacks?
2. Which option would you choose and why?
3. How would you present your selected option to the board?
4. Design a process of change to implement your selected option.

The Limerick Arena Association

BACKGROUND

The Limerick Arena Association (LAA) was incorporated in 1954 as a non-profit organization. Founded by a group of Limerick citizens, the initial purpose was to provide artificial ice in a natural ice arena which had been built in 1923.

Limerick is one of a series of communities on the outskirts of Metropolitan Toronto which have been affected by massive population growth. Originally a small farming community, it has quickly grown from a village during WWII to a town and now to a city approaching 200,000 people. This rapid growth has been both a boon and a bane to the original residents. Many have been able to ride with the change and even profit from it, while others have resisted what they see as the destruction of their way of life.

One of the changes that Limerick has resisted is the way it organizes its municipal administration. The responsibility for the LAA's operations is entrusted to a five member Board of Directors who are elected from the membership. The membership is anyone who wants to join but is automatic with user groups. In 1975, at the request of the Limerick Council, the board increased to seven with two appointees from council. All members of the board are volunteers. Limerick remains one of only two municipalities in Ontario in which the arenas are not run by the Parks and Recreation Department of the local municipal council. In Limerick the arenas are built by the council using the money collected for that purpose from the lot levies in the new construction. The administration of the arenas is then turned over to the LAA.

In 1971, the first administrator was appointed to handle all business affairs on a full-time basis. Since then, the organization has gradually developed into

Copyright © 1991, 1994 by Fred Ruemper. Based on original research gathered by Pat Thompson.

what it is today (see Figure 1 for organization charts). The LAA now manages eight arenas which range in size from small single-sheet neighbourhood facilities with almost no amenities to a large arena with seating for 8,000 spectators which is home to both a Junior A hockey team and a college hockey team. This large facility has a complete lounge and restaurant as part of its package and has a second ice surface which is suitable for practices.

The association is charged with the responsibility of operating the arenas in a businesslike manner. It provides ice time to local organized groups at rates which are competitive with those prevailing elsewhere in the general area. The local groups have first priority for available arena time. This is done while operating economically. Over 75% of the operating funds come from user-group rental fees and revenues generated from concessions. This contrasts with a provincial average subsidy for arenas of about 50%. The bottom line is very good.

Outside of the two board appointees from the Limerick City Council, the only contact between the LAA and the city council comes at budget time when the association makes its request for the additional operating funds it requires. The two councillors on the board of the LAA help to smooth this process, but since the LAA is in such good shape, there is usually little problem with their budget.

This structure of a relatively independent body having responsibility for the management of a municipal facility was common in Ontario until midway through this century. The growth of municipal services then began to require more coordination and professional management than was likely to be found on volunteer boards and municipal councils. Gradually there emerged a new form of municipal organization with a city manager or administrator at the top. While elected officials still had dealings with individual department heads, it was all funnelled through the city manager. Councils received one budget proposal, not one from each department. Interdepartmental rivalries were settled "out of court" by the manager rather than in public around the council table.

Councils also liked this new system as it usually meant that they could eliminate what they saw as rival boards and commissions. Local councils are very sensitive about the question of authority since they are the ones who must ultimately collect the taxes (and bear the brunt of the taxpayers anger about the local mill rate). They are particularly resentful if they see a local group which has a call on local funds but is not itself elected. The provincial trend for the last several decades has been to consolidate local responsibility and authority into local councils which are accountable to the electorate at regular intervals.

In Limerick this had not happened with the LAA, and the city manager often wished that he could bring them under his direct control. His problem was that the LAA had been very successful. Last year when he approached the mayor with the idea of merging the LAA into the Parks department the mayor replied, "If it ain't broke, don't fix it."

Things were different now. The city manager had kept a watching brief on the LAA, and he believed he could now show that "it was broke." The LAA board held considerable political clout since they represented the user groups for the arenas. Almost every citizen in the community had some arena connection and

FIGURE 1 ORGANIZATION CHARTS

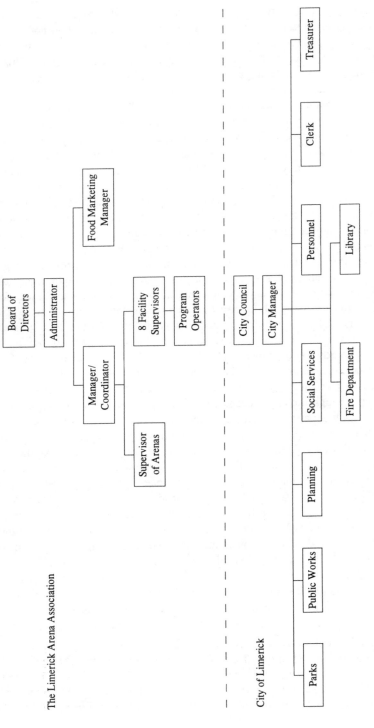

The Limerick Arena Association

City of Limerick

Separate Administrations: Police Commission, Public Utilities Commission and the Arena Association

the hockey leagues had a formidable organization. One of the reasons the mayor would have none of his merger plan was that the mayor had relied heavily on the local sports people to get elected.

The city manager had found some problems with the board. While they were nominally volunteers, he had learned that they were actually quite costly volunteers. Five years ago they had voted themselves a "stipend" of $50 per meeting which was in addition to their meeting expenses of meals and transportation. Since this stipend included meetings of committees of the board as well as the board itself, there was a pattern of double-dipping developing where committee meetings would precede a board meeting. These meetings were in addition to the regular committee meetings and were for the purpose of "checking the report." However, minutes were not available and they usually occurred over dinner in the main restaurant prior to the board meeting. Board members were also reimbursed for expenses when they visited the various facilities to familiarize themselves with issues. Their "perks" also included tickets to arena activities (one board member was known to sell his tickets) and a charge account at the lounge and restaurant at the main arena. Another board member ate lunch there every day and put it on an account that seemed to vanish before it was settled. Next month the board was to attend the annual meeting of the North America Arenas Association. This annual meeting always occurred during the arena season and always took place in a warm environment. This year it was to be in Orlando, Florida. The program was heavily sponsored by the manufacturers of arena equipment. Limerick City Council had guidelines for itself which would preclude such a junket.

The LAA administration was also in a state of turmoil and in the city manager's view it was now quite vulnerable. Last September the original administrator retired and was succeeded by the manager/coordinator. The plan was to gradually have the supervisor of arenas become the manager/coordinator and later on select one of the facility supervisors to become the supervisor of arenas. Unfortunately, and before anyone had become settled into their new positions, the new administrator was tragically diagnosed as having terminal cancer and has since gone on long-term disability. The former administrator has been retained by the board as a consultant for year-end procedures and to train the next administrator. During the interim, a few employees are forced, out of necessity, to perform tasks overlapping those of other positions and some operating problems are emerging.

ASSESSMENT OF THE STAFFING PRACTICES

Selection and promotion based on technical qualifications had been adequately practised. The original administrator was a businessman hired from outside of the organization and took a considerable period of time to attain a thorough knowledge of the operations. He was highly regarded for bringing good business practices to the running of the arenas. He was the last outsider to be hired as a manager. His successor worked his way up from Program Operator and, therefore, had an exceptional knowledge of the operations although his business aptitudes were less desirable. The present manager/coordinator also worked his way up within the organization in a relatively short period of time. While he lacks a keen business sense, his youth, eagerness, and willingness to listen and learn should help him develop into a competent administrator. The current supervisor of arenas similarly worked his way up in a short period of time from temporary status. This was done while he was obtaining a university business degree, and he is currently working on a second.

All employees' actions (i.e., conduct and performance) are monitored and controlled by their immediate supervisors. There is no separate personnel function in the organization. Each supervisor is responsible for recruiting employees to maintain the complement approved by the board. The final appointment is always made by the board and indeed it is one of their most cherished functions. A wise supervisor always informs board members of job openings.

Disciplinary procedures exist and are strictly enforced. In most cases a verbal warning is followed by a written warning. If further measures are required, a two- or three-day suspension without pay is the norm or, in extreme cases, immediate dismissal. The board is the final arbiter. There is no union in the LAA while the rest of the city employees are unionized.

There appears to be a tendency to let favouritism affect better judgment when it comes to granting promotions. Loyalty has always been a characteristic of the LAA, and it would be difficult to judge whether or not their interests could have been better served had not close relationships existed outside the boardroom.

Worker Motivation

Rewards at the LAA are both intrinsic and extrinsic. At all levels, the job provides workers with the challenge and opportunity to serve the public, so that those who enjoy their jobs will feel a sense of accomplishment and pride.

Considering that the LAA is a non-profit organization, monetary rewards are few. Upper level employees may receive cash bonuses from time to time for working considerable amounts of overtime or for saving money in unexpected areas. Operators have, periodically, received bonuses for a job well done during special events such as hockey tournaments, etc.

Recently, a program was introduced in which all employees have the opportunity to rent sections of arena boards for corporate advertising. For each rental an employee gets, they receive a 10% commission for the first year and 5% each year the rental agreement is renewed.

All employees receive praise from their immediate supervisors whenever it is due, and exceptional efforts are often recognized in monthly staff meetings.

Opportunity for promotion is increasing within the LAA since several new facilities are planned for the immediate future. The most prominent opening will be that of Facility Supervisor.

The LAA is more than reasonable when it comes to granting time off. Employees are often given three-day weekends throughout the year, provided they have time owed to them, and in some cases they are allowed an extra week of holidays. The allowances are even more flexible for management with business hours typically ending Fridays at noon in the summer months.

Raises in pay are distributed according to performance and not seniority. Fringe benefits are basically the same for all employees and include discounted or free ice time and discounted or free food.

Many of the LAA's policies lead to an increased effort. Since rewards such as pay are based on performance, an employee is likely to maintain or even increase his level of performance. To do so, he must first maintain or increase the amount of effort he puts into the job. When this happens, everybody benefits — the employees, the employers, and the public.

Communication

Monthly meetings provide feedback which is vital for an organization's effectiveness. These meetings also allow operators to make special requests and to introduce their own ideas through proper channels. Because practically every level within the hierarchy is represented at these meetings, screening is not a problem. Within these meetings, management tries to establish a comfortable environment in which to communicate while actively encouraging input from the operators; both objective and judgmental.

A friendly and trustworthy atmosphere exists separately within the management and the operators. Information is often exchanged informally via the grapevine (a form of horizontal communication) with the majority of people being "links" and very few "dead-enders" or "isolates." Being a widely used and high-profile public utility, outward communication is not a factor within the LAA.

THE CITY MANGER'S POSITION

The City Manager did not favour the current situation but had failed in his first attempt to merge the LAA within his structure. He had attempted it when the first administrator of the LAA retired. Foolishly, he had not organized the politics very well since he thought the LAA would just naturally agree to be folded into the city organization. That error was costly. The LAA was now on guard against his ambitions and would not succumb easily.

He had several reasons for wishing to take over the LAA. The first had to do with the provincial trend of abolishing such independent bodies. Their independence often caused trouble for his office and he would get the blame for their transgressions even if he had little control over their behaviour. Right now there was a problem with pay equity. The board simply refused to conform to the pay equity law. The LAA was a very traditional organization. The jobs were strictly sex segregated, women worked in the restaurant and the other food concessions and men held the other jobs. All women were paid minimum wage and most were part-time workers. Men held the other jobs including all managerial and supervisory positions.

There were also related problems with the allocation of ice time. A newly formed ice hockey league for women was complaining about discrimination. The manager had also received complaints from local families about the lack of open skating periods for families. The LAA Board of Directors included one "lady" from the main figure skating club.

While the workforce at the arenas seemed stable, there had been some rumblings about trouble. The president of the union representing the rest of the city workers had held a private conversation with him to discuss complaints she had received from arena workers and her thoughts about launching a union organizing drive. He prided himself on his ability to work effectively with unions and quite frankly thought they were a useful thing for all concerned. He would much rather deal with one union than a mob of disgruntled employees, besides, most of the complaints were screened out by the union stewards and never reached his desk. Furthermore a union pay scale was higher than a nonunion scale, and when the unionized workers got a good raise, management got at least as much.

He had another reason for wanting the merger: The Director of Parks and Recreation was one of his protegees. He did not like the fact that she only had a part of a department and believed that for career purposes she should have the experience of managing a more complete department. He felt that she could benefit from organizing the merger.

THE CITY MANAGER'S PLAN

This time he had to stay in the background. The main problem was the mayor. He treasured his good working relationship with the mayor and did not wish to ruin it over the LAA. So his strategy had to get the mayor to come on side early in the change process. His watching brief consisted of city hall gossip and a few bits of information from the two city council members on the LAA board. While useful as information, it did not provide a formal basis for action. What he needed was something external to initiate the change process, then he could step in and guide it along.

He decided to precipitate a scandal. The annual audit of the city books would soon be under way, and he could have a quiet word with the auditors about possible financial irregularities to be found in the operation of the LAA. The head of the outside auditing firm was an old school friend, and he knew he could count on his discretion. Once the report came forward, he would be prepared with a plan to save political careers and smooth the merger of the arenas into the City Parks and Recreation department. The LAA would be abolished.

His plan was to establish a merger task force representing all affected and interested parties which was to prepare a merger strategy and re-organization plan to be considered by the Limerick City Council. He would suggest that the mayor call it the Mayor's Task Force on Parks and Recreation in Limerick.

THE TASK FORCE

Chair: The Director of Parks and Recreation. This was a chance to use the skills she had developed in her business program at York University. She recognized the matrix structure of the task force and looked forward to making it work.

Other Members:

Director of Public Works: The Director of Public Works could be counted on to promote the merger. There was little sympathy to be found in that department for the continuation of a separate body.

Deputy Treasurer: The Treasury was involved because of the original financial scandal. They were definitely interested in gaining direct control over arena funds. The separate bank accounts and payroll had always been a sore point with them.

Personnel Director: The Personnel department had been taking all the heat about the pay equity problems and was keen to clean that mess up. The Director also wanted to bring arena employees into line about vacations, work routines, etc. He saw the informal style of the LAA as incompatible with good personnel policy.

President of the Union of City Employees: By including the union at this stage, it would hasten the eventual unionization of the arena workers.

Manager of the Public Utilities Commission: This appointment could be seen as a softening up process for a future merger of the PUC with the city structure. The City Manager thought this was a bit risky, but it would pay the immediate dividend of lending balance to the task force as well as possible future gains.

Librarian: The library had recently gone through a somewhat similar process. They still retained a Library Board but it had little more than an advisory role, and council appointed all of its members. The librarian was treated like a regular department head and was fully integrated into the city hall bureaucracy.

Manager/Coordinator of the LAA: Someone from the existing LAA had to be on the task force, and he was seen as the most palatable. He might see an opportunity for personal promotion in the Parks and Recreation department if he cooperated at this stage.

User Group Representatives: Three non-staff people were added to the task force to give its report political credibility. None were board members, nor had they ever been board members. The groups they represented were: Minor Hockey, Figure Skating, and the new Women's Hockey League.

QUESTIONS

1. In what ways is the LAA well-run? In what ways is it not?
2. What are the issues of power and influence both in the LAA and in the city government with respect to the proposed merger?
3. Discuss the selection of task force members. Does it seem likely that they would be pro merger? Why or why not?
4. How could the arenas be integrated into the Parks and Recreation department? Suggest a revised organizational structure and new roles.
5. Do you favour the merger? Why or why not?

The Limora Community Health Centre and the Limora Hospital

The Limora Community Health Centre (LCHC) is located in Tanzania (Africa) and is part of a 280 bed hospital. LCHC is headquartered in its own building which is located in the Limora Hospital compound.

Limora is a Lutheran church hospital and is one of three Lutheran hospitals in the diocese, all of which are answerable to Bishop Marizin, the Diocesan Bishop. The Director of LCHC is Dr. Jan MacDonald, an expatriate who was born in Scotland and trained there as a family physician. Dr. MacDonald has been living and working at Limora for the past 10 years. He started working at Limora Hospital but after three years was asked to become Director of LCHC and to take complete responsibility for the program. In the years prior to MacDonald becoming director, the community health program had a series of directors, the majority of which stayed for very short periods of time. A number of the former directors did not have any real interest or experience in primary health care and took the position mainly because they were asked to do so. The result was that for several years the community health program was in a state of "organizational drift." Staff turnover at LCHC was extremely high prior to MacDonald becoming director and the Centre continues to have difficulty retaining personnel. Many of the nursing staff at LCHC stay for a short time and then request a transfer to work back at the hospital. One of the former staff members commented:

> "the work at the Centre was interesting, but you always felt that everyone was on a different wavelength. There wasn't any sense that

people were working together as a team. LCHC seems to lack the necessary organizational glue to hold it together.

At the hospital we all share the same values, e.g., good quality patient care. At the Centre there were too many surprises! None of us really knew what we were supposed to be doing. I came out of a hospital environment, and I never really knew what we were supposed to be doing in the Community Health Centre. It was all sort of vague and indefinite. People started out with great enthusiasm but got discouraged quickly and ended up transferring back to work in the hospital or finding a job somewhere else.

There didn't seem to be very much commitment among the staff to the work at the Centre. Maybe this was because we never received an orientation or proper training for the jobs we were supposed to be doing. Several of us who came from the same village were hired, and we were expected to get on with the job.

It took me about three weeks before I began to catch on, but by that time, I had become very discouraged. I had no idea how the various parts of the job were supposed to come together.

I was never told exactly what my job was or what my duties were...everything was pretty vague and unpredictable. The most frustrating part was when we went out to the village to try to organize the local people. It was like "**the blind leading the blind.**" It's no wonder that we had so little success. It became pretty discouraging after a while.

I don't know if I just wasn't the right person for the job or did not receive the proper training. My supervisor gave me a good evaluation after three months, but I don't know why. I didn't feel I was doing a good job, but the supervisor gave everyone a good evaluation. She was very nice, and I don't think she wanted to hurt anyone's feelings or get people mad at her.

The result was that everyone in her unit got exactly the same evaluation, so the evaluation didn't really mean anything. There was one exception.

One staff member who worked extremely hard all the time got the supervisor annoyed with her two weeks before her evaluation. It was a personal thing and really didn't have anything to do with her work, but it counted against her nevertheless. Any confidence I had in the system up to then was destroyed."

There was an ongoing struggle between the hospital and the LCHC for available physical and human resources Land Rovers, which were obtained for the work of the community health unit, would end up being used by the hospital. There were a lot of times when we couldn't go out because our vehicles were being used for hospital business. There was also a fierce competition for the best nurses. The hospital matron wanted to use the best nurses in the hospital, and everyone was afraid of her, so she got the pick of the new graduates out of the Limora nursing school.

There was a lot of conflict between Dr. Taturo, the doctor in charge of the hospital, and Dr. Jan MacDonald, the Director of LCHC, over budgetary matters — LCHC is funded by money from a variety of external funding organizations. All the money goes into the hospital budget from where it is supposed to get reallocated. However, LCHC never knows where it stands financially because the hospital has been unable to provide it with a complete accounting statement on a regular basis. LCHC has tried keeping its own record of expenditures and receivables but some of these are only estimates because some of the invoices go directly to the hospital accounting department as do a lot of the cheques from the granting agencies. The inability of hospital accounting to provide LCHC with a satisfactory break-out of the budget has resulted in a deteriorating relationship between the hospital and LCHC, which is characterized by increasingly poor communication between the two units.

A further problem has developed around Dr. Kiganda, the Associate Director of the hospital, who has been seconded to LCHC for two days per week. Dr. Kiganda is a surgeon who also has a Master's Degree in Primary Health Care (PHC). Dr. Kiganda believed the work of the Centre is extremely important and that it will ultimately reduce the number of patients coming to the hospital for treatment for various recurring illnesses.

Other doctors at the hospital do not share Dr. Kiganda's view and believe that many of the resources going to LCHC would be better utilized by the hospital, including Dr. Kiganda's time. Whenever the hospital is short staffed or there is an emergency, there is a great deal of pressure on Dr. Kiganda to fill in even if he is scheduled to be working at the Centre. There is added pressure for Dr. Kiganda to be available whenever the doctor in charge of the hospital is called away on business. There are many remarks made such as: "Where is Dr. Kiganda? He is supposed to be here in the hospital when we need him, not running around the countryside. He needs to get his priorities straight."

Staff at LCHC say that they do not have the power to take local initiatives without the power of higher authorities, especially the Bishop. The Bishop, for his part, says that staff have the power to take whatever initiatives are required, but they have failed to do so.

Communication within the hospital and between the hospital and the community health centre has become strained, and there appears to be a great deal of unresolved conflict within and between the two organizations. The poor communication and the unresolved conflict are contributing to poor morale and low motivation among employees in the two units with the result that neither unit is operating as effectively or efficiently as it should.

Dr. MacDonald and Dr. Taturo both recognize the need for changes, and the Bishop has invited your group to carry out and OD intervention to assist in bringing about the required changes.

QUESTIONS

1. Identify the various management problems in the Limora Community Health Centre and the Limora Hospital. To what extent are the problems due to structural causes?
2. Suggest possible ways of solving each problem and the root causes.
3. Outline a comprehensive plan for organizational change.
4. Identify the various steps you would take to implement the plan and to monitor progress.

Mason Electric

Professor William R. Mason's original "call" system was simple. It electrically signalled the furnace room when a classroom needed more heat or had too much. Intrigued by the idea but dissatisfied with the device, Professor Mason went on to invent the first all-electric room thermostat. In 1885 he left the teaching profession and founded the Mason Electric Service Company.

The successor, Mason Electric, is a multinational corporation employing over 23,000 people in six divisions. This includes 113 branch offices in Canada and the United States and manufacturing facilities in 29 locations (11 countries) throughout the world.

The Canadian division, Mason Electric (Canada) Ltd., includes 14 branch offices from coast to coast and head office operations (administrative, research, design, and manufacturing) in Toronto. All accounting and personnel functions for Canada are handled by the head office in Toronto without much interference from the corporate head office in the US.

During the years in which the events described in this case took place, the Canadian operation showed increased profits: 17.5% for 1977 over 1976 (Figure 1) and 34.2% for 1978 over 1977 (Figure 2). The companies' forecast for 1979 was for a 20% increase over 1978, but this had yet to materialize (Figure 3).

Employee morale at the branch level is very high and this probably accounts for the continued sales activity. Unlike the "open door" type of atmosphere at the branch, the employee situation at head office seems tense and unsettled. Over the last two years, there has in fact been a steady exodus of employees from head office to the branches and other companies.

During 1978, the corporate head office in the US was alerted to a potential employee problem when two managers (each with over 10 years service) resigned. Further investigation revealed that the overall turnover rate was increasing

FIGURE 1

MASON ELECTRIC (CANADA) LTD.
Profit & Loss Statement
for the 12 Months Ended December 31, 1977
(in thousands of dollars)

	Year-to-Date		
	Actual	**Plan**	**Last Year**
Gross Sales	28,642	29,278	22,616
Cost of Sales	19,826	19,703	15,234
Gross Profit	8,816	9,575	7,382
% to Sales	30.8	32.7	32.6
Selling-Adm. Exp.	6,158	6,319	5,175
Operating Profit	2,658	3,256	2,207
Other Income (expense)	80	80	124
Pre-tax Income	2,738	3,346	2,331
% to Sales	9.6	11.4	10.3

FIGURE 2

MASON ELECTRIC (CANADA) LTD.
Profit & Loss Statement
for the 12 Months Ended December 31, 1978
(in thousands of dollars)

	Year-to-Date		
	Actual	**Plan**	**Last Year**
Gross Sales	32,979	34,164	28,642
Cost of Sales	22,773	23,353	19,793
Gross Profit	10,206	10,611	8,849
% to Sales	30.9	31.1	30.9
Factory Profit Realized	567	659	680
Manufacturing Variances	(471)	(499)	(713)
Gross Profit	10,302	10,771	8,816
% to Sales	31.2	31.5	30.8
Selling-Adm. Exp.	6,964	6,989	6,158
Operating Profit	3,338	3,782	2,658
% to Sales	10.1	11.1	9.3
Other Income (expense)	336	(115)	80
Pre-Tax Income	3,674	3,667	2,738
% to Sales	11.1	10.7	9.6

FIGURE 3

MASON ELECTRIC (CANADA) LTD.
Profit & Loss Statement
for the 10 Months Ended October 31, 1979
(in thousands of dollars)

| | Year-to-Date | | |
	Actual	Plan	Last Year
Gross Sales	21,593	25,755	22,762
Cost of Sales	15,262	17,640	15,881
Gross Profit	6,331	8,115	6,881
% to Sales	29.3	31.5	30.2
Factory Profit Realized	447	560	329
Manufacturing Variances	(306)	(545)	(523)
Gross Profit	6,472	8,130	6,687
% to Sales	30.0	31.6	29.4
Selling-Adm. Exp.	6,217	6,620	5,503
Operating Profit	255	1,510	1,184
% to Sales	1.2	5.9	5.2
Other Income (expense)	206	(180)	386
Pre-Tax Income	461	1,330	1,570
% to Sales	2.1	5.2	6.9

drastically and the profit/loss picture was trending to less satisfactory levels. The corporate heads reacted by appointing a new Canadian president.

The new president was renowned for his successful managerial practices in other areas of the company. Within four months of his appointment, the executive committee had four new faces. Most of these new faces came in the form of successful, former branch managers, whose newly vacated positions were, in turn, filled by the displaced members of the executive committee.

The Toronto head office consists of 155 employees. Of these, 48 are production workers and another 107 are in engineering, design, accounting, etc. (See Figure 4.) There have been 22 terminations and two transfers from the production floor (approx. 45%). From the 107, there were 24 terminations (approx. 22%) and 12 transfers. During 1979, a staggering number of head office employees left for greener pastures.

The chief problem that faced the new top management in mid-1978 was the disorganization caused by employees leaving their positions. In some departments the turnover rate was so high that people never had time to adjust. This was creating problems with the branches, which require quick and accurate product information if they are to remain competitive.

The president realized that it would take time to get to the heart of the turnover problem. Meanwhile he must change the structure of his departments so

FIGURE 4 FORMAL ORGANIZATIONAL CHART OF THE TORONTO HEAD OFFICE OF MASON ELECTRIC (CANADA) LTD.

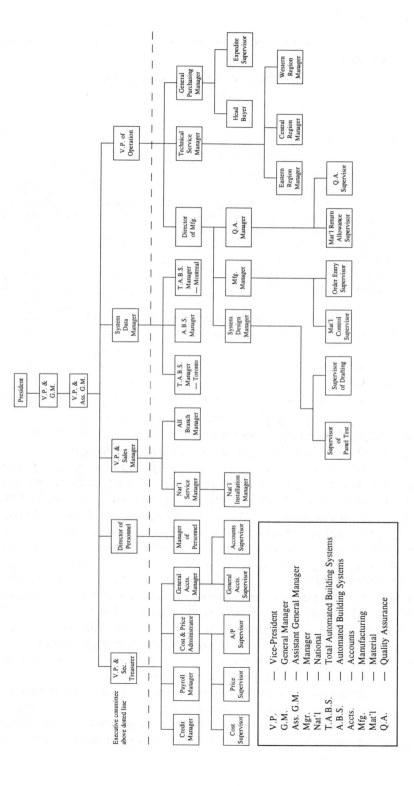

FIGURE 5

Inter-Office Correspondence

DATE	October 19, 1979
SUBJECT	Performance Appraisals
FROM	D.A. Bigler — Toronto
TO	Branch/Department Mangers, Department Heads

Further to my letter of June 4, 1979, we wish to remind you that a copy of performance appraisal form #6101 must be submitted for each employee who is being considered for a salary increase associated with our 1980 general salary review.

These forms are to be received by the Personnel Department by November 1, 1979.

During a recent study concerning exit interviews with terminating employees, it was learned that one of the main dissatisfiers was that the employees were never afforded the opportunity to discuss their performance with their supervisor.

Please do not let this happen to us!

DAB:dm

that, if any department member left the company, his or her job functions could easily be taken over by someone else.

Department heads were then given specific instructions, and they in turn passed down specific task directives to their subordinates. "Standard Practice Instructions" manuals were developed and specific job functions established throughout each department. Now, if someone left, there would at least be detailed standard written instructions of his or her job function within the organization.

This procedure did decrease the disruption caused by the high level of employee turnover, slightly improving the overall efficiency of the departments. However, it also tended to make the employees' roles quite rigid. The program was supposedly a temporary measure to buy some time to tackle the root problem. While the middle managers and supervisors were busy implementing this new approach, top management was busy sending out "feelers."

One step taken by top management in an endeavour to locate the cause of the high rate of employee turnover was to request that all terminating employees fill out a questionnaire. Basically it asked, "What made you dissatisfied with your job?" and "What changes would you recommend?"

At first, the completed questionnaires were not taken seriously because some of the comments written for the latter question were apparently quite facetious. However, a distinct pattern started to emerge from the comments to the former question. (See Figure 5.) The results indicated a communication

FIGURE 6

Employee Self-Evaluation

NAME
JOB TITLE
BRANCH
NO. OF YEARS IN PRESENT POSITION
DATE

1. Do you basically agree with your job title?
2. In what areas are you satisfied with your performance and growth this past year?
3. What do you feel are your strengths?
4. In what areas are you not satisfied with your growth and performance this past year?
5. What do you feel are your weaknesses?
6. What personal goals were achieved this past year?
7. What personal goals were not fulfilled?
8. What are your goals for the year ahead?
9. What are your long range goals?
10. What obstacles do you see which might keep you from achieving your goals?
11. How do you feel your department can become more effective and efficient in the year ahead?
12. Do you know what objectives of your department are for the year ahead?
13. Are you happy in your present position? If not, why?
14. Please describe briefly how you feel the department performed this past year outlining strengths and weaknesses.
15. What are your expectations for the performance of the department for the year ahead?
16. Do you feel you are being adequately trained?
17. Do you have any responsibilities outside the department office which affect or contribute to your position at MEL?
18. Are there any other items you feel need to be discussed at this time?

(Answer questions on separate sheet)

problem with regard to the evaluation of an employee's performance. The upward communication link was suspect. Therefore, policies were considered to establish closer links between subordinates and their supervisors.

These conclusions took many months to form. During this time, the downward communication channel was becoming well established. Job descriptions in the form of specific task directives were flowing downward, along with information on organizational practices and procedures. Rigid instructions became the measure of the day. Meanwhile, the employee exodus continued.

Three programs were developed almost simultaneously by three department heads (accounting, personnel, and manufacturing) to foster upward communication. An employee self-evaluation questionnaire (Figure 6) for use by supervisors and their superiors; a job appraisal form (Figure 7) that a supervisor used to rate an employee's performance; and last but not least, a committee called ICC (Interdepartmental Communication Committee) was formed.

These attempts to institutionalize the feedback had, to the latter part of 1979, failed miserably. The self-evaluation form was to be handed to an employee's immediate supervisor. Many employees, especially those that had not been with the company long, were very intimidated by the questions asked. As a result, they were reluctant to write what they actually felt for fear of recrimination or reprisal. The information collected from this type of census becomes what employees feel their bosses want to hear. There were not too many people who wished to discuss their weaknesses (question 5 of Figure 6) or how they feel their department performed this past year (question 14). The latter question hints at an assessment of the competency of department heads of supervisors.

Another weakness with this evaluation was the insistence on determining the employees' personal goals (nearly one-third of the questions pertain to this). If an employee was planning to quit the company within the next year, the chances were nil that he would have highlighted this as his future goal.

The job appraisal form was a summary of an employee's performance. It placed numbers (one is outstanding and five is unsatisfactory) on a person's performance, and this rating was completed by an employee's immediate supervisor. The supervisor then allowed his subordinate to see the appraisal and sign that he has seen it. This tended to place supervisors in a vulnerable position and, in some cases, has caused outward hostility by an employee toward his supervisor.

The Interdepartmental Communication Committee was established as a back up to the other programs. Its function was to supply verification for the self-evaluation form and to hear the needs of the employees. Unlike the other institutionalized programs (self-evaluation and job-appraisal) the ICC idea could potentially supply a more personalized form of communication with the potential to establish a natural upward flow. The shortcomings of this committee are twofold. First, the committee had as its chairman the payroll manager who answers directly to a member of the executive committee (vice-president and secretary-treasurer). Second, top management has (by November, 1979) yet to interpret the information collected by the ICC in a serious manner. Many managers actually condemn the idea of the committee. They feel they are being talked about and declare that the committee meetings (once a month for two hours) cut into valuable working time.

The committee was to have voluntary membership, with a limit of one representative from each department. Members were not to be appointed by department heads, but picked by their peers to act as representatives. Since the committee was not taken very seriously, it was not seriously supervised by top management. As a result, committee members were appointed by their department

FIGURE 7 · SUMMARY PERFORMANCE APPRAISAL FORM

Employee Name	Social Security No.
Location Name	Location No.
Position Title	Payroll (Check One) ☐ 2 = Weekly ☐ 3 = Monthly ☐ 4 = Part Time
Appraisal Covers Time Period:	From To

☐ **Annual Appraisal** — years in current Job _____

Complete this section if this is an Annual Appraisal (for employees who have completed their probationary period):

Overall Performance

Review the entire performance appraisal and judge the employees' overall performance in current job. Place the appropriate number of the rating in the box to the left.

	Outstanding		High		Competent		Needs Improvement		Unsatisfactory
	1	Far exceeds overall standards for this job	2	Exceeds overall standards for this job	3	Meets overall standards for this job	4	Needs improvement to meet standards for this job	5	Fails to meet standards for this job

Continued…

FIGURE 7 SUMMARY PERFORMANCE APPRAISAL FORM (Continued)

Overall Potential

Judge the employee's capacity and ambition for future advancement, both within the current department or branch and within MEL. Place the appropriate number of the rating in the box to the left.

1	Outstanding candidate for future development. Could be expected to go far
2	Capable of developing beyond current position
3	Has probably reached most suitable level of work
4	Uncertain at this time

☐ **Probationary Appraisal**

Complete this section if this is a Probationary Appraisal (for employees currently in or completing their probationary period including new employees and recent transfers or promotions).

Overall Performance

Review the employee's overall performance since starting work. Judge performance against standards for a trainee. Place the appropriate number of the rating in the box to the left.

1	Performance has been adequate or better than expected for a trainee END PROBATION
2	Performance has been only minimally adequate for a trainee. Certain areas need improvement EXTEND PROBATION
3	Performance has been less than satisfactory TERMINATE or DEMOTE and EXTEND PROBATION

Continued…

FIGURE 7 SUMMARY PERFORMANCE APPRAISAL FORM (Continued)

Complete this section for all employees:

1. What are the employee's major strengths?

2. What areas need improvement? What actions are being taken to rectify the situation?

3. General Remarks: Indicate any comments to further clarify this evaluation.

_____

To the employee — Please sign below to indicate that you have seen this appraisal.

Employee's Signature _____ Date _____

Supervisor's Signature _____ Date _____

Branch Manager's Signature _____ Date _____
(If different than Supervisor)

Regional Manager's Signature _____ Date _____
(If different than Supervisor)

heads. This was the very situation that the committee was trying to avoid (usually the appointee was one in favour with his/her supervisor).

Some departments did, however, choose their representative by the democratic process. In some of those cases, the manager or supervisor was chosen. However, other managers and supervisors tended to shun those elected by their subordinates.

The format of the committee is fairly simple. One week prior to a meeting, departmental representatives submit topics for review (these topics should stem from discussions by employees and the ICC representatives in individual departments). The chairman then publishes an agenda with the topics in a priority ranking. His bias, of course, determines the ranking. Since meetings to date have lasted only two hours, the lower priority items were usually postponed to future meetings. This set up some hostility among certain departmental representatives. The downfall of the committee was becoming more evident with every new meeting. In December 1979, just 16 months after its first meeting, there are only six departments remaining with representation (out of 13). For this reason, there is a lot of destructive criticism regarding the committee's future function.

The chief cause of the committee's downfall began last year when there were rumours within the company that a new benefits package was being considered for 1980. The ICC felt that this would be an excellent opportunity to show how effective it could be. Permission was eventually granted for the committee to carry out an independent survey on certain benefit proposals. The following is a description of the meeting that proposed the survey.

Since all departments were concerned about the benefit package, it obtained a high priority on the upcoming ICC meeting scheduled for May. The idea of the survey was first introduced by a member of the cost accounting department. Her motion was seconded and accepted by a majority (nearly unanimous) vote.

The existing benefits package was discussed and from certain ICC observations, preliminary questions were prepared. This took the form of a questionnaire (Figure 8) that would be handed out with the pay cheques and collected by means of a suggestion box. (The committee actually killed two birds with one stone; the company never had a suggestion box prior to this survey.)

The company's existing benefits included two weeks' vacation for service up to seven years. After seven years' service the employee would receive three weeks; after ten years, four weeks; and after fifteen, six weeks. Medical insurance would be paid for by the company after one year's service, but there was no dental plan. There was a salary continuation program for which each employee paid a weekly amount. Hours of work were 37.5 a week for administration, and 40 for the production group.

The results of the benefits questionnaire were summarized and submitted with recommendations to the personnel director. The majority of workers were not in favour of a shared cost dental plan. About 30% were in favour of a profit sharing plan in the form of an RRSP, based upon the company matching an employee's donation from company profits (if over 20% for the past year). The topic that raised the most concern was the vacation allowance. An overwhelming

FIGURE 8

Employee Survey

The employee is asked to fill out with his benefit in mind, the following questionnaire.

No names are to be given and try to give comments where instructed. It is in your best interest to give accurate and honest answers.

Please print all comments.

Thank you.

1. Are you satisfied with the company's present program?
   ☐ Yes   ☐ No
   Comments:

2. Were you satisfied with your last pay increase?
   ☐ Yes   ☐ No (if no, give reasons)
   Comments:

3. Are you in favour of a dental plan?
   ☐ Yes   ☐ No (if no, give reasons)
   Comments:

4. Are you satisfied with the vacation schedule?
   ☐ Yes   ☐ No (if no, give reasons)
   Comments:

5. Do you understand the profit sharing concept?
   ☐ Yes   ☐ No (if no, please consult your supervisor)

6. Would you be in favour of investing in a profit sharing program (similar to an RRSP) with the company?
   ☐ Yes   ☐ No (if no, give reasons)
   Comments:

7. What is your main complaint with the present benefit program?
   ☐ None   ☐ Other (if other, give explanation)
   Comments:

majority was in favour of three weeks after three years and four weeks after seven. The ICC felt it had contributed effectively to the needs of the majority of employees and hoped that the top brass would treat their recommendations and findings seriously.

The new benefits package was presented to the employees in four groups on four different days. Expectation was high until word got out after the first group had received the presentation. The vacation schedule would remain the same; a dental program would be established providing there was 40% membership; and the company was offering the new profit sharing program.

After the deadlines for enrolment into the different programs had passed, a newsletter was sent out to all employees. There would be no dental plan (only about 28% enrolment) and the profit sharing plan only interested 18% of the employees (down from about 30% when the survey was taken). The disastrous profit sharing plan (the committee feels) was the result of retaliation for the insensitive decisions of top management. The ICC lost most of its integrity that day.

From then on, membership in the committee fell and general morale dropped to an all time low. In fact, the committee was to have only one small victory. For years the company parking lot had not been paved, and in winter many cars would get bogged down in the snow. Two months ago, the lot was paved after an ICC recommendation.

The committee's recommendations for combined break and lunch hours, summer hours (working extra time each day for one Friday off a month), a bowling league, and a social club have been ignored. Proposals to remove names from evaluation forms and to have an outside chairman for the committee have fallen on deaf ears. In fact, most people have come to the conclusion that the committee is a waste of time and soon will be dismantled.

Office personnel are still encouraged to take their breaks and even lunch at their desks. There are three different breaks and lunch periods as well as two starting and quitting times. No socializing between departments is allowed without good reasons, and socialization at lunch (bowling at nearby lanes) is discouraged with punctuality as the main reason.

The ICC was comprised of secretaries, clerks, supervisors, foremen, and a manger. Even with this cross section, they could not influence top management. The most recent proposal was for a reward (in the form of cash bonus) for developments or innovations that benefit the company. Again, the committee was shocked at a refusal based on, "people would be going off on all kinds of tangents."

The "temporary" rigid job descriptions now seem to be here to stay, and they are creating alienation. More and more, there is a race for the door when quitting time comes around, and people are generally doing only what is required to get by. The relationships between roles and employees have become more formalized. As a result, the organization is becoming less dependent on the services of particular individuals. The system, as it now stands, is barely coping with a high turnover and has become only partially successful as a coping mechanism rather than as a preventative check.

At the next ICC meeting on December 7th, the committee will put forward the following suggestions:

1. That every department be represented by a nominated employee.
2. That an outside neutral party be hired to chair the committee and that he or she will report to the president.

3. That the committee meet on a regular basis.
4. That top management take turns (when the need arises) in attending the committee meetings.
5. That management consult the ICC regarding any planned changes in company policy concerning benefits, job descriptions, and working conditions.
6. That employee's identification on self-evaluative or opinion forms become optional or that the forms be eliminated.
7. That employees be encouraged to use the suggestion box through a system in which innovative employees are formally recognized or rewarded.

QUESTIONS

1. (a) What are the problems faced by Mason Electric (Canada) Ltd.?
   (b) What are the root causes of the problems you have identified?
   (c) If these problems and root causes were solved, what would be the **first** indicators of this change?

2. Assess the function of the Interdepartmental Communications Committee, highlighting the factors that are necessary for its success.

3. What levels of management would be most threatened by an effective ICC?

4. Evaluate the policies put into effect to deal with high turnover.

5. Will the suggestions proposed for the December 7th meeting, if adopted, significantly improve the situation at Mason Electric?

6. If you were the president of the company, what would you do?

Metropolitan General Insurance

This case depicts events at an Oshawa, Ontario, branch office of a large international insurance company, Metropolitan General Insurance Co. It is one of the top 15 general insurance companies in Canada with annual premium income of almost $200 million. Although its head office is located in Toronto, the company transacts business through independent insurance agents and brokers right across Canada through 20 branches.

Metropolitan General is committed to a decentralized operating structure with the various branches having autonomy for their daily operations, including types of business written, agents to deal with, selection and utilization of staff, and a full branch operating budget. Head office is used as a resource centre in the financial area (investment planning and control) and also provides technical expertise (e.g., the various product line managers provide guidance and knowledge to the branch staff). The company has out-performed the industry over the past five years in the areas of underwriting profit and premium income growth. Ultimately, this was not the case at the Oshawa branch.

THE OSHAWA BRANCH

This branch employs 30 people, including the branch manager and the various department managers (see Figure 1 for the organization chart). The branch was opened seven years ago to take advantage of the growth opportunities that were developing east of Toronto in the areas of personal insurance and commercial insurance (i.e., fire, liability, and casualty insurance for commercial enterprises).

FIGURE 1   ORGANIZATIONAL CHART OF THE OSHAWA BRANCH OF METROPOLITAN GENERAL INSURANCE

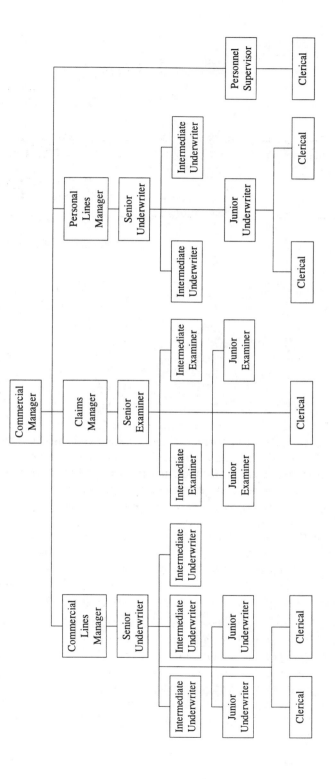

The staff complement of 30 is made up as follows:

1	branch manager
3	department managers
1	personnel supervisor
3	senior underwriters/examiners
7	intermediate underwriters/examiners
5	junior underwriters/examiners
10	clerical staff

The staff are divided into four departments in order to facilitate the overall branch operation. These departments and their staff complements are as follows:

Management/Administration	7 staff
Commercial Lines department	9 staff
Personal Lines department	7 staff
Claims department	7 staff

The various departments operate almost independently of each other. Coordinating them is the responsibility of the branch manager and the personnel supervisor.

The branch transacts business through an independent agency network consisting of 152 brokers located throughout its five territories (running east of Toronto to Kingston, as well as recently acquired territory north of Toronto to Barrie). The branch had premium income at the end of last year of $8.5 million and an underwriting loss (excess of claims paid out over premiums paid in) of $1.1 million. Its projected premium income for this year is $7.6 million, and it hopes to "break even" with respect to underwriting profit/loss.

Following is a brief description of the managers and other key staff members within the Oshawa branch:

Branch Manager — Larry Gelbart   Larry is 43 years old and has been a branch manager for 10 years. He has been with Metropolitan General for over 25 years and has worked his way up through the ranks to the branch manager position. Gelbart was given the job of opening the Oshawa branch. (He had previously been manager of a smaller branch in another province.) The position was awarded on the understanding that significant growth and profit would enable him to progress further up the corporate ladder to the executive level at head office. He is considered to be a close friend of the company president, having worked with him as a department manager. However, he is not well liked by many of the other senior executives in the firm because they consider him "pushy." Branch employees, on the other hand, feel that they hardly know him.

Commercial Lines Manager — Sadie Tompkins   Tompkins is 29 years old and has held this position for approximately one year. Prior to being appointed Commercial Lines Manager in the Oshawa branch, she had been an assistant to one of the head office line managers for two years. There she dealt very effectively with the paper flow, but rarely with people. Tompkins has been with Metropolitan General for almost 8 years and had worked, prior to her most recent appointment, purely in a technical underwriting capacity. Her staff see her as quite demanding — sometimes unreasonable.

Claims Manager — Harry Higman Harry is 55 years old and has been in the insurance business for over 35 years (the last 11 with Metropolitan General). Prior to becoming Claims Manager in Oshawa, Harry had been a senior examiner in a larger branch in Ontario. His appointment to department manager was somewhat of a surprise to the others. He had not previously exhibited any management ambitions. Higman is considered to be technically competent by the line managers he deals with in head office. However, he considers that the head office is interfering in his department whenever they query anything. Problems among his staff make him feel uncomfortable.

Personal Lines Manager — Connie Burns Connie is 27 years old and has held her present position for only two months. She was appointed from within the Oshawa branch to replace an incumbent, Bob Hood, who had been promoted to the position of senior underwriter within the branch. Previously, she had spent one year in the Oshawa branch as a commercial lines underwriter, and five years in other branches in the Personal Lines area. She is well regarded in the head office, particularly for her "people skills." Her appointment as a manager in Oshawa was looked upon very favourably by the rest of the staff.

Personnel Supervisor — Ruth Burkholtz Ruth is 34 years old and has held her present position since the opening of the Oshawa branch, when she was hired by Metropolitan General. She had had no previous experience in personnel but has learned well on the job. She is a close confidant of the branch manager, Larry Gelbart, and he relies upon her input in his decision making. She has tended to be jealously protective of Gelbart. She occasionally restricts input and access to him by other staff, including managers.

Senior Underwriter, Personal Lines — Helen Whiteface Helen is 54 years old and has been with Metropolitan General for 28 years (seven years in her present position with the Oshawa branch and 21 years in a similar position in another branch). She is considered to be very technically sound and she enjoys the confidence of Gelbart who had worked with her previously in another branch. He had specifically requested her for Oshawa. She is seen by some of the junior staff as a benign matriarch. That is a perception that pleases her and she does nothing to discourage it. She views herself as the expert in Personal Lines and the anchor for the department over the past seven years. She is often the focal point of small groups of staff during lunch time and coffee breaks.

Senior Underwriter, Commercial Lines — Bob Hood Bob is 41 years old and has been in the insurance business for 17 years. He was hired by Metropolitan General three years ago to fill his present position in the Oshawa branch. Hood is considered technically expert in his line but is seen as somewhat reluctant to make decisions and often appears disorganized. He had been promoted briefly by Gelbart to Commercial Lines Manager. However, he was quickly and quietly demoted when he encountered problems and complaints from some brokers. Hood has become somewhat resentful of both Gelbart and the company.

THE PROBLEM

The branch has been realizing less premium income for the past five years. The following is a breakdown of annual premium income:

Year 1	$7.6 million
Year 2	$7.2 million
Year 3	$6.3 million
Year 4	$5.1 million
Last year	$8.3 million*

* growth last year is the result of the transfer of the territories north of Toronto to the Oshawa branch. The total volume transferred with these territories was $3.5 million.

The projected volume for the end of this year is $7.5 million including the new territories, and this projection may be difficult to achieve in the currently competitive market.

The staff turnover in the branch has been in excess of 20% each year for the past three years. Recently, one intermediate underwriter and one junior examiner resigned. Another junior underwriter was fired after 16 months in the branch. As well, the recent changes in the Personal Lines manager's position (with the incumbent being demoted to a senior underwriter's position within the branch) has created some resentment among the staff in general.

Productivity levels have dropped significantly, and this has adversely affected the level of service and the attitude of the branch's independent brokers. When Larry Gelbart held a marketing meeting recently for his senior staff, his response to the question of broker alienation was, "They are going to regret treating us this way. If they don't want to do things our way — then to hell with them!"

The quality of underwriting in the branch has also deteriorated, resulting in the acceptance of substandard risks. Because of this, the branch has lost money in each of the past three years. This unprofitability has been of great concern to the corporate head office. Also, in light of the loss in premium income, the viability of maintaining this branch has been under examination.

At a recent meeting of the branch management and senior staff held to discuss branch problems, the following series of exchanges took place.

Larry Gelbart: I know why we keep losing business. The territories we service are the most competitive in Canada and head office won't give us competitive price on our products.

Connie Burns: But our brokers say that we're competitive at least in some products. It's a case of us not providing the service and backup that they need. They tell me that when they phone in for a quotation, the staff doesn't really seem interested in handling their requests.

Helen Whiteface: You haven't been here long enough, dear, to realize that we've done everything we can for these brokers. You can't expect us to work 24 hours a day just to satisfy them! I'm sure that our people are doing their best. And I should know by now.

Larry Gelbart: That's right, we run this branch, not those brokers. If we could give them better service with the staff we have, we would. We sure pay them enough. And didn't we just move you into your job in an effort to improve things, Connie? Anyway, I'm not aware of any one acting like that.

Harry Higman: Besides there's only so much that we can do. We have to satisfy head office all the time, and they're even more difficult to deal with than the brokers. If we try to change too many things, head office will be on our backs again looking for information and asking questions. I say: Let sleeping dogs lie!

Sadie Tompkins: I'd have no problem giving these brokers the service they want, if only I had some time to do some underwriting. Every time I sit down to move some paper my staff keeps interrupting me with their problems! How am I supposed to get anything done in that situation?

Ruth Burkholtz: I know what you mean Sadie, Larry faces the same problem every day. Fortunately I've been able to reduce the interruptions somewhat and this allows him to get on with the work.

Larry Gelbart: I appreciate your efforts, Ruth. The problem for you, Sadie, may be solved if you had someone to run interference for you in your department. Perhaps Bob here could act as your screening mechanism to give you time to get some real work done.

Bob Hood: I could do that if you want. Of course I'd need a little help in determining which items or people should be passed on to Sadie and which items should be dealt with elsewhere. And I assume that this would mean some relief from my more routine work — not just more work added on. You know, the usual policy is to load it all on "Old Bob." Anyway, I could check this out with you later and we can decide something then.

Sadie Tompkins: Fine Bob, then maybe I can give some of these brokers the service that Connie was talking about!

Larry Gelbart: Well, I'm not to sure that we can do much in that area myself; not with the pricing structure head office has saddled us with. However, see what you can do, and let me know. I appreciate that feedback, Connie. But I also think Helen and Harry may be right.

Helen Whiteface: It's just those damn brokers! If they weren't so demanding with their 'I need this quote yesterday' stuff, we could organize our workload and get things done in an orderly way.

Ruth Burkholtz: You can say that again. You should hear the way they talk to me when they have some complaint and are trying to get hold of Larry. It's all I can do to convince them to deal with the right person instead of screaming in Larry's ear.

Larry Gelbart: Maybe I should let you people in on a rumour I've heard — that head office is sending down a 'troubleshooter'. I understand that he's either going to help us turn around the profitability of the branch or maybe even decide to shut us down. I guess there is not a hell of a lot we can do about it except work as best we can. What a situation! Well, I suppose that's all for now...

Connie Burns (looking alarmed):   Wait a minute, people. We can't just do nothing and watch our jobs go down the tube!

Sadie Tompkins: Gee, I didn't know things were that serious. I better start leaning on my staff to work harder.

Harry Higman: Oh, calm down ladies. It's just the usual sort of nonsense handed out by head office to keep us off balance. Right, Larry?

Bob Hood: Yeah, don't worry. We all know who the 'fall guy' is going to be — AGAIN.

QUESTIONS

1. Under the headings of motivation, communication, and leadership discuss the root causes of the performance problem at the Oshawa branch office.
2. To what extent are interpersonal relationships and branch office structure responsible for the branch's problems?
3. In what ways is the branch office "culture" preventing an improvement in performance.
4. What should Connie Burns say next? (The meeting may be continued with the roles being played by participants in the case discussion.)
5. As the 'troubleshooter' from head office, what recommendations would you make to Larry Gelbart if the situation did not improve? What recommendations would you make to head office?

Multi-Bake Corporation

With annual sales exceeding $100 million, Waterloo, Ontario-based Multi-Bake Corporation ranks as a strong competitor in the bakery sector of the Canadian food industry. Its subsidiaries manufacture and market a variety of goods, ranging from frozen foods to specialty bakery products such as Christmas cakes and sweet goods. Recently, the company expanded beyond Ontario and into Québec when it acquired the controlling interest in a number of French-Canadian bakeries. Multi-Bake now has five production plants; three in Kitchener–Waterloo and one each in London and Ottawa. Each of these plants supports numerous sales areas. The company's Ottawa operation was expanded by the addition last year of the B.I.T. Buns Company. This acquisition increased Multi-Bake's share of the Ottawa market but also added to the company's headaches. In addition, the company now has the recently-acquired Québec bakeries.

ORGANIZATIONAL DETAILS

The organization chart shown in Figure 1 sets out for Multi-Bake the top management structure and the reporting relationships in the area of finance and accounting from the accountants up to the president.

About a year and a half ago, John Stone was promoted to the position of Corporate Controller reporting to Don Keyes, the Vice-President of Finance and Information Systems. Stone's background in the auditing field with a large retailer had brought him to Multi-Bake some years ago to fill the position of Manager of Internal Audit, whose incumbent also reported to Don Keyes. John Stone had been able to learn about the various facets of the bakery business through his various auditing activities. His easy-going manner and friendly disposition had also gained him many friends, not only in the sales and marketing groups, but also in the production and distribution areas. In the relatively short time that he had been Controller, John had gained respect from his staff and was well regarded by his

FIGURE 1 ORGANIZATIONAL CHART FOR THE FINANCE AND ACCOUNTING DIVISION OF MULTI-BAKE CORPORATION

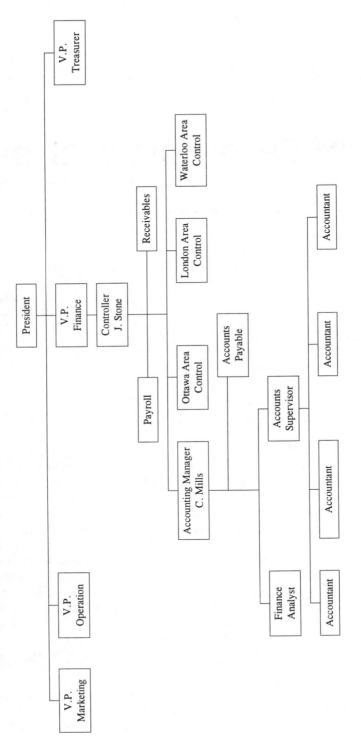

peers. John's political savvy in the organization and his shrewd manoeuvres made him a valuable ally. When the workload slackened, John was often found with the accountants discussing the football pool and hockey standings. Aside from his suit and age, there was very little to distinguish this boss from his subordinates. The camaraderie that existed bound the group together. And it was very useful when upper management pressured him for some fast analysis and when individuals at the branch level demanded financial explanations.

Explanations and analysis were a routine part of the accountants' workload. However, in recent years, the increased amounts of information that needed to be processed, coupled with human error, had resulted in more and more reports that were incorrect in amounts or late in preparation. For example, the sales route accounting system developed for the company many years ago had been adequately designed for the recording of sales, discounts, and receivables information. However, as the company had grown, the system needed to be upgraded. In fact, what had happened was a series of band-aid solutions which were only to cause many more problems in the future.

Under the system that had been originally designed, each sales area was divided into various routes serviced by a company route salesman. Each route consisted of many customers. At the beginning of each day, the salesman picked up his daily standing orders for delivery and his route number was charged with the amount of product that was loaded for the day's deliveries. At the end of the day, the route was credited with the amount of sales and product returned. The information was then totalled for all the routes in a sales area and a consolidated route accounting report prepared. Originally, the route statement for a sales area allowed for a maximum of $999,999.00 in sales, both cash and receivables. For anything over $1 million, the computer dropped the seventh digit. This caused many problems for the accounting department when various sales areas started to record sales of over $1 million — only one of the many problems that lack of foresight had caused.

THE PROBLEM

From the first day that John had become Corporate Controller, he had been saddled with the problems arising from the B.I.T. Buns Company acquisition. No one had stayed in the position of Area Controller for the company's Ottawa area for more than nine months. John's most recent recruit, Jerry Farrell, gave John a month and a half's notice, which should have been sufficient to find a replacement. In the following weeks, John Stone and Cecil Mills, the Corporate Accounting Manager, had many discussions about finding a replacement for the area controllership position.

During this same time, there was a change in John's reporting relationship. Don Keyes, whose reputation preceded him wherever he went, contributed to his own demotion through his lack of social graces, his lack of tact, and moreover his incompetence in his area of responsibility. The area of finance was removed from his jurisdiction. John was to report directly to the president. It was speculated that John Stone would be made Vice-President of Finance at the next general meeting of the shareholders. By that time, many hoped that Don Keyes would have left the company and that the area of Information Systems would also be given to John Stone. This would facilitate better cooperation between the Data Processing department and the Accounting department.

John's philosophy was not to be overly optimistic; he would wait and see. Cecil Mills, the Accounting Manager, knew full well that should John become vice-president and move upstairs to the executive row, his chances of getting the corporate controllership position would be greatly improved. Company history had shown that the average tenure of a controller was about a year and a half. In the five years that Cecil had worked in the Accounting department, three different controllers had occupied the office with the door; the third being John Stone. Cecil's experience and ambitions had now placed him one step away from the controllership position he had wanted for so long. He had been overlooked three times because, so he believed, he was not close enough in his education to a professional designation. Yet his long experience in the department had made him invaluable to each new controller in his or her initial months.

During the last two years, Cecil's work had centred on the mass conversion of an older accounting system to a newly acquired computer system. His involvement in this particular project made him almost irreplaceable. No other person in the company had such an extensive knowledge of the new accounting software system. This advantage would be a bargaining point for Cecil during reviews. Because his position in the company was not a highly visible one, Cecil's accomplishments in this area had gone largely unnoticed, which had made him feel even more frustrated.

"If only they knew what I could do...with one instruction I could scramble the entire system... but they really don't know," Cecil confided to a close friend. Cecil's frustrations came to the surface in occasional bouts of depression and temper. However, this behaviour served to reinforce John's feelings that Cecil belonged where he was. At least there, his outbursts would be confined to the department and would not jeopardize relationships with upper management or other departments.

With Don Keyes's demotion, John became more accountable for the Ottawa problems. These were problems that had arisen from poorly trained staff, lack of continuity of management, and ill feelings between the formerly B.I.T. Buns Company employees and the Multi-Bake Ottawa employees. In the last year or so, efforts to amalgamate both companies' operations had been hampered by a lack of accurate information. A main contributor to this problem was the reluctance of the B.I.T. Buns Company employees to conform to Multi-Bake's reporting procedures. The problem was further compounded by the fact that there had been no area controller in Ottawa to see the problems through to a solution.

Jerry Farrell's replacement would have to commit himself or herself to seeing those same problems through. Choosing a replacement was not an easy task. John felt that the replacement should come from within the organization. There was no lack of qualified people in his department, but there was lack of desire on the part of any of them to go to Ottawa for a lengthy period of time.

The Ottawa controllership position provided front-line training that would have given the person appointed an opportunity to see operations at the depot level and to see the information being amalgamated into a comprehensive reporting package. The primary responsibility of an area controller was to ensure that the information transmitted to head office was accurate. How that controller arrived at that goal was up to the individual. Each controller had favourite methods of scrutinizing and controlling the flow of information. For the ambitious, this position would have offered invaluable training for a more challenging management position at head office.

"We are running out of alternatives, John," Cecil pointed out, "Joyce and Patrick won't consider this assignment without some guarantee that they will be brought back to Waterloo within a year and a half. You know, as well as I do, that it may take years in Ottawa to straighten out the mess that we bought."

"We can offer it to Hilary, Cecil, she would take it without any strings attached. Besides, the change would do her good."

"You must be joking, John, Hilary might do more damage than you think. You know she's not discreet about anything, least of all her personal life."

"I don't understand what you mean, Cecil, her personal life has no bearing on her work. The facts are: she has no family, therefore, she would have no qualms about working late; she has worked in receivables for months now in a position of relative authority; she's been a good supervisor; and her experience in data processing would be an asset. Hilary would not find another position comparable to this anywhere else. It's time we addressed the problem of turnover in that position."

"Alright, John, if that's what you want, I'll speak with her in the morning. But I advise against it," Cecil said flatly.

"It will work out fine. Besides, if it doesn't, you'll make it right," John chuckled.

Hilary Oates was 40 years old, divorced, and had no children. She had been with the company seven years in various capacities: in the marketing department, data processing, and most recently held the position of accounts receivable supervisor. Her performance was quite satisfactory. It was her lack of formal training that prevented her from going much further in the company. On John's insistence, Cecil offered the position to Hilary the following morning. The offer was promptly accepted and two weeks later, Hilary was on her way to Ottawa.

From the first day onward, it was an uphill fight to gain acceptance and respect. On the first day, Hilary held a general meeting for all the staff at the Ottawa office. After the initial introductions, she began: "When I accepted this position, I knew, as the entire company knows, that this office and this entire area of the company has been running haphazardly. Mistakes that result from carelessness are inexcusable. We are responsible adults and from this day onward your work will reflect this attitude. We are paid to do a job and I have a big job ahead of me. With or without your cooperation, this operation is going to be cleaned up. Tardiness and absenteeism will stop, those guilty will be dealt with promptly. Needless to say, your cooperation in his matter will make things easier for everyone concerned. If there are no further questions...we will return to work."

From that point onward, the staff knew that what was ahead of them was not going to be easy for anyone concerned. And in the following months, Hilary's attempts to resolve some of the Ottawa problems seemed only to increase them. The atmosphere of the office was tense and hostile. The staff were always on the defensive, wary of her every move and question. They were uncooperative and suspicious of her intentions.

"She's constantly breathing down your neck...questions, questions, and more questions about everything I do or don't do. She's probably looking to replace me, you know; I feel it in the way she treats me.... If you ask me, I think she's going to replace all of us," one woman complained.

"She doesn't leave for her two-hour luncheon dates until we've all returned from our half-hour breaks. She must think we're blind. I have heard all about her meetings at lunch, and let me assure you that I could write a book on her exploits," gossiped another.

"Wouldn't it figure that head office would send a woman to do a man's job. She doesn't know much...she's created more work for me than I can handle. I don't have time to explain everything I do to her. She's got more nerve than brains. I don't know how much more I can take of her and her condescending ways. 'Do this and do that,' as she's peering down the end of her nose at you."

Such comments and complaints were commonplace in the Ottawa office, and the situation was not improving. Also, positive results were not coming as quickly as some of the executives had hoped. Suggestions were being made at head office that John did not have a handle on the Ottawa situation, and this placed even more pressure on him to show results. Hilary was made aware that the situation had to change and quickly.

Hilary believed that the staff did not take her threats seriously enough in order for her methods to be constructive. The following day provided her with an opportunity to show that she meant what she said. Hilary and the sales manager worked late that day reviewing sales data. They had used the terminals to access the information. In order for them both to view the screen properly, the equipment was somewhat rearranged. The equipment was left until the next morning when Leah Goldman, the terminal operator, arrived at work. Leah was an established member of the Ottawa staff. With her experience and seniority, many people turned to her for direction and guidance in procedures. Even though her expertise was limited, her intentions were good. She organized the children's Christmas parties, the social events, and the hockey pools, etc. She was generous with her time as well as her criticisms. Leah's tongue was sharp, but her temper was short-lived.

On that particular morning, Leah was upset that the equipment had been moved around and not returned to its proper position after being used. Upon further investigation, Leah learned that it was Hilary and Johnson, the sales manager, who had been using the equipment. Leah had had enough of Hilary by then and commented sharply: "Common courtesy would have made me move the equipment back to the place I found it. I don't have time to rearrange everything after anyone who uses it...least of all people who don't even ask for my approval to use the equipment I'm responsible for!"

"Your approval, Miss Goldman?" Hilary sneered, "You seem to forget that you work for me. I don't need your approval or anyone else's approval to get some work done in this office. I would strongly suggest you change your tone of voice when speaking with me. You may find yourself short of a job. Everyone is dispensable...even you."

"You're wrong, Miss Oates...I used to work for you! I quit!"

"Correction...you're fired!" Hilary had found her example. Surely, the staff would cooperate now. Unfortunately, her firing of Leah only served to bind the staff together more firmly against her. Rumours of her iron hand and the resulting discontent filtered through to head office. John began to have serious doubts about the entire situation. Perhaps, Hilary was not the right person for the Ottawa area. He decided to send Cecil to Ottawa to investigate the situation and provide some recommendations on how to resolve it. Cecil's knowledge of the reporting systems would enable him to pinpoint the sources of the inaccurate reporting. Moreover, it would give him an opportunity to show that he could deal with interpersonal problems as well.

When first approached, Cecil had chosen to decline the assignment. The Ottawa situation was not one of the easiest to deal with. But top management was impatient for results and were carefully watching any new developments. Using a different approach, John tried once again to encourage Cecil to take up the challenge.

"Cecil, you know that the spring annual meeting is not that far away. If all goes well, I may be on the 12th floor and my office will be unoccupied. Your assistance in resolving this problem can be a great selling point when I go to bat for you. You know how highly visible this problem is...it will give you the kind of exposure you need. Show me results, Cecil, and you could well have my office in the spring."

Knowing that he was seriously being considered for the corporate controllership position, Cecil finally decided to give the Ottawa crisis a try. Cecil already knew what the problem was. After all, he had tried to tell John from the very beginning that Hilary was not the right person for the job. Cecil left for Ottawa two days later.

His arrival in Ottawa was perceived by Hilary as a reinforcement sent from head office to help her in her crusade against insubordination. It was quite obvious that the atmosphere in the office was uncomfortable. Hilary seemed to try to discourage Cecil from having any prolonged contact with any of the employees. Consequently, Cecil soon realized that to get any feedback from the staff, he would have to approach them informally after work. So he invited a few of the staff up to his room after work for a few get-acquainted drinks. Before long, he was receiving an earful of complaints and comments.

"Let's not be naive, Cecil, everyone knew that the only reason Hilary got the job in the first place is because she slept her way here. It's common knowledge that John Stone and Hilary Oates have been having an affair for years. It's no wonder she gets away with everything."

"I can't understand her attitude. She's always so condescending — as if we weren't even people," another offered.

"I gather then, that you would want her out of your lives?" Cecil asked. "Have you considered that she may really be trying to do her job?"

"Do her job? She doesn't arrive until 10:00 AM but she'll be the first to point it out if you are late. She takes lunch from 12:30–2:30 PM, but if we're late coming back, even five lousy minutes, she'll be calling you in for a "talk." She's got everyone running around doing things that have already been done. Creating work for you even if it serves no purpose...you call that doing a job?"

Cecil felt that with the ill-feelings that existed, Hilary would never be able to gain acceptance. Her recent move in firing Leah Goldman, so it seemed, had permanently alienated her. There seemed to be few options left. If action was not taken immediately, the company would be faced with the possibility of losing the entire Ottawa office staff. On the same afternoon that Cecil returned from Ottawa, a petition arrived addressed to the president of the company with copies to the Director of Employee Relations and to John Stone. It was a petition demanding that Hilary Oates be removed from the Ottawa office and that the situation in Ottawa be given greater attention. It charged that John Stone was ultimately responsible for the problem. It was signed by almost all of the Ottawa staff. That same afternoon, two resignations arrived from two key members of the Ottawa staff.

CONCLUSION

Early in the afternoon, Cecil submitted his recommendations to John which were as follows:

1. Hilary Oates should be removed from the position of area controller for the Ottawa area.
2. The London area controller should be given the assignment to clean-up the operation in Ottawa with the full cooperation and support of the head office personnel. (The London area ran like clockwork and had become the standard by which all areas were compared and measured.)
3. The position of area controller for the Ottawa area should be filled by a replacement from outside the company, preferably from the Ottawa-Hull area.

At 4:00 PM that same afternoon, the first of Cecil's recommendations became unnecessary. Hilary Oates submitted her resignation.

QUESTIONS

1. Under the headings:
   (a) leadership
   (b) motivation
   (c) bureaucratic structure

   discuss why Hilary Oates failed to be a successful supervisor.

2. Was Hilary a victim of sexual stereotyping? If she had been a man and behaved similarly, do you think the results would have been as bad?

3. Discuss the organizational problems that exist at this stage of Multi-Bake's expansion. Identify problems unique to mergers.

4. Comment on the behaviour and performance of John Stone and Cecil Mills as managers, indicating the various forces that govern their relationships and decision-making roles.

5. Would you consider that John Stone's and Cecil Mills' actions were optimal concerning the Ottawa situation? What would you have done differently from the beginning up until Hilary's resignation, and why?

Multi-Store's Imaging Department

Multi-Store, one of the largest organizations in the country, was highly successful. Its success was based on innovations. One of those innovations was the creation of the Multi-Store Credit Corporation in 1991. This was followed by the formation of a new department, the Imaging Department.

Image processing is the ability to replace paper documents with an electronic likeness, and then store, retrieve, display. process, distribute, and print the information. Image processing is accomplished by feeding a paper document into a scanner which digitizes and captures an electronic image of the document. This image contains all the information that appears on the original document. Images can also be created from faxed-in forms. The effect is to eliminate paper files.

The Imaging Department consisted of nine full time workers and fifteen part-time workers. They had originally been located in the New Accounts Department where they were Credit Assessors who evaluated customer applications. There they had enjoyed their responsibilities until the company decided to divide the department functionally. The chosen, decision-making people remained in the New Accounts Department, while the others were relocated into the Imaging Department as Imaging Operators or Verifiers. They lost their decision-making function and concentrated solely on imaging and checking the credit applications.

The basic functions of a Credit Assessor had been to verify and evaluate credit card account applications. To qualify for such a position, applicants had to possess good communication skills, pleasant telephone manners, keyboard and typing skills. At the start of their employment with the company, they were

Adapted by Randy Hoffman from a paper by Dennis Woo. Copyright © 1994 by Randy Hoffman.

enthused as they perceived their new positions to be a challenge and a situation where they would be able to gain valuable experience. Then, electronic imaging was introduced and about 60% of the Credit Assessors were shifted to relatively structured jobs with no customer contact or decision-making opportunities. Comments from these seemingly down-graded employees were as follows.

Fawzia: Imaging Operator   "I think the tasks given to us are a waste of time. Why don't they teach us to do the whole functions? We're supposed to be Credit Assessors. We should be credit assessing. Before, the quality of our work was important. Now, it's the quantity. I think maybe they think we are not competent enough to do the whole job. They even brought someone in from another department and gave him the customer contact responsibilities. It seems unfair. We are the ones who have more experience in the department. It doesn't make sense. He had to learn from scratch. I'm not really motivated at work. I know I'll be doing the same thing everyday. The job's OK, — better than being on the streets — but no future. There's not much room for advancement in the company. Once you are given the job, that's it. If I stay here for 20 years, I'll probably still be in the same position as I am now. I'd like to see employees have more say. Management decides something and then they impose it on us. That's all. It's like being treated like a machine."

Wilson: New Accounts Clerk (Verification)   "Even though they assign you specific tasks, they are not really saving time. Work gets passed on to someone else and if it needs more looking into, it gets passed on to another person, which is a long process. I think that they should give people more responsibilities, have more faith in their employees. I was first hired as a credit assessor. Two months down the line, I was thrown into doing only verification. No one asked me what I thought about it. There were other people here and they could have chosen them. Initially, I didn't mind because it was better than imaging. Verification is not that bad. There's a bit more decision-making on approval of applications. It has a bit more variation, less boring. But I'm still dissatisfied. It's not really that challenging. To me, anyone can do this. Anyone can sit down and phone and verify employment or bank records. All you need to know is how to write and speak English. I can't see any challenge in this type of work unless you are in the upper management level."

Sylvie: Imaging Operator   "It's not a bad job, but it's not one for me. I like to use my mind when I'm working. This job doesn't require thinking, but it is a job somebody has to do and it just happens to be me. A lot of time they hire you for a particular job and that's what they hire you for. Why should you do something different. I'm not really motivated at work. When I wake up for work, I don't feel like going. I always look forward to the weekends."

More recently, even those who retained the credit assessment function were affected by technological change. Artificial intelligence had taken over human decisions. Previously, the computer's function was to trace the involved applicant's credit history. The assessor would then base her/his decision on the information given. However, the computer system has now been modified to a point where the computer, itself, can assess the data inputed and make the decision. This upgrading of the software downgraded the jobs.

The Multi-Store Credit Corporation had spent over a year and many dollars in the development of the new imaging system. But, after all this effort, it was still very much in doubt whether the concept of imaging was valid; whether the new system could gain the market that had been anticipated for it; and whether it was reliable. Errors had been made in the credit approval process that seemed to stem from "bugs" in the software. But, as one of the Directors of the Corporation indicated: "The rate of change is accelerating, only adaptable companies will be the ones who survive. We must recognize the need to change, be receptive. Changes in the service sector must be accompanied by technology." Hence, the reason for imaging.

QUESTIONS

1. What were the motivational and attitudinal differences among the three employees who were quoted in the case?
2. For Credit Assessors who become Image Operators or Verifiers, in what ways did the extrinsic and intrinsic factors of the job change?
3. In what ways were the introduction of imaging mismanaged by Multi-Stores? Suggest a different change process.
4. Must automation of this nature always lessen the challenge in jobs? Why or why not?

Case 33

Newton College

BACKGROUND INFORMATION

Newton College of Applied Arts and Technology is a multicampus educational institution serving Toronto and surrounding regional municipalities. Founded in 1970, the college first operated out of various rented facilities with an initial enrolment of 852 full-time postsecondary students and 1,067 part-time registrants. Enrolment figures for 1991 show 9,500 full-time and 28,540 part-time students.

In its relatively short 20-year history the college has a host of program offerings. The college now offers a wide range of educational opportunities; from Business Studies to Early Childhood Education, from studies in Technology to Recreational Programming, and from Liberal Studies to Law Enforcement. The studies include both full-time day diploma programs for graduating high school students and a multitude of continuing education programs for the community at large.

To service student requirements for 1991, Newton employs 1,500 people: 700 faculty members (professors) who are directly responsible for teaching, 600 support staff (clerks, typists, maintenance) who respond to faculty and administrative needs, and 150 administrators (chairpersons, deans) who oversee the whole operation. This compares to 1970 employment figures of 100 faculty, 80 support staff, and 20 administrators.

ORGANIZATIONAL CULTURE

Newton's raison d'être is summarized in its 1988 Mission Statement.

"Newton College stands committed to training and education that will enhance effectiveness in the workplace and quality of life for all. In this continuing endeavour, the college shall ensure excellence in teaching and learning for its communities. Students will participate in programs dedicated to relevance, social responsibility and lifelong learning."

To achieve this mission, the college in that year also established primary objectives which emphasized quality education, student achievement, and employee development.

The stated objectives were:

To offer academic programs which are excellent and relevant to the needs of the communities which Newton College serves.

- To improve the quality of student life, in co-curricular and extra-curricular activities.
- To enhance current relationships and develop new relationships with the many communities which the college serves in order to: ensure greater understanding of college issues and greater awareness of college programs, courses, activities, and services; and to address current issues and local needs as perceived by these communities.
- To contribute to student achievement through the provision of effective counselling, recruitment, admissions, and placement services.
- To ensure the continued support and development of all employees and the enhancement of the quality of employee life in an environment conducive to growth and well-being.
- To contribute to the achievement of academic excellence through providing appropriate and well-maintained physical resources and appropriate administrative support services for all programs and service divisions.

EMPLOYEE RELATIONS

The second decade of Newton's existence has been turbulent to say the least.

A number of indicators leads one to believe that the quality of working life of faculty members at the college — as indexed by job satisfaction — is in decline: a first strike (1984) in the college's history, which lasted almost one month and resulted in faculty being legislated back to work; the large number of faculty grievances which have increased annually to their formation of divisional associations independent of the union to press for workplace changes; poor faculty response in applying for positions of promotion; faculty 'self-actualizing' outside of their work place; poor after-work-hours relations with the college; poor volunteer rate for college committees, graduation ceremonies, and external liaisons (high schools, student employers); and disrespect for management in the form of open letters of criticism to the public and press constitute a few of the more measurable examples of dissatisfaction. Feelings of distrust, mistrust, hopelessness, and anger exist also, and, while more subjective, these feelings are no less important as indicators of a degraded quality of work-life situation.

The issues of job dissatisfaction in the college, however, are not as clear cut as they appear at first reading, since certain ambiguities and paradoxes cloud the situation; for example, there have been relatively few resignations among tenured staff, who enjoy a high degree of job security, an excellent paid vacation and holiday schedule, a complete benefits package, and a very competitive (with industry) salary. Furthermore, the union which represents faculty members has in place a system of automatic dues deduction, membership in several college decision-making labour-management committees, an input into staff layoffs, and a well-established grievance procedure. While these **basic** quality of work-life arrangements appear to have been implemented early in the life of the college and have perpetuated, an examination of the current situation reveals a second strike in November 1989, continued bitterness, frustration, and increasing anxiety among many of the organization's members.

EMPLOYEE ATTITUDE SURVEY

In April 1990, a survey questionnaire was distributed to the three major employee groups at Newton, asking them to provide input with respect to their attitudes towards the college in several areas, e.g., as an employer, issues of career development, and attitudes towards jobs, etc. Table 1 details a summary of responses to that survey.

Of the 729 respondents, 260 were support staff, 344 were faculty, 85 were administration, and 40 employees who answered the survey did not state their employee group.

The percentage given in this summary table are column percentages. For example, 10 percent of support staff felt that Newton is better than it was three years ago, while 23 percent of support staff felt that Newton does a good job in planning.

PRESIDENT'S SUMMARY REPORT

The President of Newton College, A. R. MacDonald communicated his response to the Employee Attitude Survey in a Summary Report:

> "I am pleased to forward to you an Executive Summary Report and to indicate that copies of the full report will be forwarded to each College Resource Centre, as well as each divisional office, in the event that you wish to review the report in its entirety.
>
> Attitudes are usually based on perceptions. While perceptions are not in themselves either right or wrong, they are real. If perceptions are built on lack of information, misinformation, or worse still, rumours, then it is important that better communication efforts to be put in place if one wishes to have people perceive things as they really exist.
>
> For example, much of the time of the college's senior management has been spent **addressing** both short- and long-range planning, as well as the current issues facing all Newtonians. However, if people perceive that no planning is underway as is indicated in the survey responses, then this indicates a breakdown in communication with respect to the information flow from top to bottom and, conversely, from bottom to top. This is only one of the areas identified by this survey that can be addressed immediately.

TABLE 1   SUMMARY OF RESPONSES TO THE SURVEY QUESTIONS

	Support	Faculty	Admin.
		(percentages)	
Newton is better than it was 3 years ago.	10	12	13
Newton does a good job in planning.	23	14	17
Newton is well managed.	27	15	25
Newton provides adequate facilities.	43	22	31
I would attend more social functions at Newton.	51	23	41
My Dep/Div is above average compared to others at Newton	33	43	71
My Dep/Div is better than it was three years ago.	17	23	35
I think my Dept./Div. is Excellent/Above average in terms of:			
• management	35	34	64
• reputation in the community	38	58	61
• planning	29	29	39
• interest in employees' ideas and opinions	32	36	67
• attitude toward students	39	58	54
• providing working hours that are convenient for me	56	71	60
• having enough people to do the work in my area	21	21	15
My job makes good use of my skills and abilities.	72	86	81
My work makes a contribution to the educational process.	70	81	77
I agree that extra work and exceptional job performance lead to advancement.	30	21	48
I know what is expected of me in my job.	88	79	80
I am adequately informed about the college's policies and procedures.	60	50	75
I have opportunities for career development within Newton College.	52	36	54
The people I work with cooperate to get the job done.	73	72	90
The machinery and equipment I need to do my job is available.	68	43	64
I feel I have job security at Newton.	76	59	60
The promotional system rewards the best qualified.	16	9	23
I am informed about salary and benefits.	90	82	85
I am satisfied with:			
• the recognition I receive for the work I do	55	49	60
• the people I work with	78	77	91
• the work I do on the job	82	95	87
• the pay and fringe benefits	49	72	69
I am satisfied or very satisfied with:			
• working conditions	59	50	74
• my job as a whole	70	81	84
• life in general	89	97	87
There is another job at Newton I would prefer.	54	22	42
Supervisor is Excellent/Above Average in:			
• knowing his/her job	60	48	74
• giving regular feedback	38	27	44
• giving me the information I need to do my job	39	33	55
• listening to what I have to say	?	?	?
• informing me of college policies/procedures	36	33	57
• solving problems	38	36	66
• appraisal of my job performance	41	26	48
• developing teamwork	31	25	51

Continued...

TABLE 1   SUMMARY OF RESPONSES TO THE SURVEY QUESTIONS
(Continued)

	Support	Faculty	Admin.
		(percentages)	
Supervisor is Excellent/Above Average in:			
• providing information on opportunities within Newton	22	18	35
• being available to discuss a problem	54	53	57
Advertised positions are truly available.	18	14	27
The college has a great deal of interest in my career.	7	7	12
My Dept./Div. has a great deal of interest in my career.	19	17	28
The most important factor which would influence my decision to go through a training/development program:			
• to get a new position	25	7	14
• self satisfaction	41	64	61
• to get a pay increase	16	5	5
The factor which counts the most in getting a promotion:			
• education	11	6	4
• work experience	11	3	8
• skill and knowledge	16	7	18
• relationship with your supervisor	11	16	11
• who you know	32	38	30
• quality of work	3	3	10
My salary is fair in relation to other jobs at Newton.	38	80	56

The Committee working on this study met last week and looked at several things that could be done immediately to respond to the findings of this survey. They are as follows:

1. **The introduction of 'Newtonians Update':** This internal document will be distributed to all Newtonians and will cover, in capsule form, the myriad of activities taking place within the college on a daily basis.

2. **Management training:** In response to the request for and the perceived need for additional management training, the Professional Development department has been asked to identify a "core program" that will be mandatory for all administrative personnel. With the exception of a few seminars, in the past two years most administrative staff professional development has been self-directed. This core program will ensure that we are all working from a common base.

3. **Excellence Awards:** Consistent with the recommendations that are now approved by the Board of Governors for the establishment of Excellence Awards, the college will proceed immediately to form the local structures that were recommended to address issues that enhance and/or restrict the achievement of excellence at each of our campus locations.

4. **Communications:** The survey produced some surprises for those of us who have tried to work diligently to ensure that policies and

procedures are in place to address many of the areas questioned in the survey. As stated earlier, it became very evident that information is not flowing up or down within our organization as we would hope. Many of the written comments indicated that people did not know where to turn or how to convey their feelings if they had what they thought was a good suggestion and/or concern about current issues of their work environment.

The Committee has recommended the establishment of a method of communicating your concerns and/or questions to the appropriate source. Therefore, the following is to be put into effect immediately:

• A 'hot line' telephone, local ext. 0001, has been established in my office which will be monitored daily, and your questions or suggestions will be forwarded promptly to the appropriate person.

• The Professional Development department is committed to conducting a second survey within the next two years to see what changes have taken place.

• To those who participated by filling out the questionnaire in order to help with this project and to those who worked to prepare and collect the data, may I say thank you on behalf of the college. This type of information is meaningful only if you act upon it. As someone once wrote — and I quote loosely — it is not where you stand on an issue but more important is the direction in which you are moving!"

QUESTIONS

1. Provide a summary report detailing problems **you** feel currently exist at Newton.
2. Comment on President MacDonald's proposed solutions: are they appropriate and sufficient?
3. Will the attitudes of Newton's employees impact on the organization's stated objectives? How, and to what degree?
4. A second survey will be conducted within the next two years. What changes would you expect to see in employee attitudes, and how would they be reflected in the Summary of Results?

Portrait of a Canadian Advisor

Results of this study provide a revealing portrait of the Canadians who work as advisors on CIDA-sponsored projects. From interviews with advisors, spouses, colleagues, and national counterparts the following profile emerges of a typical Canadian advisor.

The typical Canadian advisor is a male between the age of 40 and 50. He was born in Canada, where he has lived at least five years of his life. His mother tongue is English (47 percent) or French (44 percent). and he is well educated, having at least one university degree. He is married and is accompanied on this assignment by his spouse.

Our advisor is a professional working for a private Canadian firm that is under contract to CIDA. No stranger to the developing world, he has had at least one previous overseas posting and has spent at least two years working in developing countries. On this assignment, he is working in an urban setting as part of a team. He will be working directly with a counterpart from the country of assignment in a management capacity. He sees his role as an advisory one involving training and the transfer of skills and knowledge.

Our advisor approaches this assignment with confidence. His interest in the host country is high, and he is not worried about his ability to adapt. He is confident that he will do well on the assignment and that he can make a significant contribution to development efforts in the country. He feels he has better than average interpersonal and communication skills. And although he considers

Daniel J. Kealey, "Cross-Cultural Effectiveness — A Study of Canadian Technical Advisors Overseas," 1990, pp. 32–33. Published by Canadian International Development Agency. Reprinted by permission of CIDA Briefing Centre, Hull QC and Daniel J. Kealey.

himself to have a high sense of adventure and altruism, he is concerned about his security and places a high value on upward mobility.

A desire to give and/or learn lies behind our advisor's acceptance of the overseas assignment. His attitudes on development are fairly conservative, and he views the transfer of technology as the key to improving economic prosperity in the developing countries and to narrowing the gap between rich and poor nations. He sees no need for the developed world to limit its standard of living and supports Canada's policy of tied aid, which requires that the majority of our development dollars be spend on the purchase of Canadian goods and services.

On assignment, our advisor expresses a great deal of satisfaction in his personal, family, and professional life and experiences a high degree of involvement in the local culture. In his mind, the process of adaptation has been a smooth one involving little culture shock, and he feels more satisfaction with his life overseas than he did previously in Canada.

On the job, he feels that his terms of reference are well defined and understood and that both he and his colleagues have been highly effective in the task of transferring skills and knowledge to their national counterparts. Although status differences exist between himself and his counterpart, he does not see this inhibiting their working relationship. And while he feels that his living conditions are generally less comfortable than those in Canada, he does not see this as an impediment to his assignment.

DIFFERING REALITIES

The views and attitudes expressed above are the advisor's perceptions of himself. A different and less optimistic portrait emerges, however, from field interviews with spouses, colleagues, and counterparts as well as observations made by field researchers. As seen by others, our advisor has minimal involvement with the local culture, preferring instead to spend his leisure and social time in the company of other Canadians and expatriates. He has made little effort to learn the local language and is likely to spend little time outside the job with his counterpart or other nationals. Although he is able to accurately identify the key factors which promote success on a development assignment, he is less able to actually demonstrate the required skills and interest in his own behaviour. What people say and what they do are often inconsistent. How an individual sees and assesses himself often bears little resemblance to how he is seen and assessed by others.

QUESTIONS

1. Why is the gap between the typical Canadian advisor's self-perception and the perceptions by others likely to be greater in a foreign environment? Would similar gaps exist in a domestic environment?

2. How is this gap likely to affect the advisor's performance?

3. What measures would you recommend to improve the accuracy of the advisor's self-perception and performance?

Reduced Hours

Fraser Shilling, the manager of the head office training department of a large insurance company based in Calgary, is reviewing a proposal submitted by Nairobi Hanson, who occupies a mid-management position.

Nairobi is a female in her late 30s who has decided to return to university part-time to complete a B.A. degree with a major in Fine Art that she had begun some 20 years earlier. There is no overlap between her career and her chosen area of study. Her job entails analyzing the training requirements of employees at various levels across the organization and designing training material appropriate to their needs. Each of her peers in the department manages their own project(s) and deadlines are set according to the scale of each individual project. There is only an occasional need for cooperation among department staff members.

The organization's policy regarding continuing education is proactive, provided the studies are job-related, and would develop skills which enhance on-the-job performance. Courses falling into this category are paid for in full by the company.

In this particular case there is no perceived benefit to the organization by this employee pursuing studies in fine arts. The work arrangement which she proposes includes covering the cost of the course(s) herself and working a three-day week at 60% of her regular salary. She will continue to work on the projects currently assigned to her, however, deadlines will have to be extended to accommodate the reduced work week. The work arrangement is to remain in effect for an indefinite period.

Mr. Shilling is quite well-disposed towards Ms. Hanson's proposal. She is one of the most productive members of the department, and he fears that she might leave entirely if refused.

In addition, he is quite supportive of a more flexible approach to employer-employee relationships. His regret is that the courses she intends to take will not be professionally oriented. Fraser Shilling believes that a career can and should be developed through a life-long commitment to supplementary education.

Nairobi's peers are not unanimously supportive of her proposal. There is the suspicion that although her attendance will be reduced and her salary will be pro-rated, her performance and output might be undiminished. This would make everyone who is remaining full-time look very unproductive. Two of the people who felt this way have already spoken to Fraser Shilling and said that they thought a person should have the right to a full leave for a period of time, but that the job could not be properly done part-time. They also indicated to Nairobi that it would be "difficult" to cooperate with her once she began her reduced hours.

QUESTIONS

1. Is Nairobi Hanson's proposal a reasonable one? Would it be a better proposal if the educational program was professionally related?

2. Assuming that he was willing to approve the proposal, should Fraser Shilling attempt to deal with the concerns of the other staff members? In what way?

3. Should Nairobi try to restrict her output to about 60% of its former level once she goes on reduced hours?

4. Should Fraser Shilling accept the proposal:
   (a) as it is?
   (b) with qualifications? State any that you believe are warranted.

The Reorganization

Lilly Jones has been with the Department of Regional Industrial Expansion for four years. During this time she received several pay increases in recognition of her superior performance as a Economic Analyst and as Manager of the Economic Analysis unit. Recently she was promoted Director of her branch in the Economic and Regional Policy Division of the department which employs some 250 people, most of whom are professionals: economists, sociologists, lawyers, and accountants.

As Director, Ms. Jones has three unit managers reporting directly to her: Charles Thompson, Strategic Policy Analysis; Karen Smith, Economic Analysis; and Stan Cooper, Regional Policy Analysis. The Strategic Policy Analysis unit has the most employees with over 120 analysts whose function is to process private sector applications for regional development grants and subsidies. Economic Analysis is the smallest unit with about 30 employees who study economic trends to ensure that the department is aware of the developments in national economic conditions. The Regional Policy Analysis unit evaluates projects to ensure monies have been properly spent and assesses the effectiveness of the development policies of the department as determined by priorities established by the Economic Analysis unit.

Ms. Jones worked closely with Ms. Smith in the past and was instrumental in her appointment as manager to succeed Ms. Jones as head of the Economic Analysis unit. Ms. Smith's promotion, however, has caused resentment among some of the professional staff of the Economic Analysis unit. Some of them feel that Ms. Smith was promoted because she is a woman and worked closely with Ms. Jones.

Mr. Thompson, on the other hand, resents Ms. Jones' recent appointment because he feels he deserved the director's position in the branch by virtue of his senority and breadth of experience. Mr. Thompson has worked in the department for the last ten years, has contributed to the success of many projects, and has served on various interdepartmental committees during this time.

Mr. Cooper is one of the longest serving members, not only in the branch, but also in the department and is close to retirement. For this reason he did not expect to be appointed to the director's position and, in fact, had lost interest and enthusiasm for his job some time ago. This was evident to most of the staff in the Regional Policy Analysis unit who thought he would coast for the next few years before he retired. Accordingly, many of the more ambitious types in the unit were "jockeying for position" in the hopes of succeeding Mr. Cooper in the manager's office.

The other day Ms. Jones received a directive from her assistant deputy minister that an impending budget cut would require the department to cut $50 million annually and a minimum of 35 PY (Person Years). The bad news was that her own branch would have to take the lion's share of the personnel cuts because of a pending internal reorganization of various branches of the department. As the director of the branch, Ms. Jones had to recommend the reallocation or dismissal of 35 PY, of which at least two would be in the management category, and the cut of up to $15 million from her branch's current year budget.

The assistant deputy minister (ADM) of the division called Ms. Jones to his office this morning to discuss the reorganization of the department, the effect of the required cuts to the branch, and its possible impact on the division. During their meeting the ADM made it clear that Stan Cooper was one of his old friends and was personally close to the Deputy Minister as well. The ADM then made it clear that Mr. Cooper should perhaps be allowed to stay on for the next several years in order to qualify for his full pension. The ADM also said a number of positive things about how "Charlie" Thompson had been such a hard and dedicated worker for the department over the years. This left Ms. Jones with the distinct impression that perhaps Mr. Thompson should also be spared from any impending cuts in her branch. The ADM concluded their meeting by saying that he would like to see her preliminary recommendations on how the impending cuts to her branch should be handled by 10:00 AM tomorrow.

QUESTIONS

1. What are the moral, ethical, and organizational issues in this case?
2. Is the ADM acting properly when implying that Mr. Cooper and Mr. Thompson should be spared from the cuts?
3. What do you recommend that Lilly Jones put in her preliminary recommendations?
4. What will be the consequences of your recommendations?

Ridgway Furniture Limited

Ridgway Furniture Limited started manufacturing on a small scale about 20 years ago but now employs over 700 people, producing a wide range of wood and metal home and office furniture. The firm enjoys a good reputation in the furniture industry and its products, sold in the medium-to-high price range, are considered good quality products by the general public. The firm is also recognized for its own special furniture stylings. To produce its furniture, the firm uses the latest in modern technology. The firm's most rapid expansion took place in its first 10 years of operation. However, although the firm has kept growing since then, the rate of growth is now much slower.

Donald Carson, who has been with the company since it started, is the head of the Furniture Design department. Dick Prindles, who also joined the firm at that time, is now the company president and Donald's boss. Both are good friends and have together witnessed the company's growth to its present size.

Carson is regarded as one of the pillars of this organization because of the many contributions he has made towards the growth of the enterprise. He is well recognized for his creative abilities which have led to the firm's unique furniture designs, one of the hallmarks of the company.

Until five years ago, Carson had a small staff of eight employees engaged in the task of creating new furniture designs. Five of them were male and three female. They were all hand-picked, bright, young individuals. They were all highly creative, and most of them had received formal training in the art of furniture design at various community colleges. Carson rated them as "high performers."

Carson's department has expanded considerably, and the number of employees engaged in designing had jumped from eight to nineteen, which included two

By Anwar Rashid. Copyright © 1991, 1994 by L & S Management Publications.

clerical employees and a secretary to the head of the department. In addition to these 19 employees, Carson had hired John Gilbert as his assistant. His title was somewhat vague, but it is believed that Carson created this position so that the new person could assist him in running the department. Carson's workload had become unusually heavy, and John Gilbert's appointment came in response to this problem. It was expected that Gilbert would relieve Carson of much of the supervisory work and also take care of many administrative details, thus releasing Carson to perform developmental work, relate to customers, and plan for the future. John Gilbert was hired from outside the firm and was regarded as particularly suitable for the position because of his supervisory experience as well as his knowledge of furniture design. He shared a large office with the other artists and designers.

The relationships in the department were very informal and people felt free to approach Carson any time. Carson's office door was always open. The employees liked him as a boss and many admired him. Carson was always willing to listen to their ideas as well as their problems. Quite often they discussed their personal problems with him, and they never failed to get "good advice." They even had his home telephone number so that they could reach him after office hours in case of emergency.

Three years ago Carson decided to hire another supervisor who would look after the specialized work being done by a group of six designers involved in the development of "modular furniture." A young and dynamic person by the name of Martin Starke was chosen for the newly created position. Starke was respected in the industry for his designing ability and had come to the company with excellent credentials. It was believed that he would bring new vitality to the group and would be responsible for the training of his workers. It was also expected that his work group would gradually increase in size since there appeared to be a strong demand for the kind of furniture they were designing. In the new organizational structure, Starke was responsible to Gilbert for his work, but he would have free access to Carson, the head of the department. It was assumed that the other employees would report to Gilbert and receive their instructions from him.

During the next two years, new practices and patterns of relationships developed in this organization. While it was understood that some of the employees would report to Gilbert and some would report to Starke, it did not work that way in practice. The designers had acquired the habit of keeping in touch with Carson for almost everything they did, and they looked to him for all sorts of decisions. They even approached Carson with work-related problems which could have been handled by Gilbert or Starke. The six designers working under Starke went to Carson for every detail. Perhaps for reasons of expediency, Carson went along with this. He never turned the designers away or referred them to the supervisors concerned. Perhaps because he had been hired by Carson, or because he was easier to talk to, Starke also frequently approached Carson directly with his problems, rather than going to Gilbert.

As time passed, Gilbert began to show strong signs of resentment towards Carson's policy of discussing work with the designers, but he never lodged a formal protest or confronted Carson with his "beefs." Since Starke was still fairly "new" to the company, he preferred to lie low and adopt a do-nothing approach. In fact, he had never seriously tried to assert his position as a supervisor, except recently when he had a showdown with his group who were now openly defying his authority. As a result of this incident, Carson arranged a meeting with the six designers, Starke, Gilbert, and himself. During the meeting Starke was accused by the designers of "not being around" when help was needed! They also complained that Starke had made very little effort to train them in design techniques. Two of them complained of not getting straight answers from him to any of the questions they had raised in the past. Starke responded by saying that he was involved with a lot of other work which caused him to overlook some of the routine activities. He apologized to the group and promised to develop a "think-tank" type of training program for his designers. Starke took a defensive approach during this meeting. Gilbert never said a word. Carson pointed out to the designers that in accordance with the organizational structure, they were responsible to Starke and they should go to him with their problems. He also suggested that another meeting should be arranged to be attended by the remaining employees, Gilbert, and Carson to clarify departmental policies.

In the meantime, another development had taken place. The president had informed Carson that the company would soon undertake a major expansion program, creating an additional position for a vice-president. Prindles had made it clear that he would like Carson to take over the new position. But Carson realized that if he were to move into the vice-president's office, a gap would be created in the Design department because, in his estimation, Gilbert was not ready to assume the responsibility of department head. Carson felt that Gilbert had lately become quite uninvolved and disinterested in the affairs of the department. It was Carson himself who was dealing with all the administrative work as well as carrying out the necessary supervision of the employees. The only things that Gilbert attended to were those of a semi-clerical nature and, on occasions, answering simple questions raised by some of the customers. It seemed to Carson that, because of Gilbert's apathetic attitude, the employees preferred to come directly to Carson. Also, they seemed to be satisfied with the answers he gave them. However, Carson was now spending too much time supervising the tasks being performed by various people in the Design department. In fact, some of them should have been dealt with by Gilbert and some by Starke. Together, these two should have run most of the departmental activities, leaving Carson free to attend to other developmental type of work. Carson realized that there was something wrong with the organization of this department, and some action had to be taken to rectify the situation. He decided to have a quiet chat with Gilbert as well as with Starke to remind them of their responsibilities and of the fact that the morale of the entire department was being affected. He told them over coffee to assert the necessary authority over their subordinates and insist that they come to them for instructions and decisions and not to Carson. Both the supervisors gave certain reasons for their present dilemma or predicament and promised to "put things into harness" for the future.

Over the next few months, Carson failed to perceive any change in the prevailing practice followed by the Design employees nor did he notice any change in the attitudes of Gilbert and Starke. Employees continued to come directly to Carson and when he tried to discourage them, they explained that "they had come to him after failing to get a satisfactory answer from the supervisor." Motivation and morale had gone down considerably in the past few weeks. It was virtually impossible for Carson to deal with his own departmental work, which had been increasing all the time, and to relate to market developments and at the same time be involved in organizational changes. He had to make his choice now and set priorities that would be acceptable to himself as well as to the others. He had to encourage Gilbert to use discretion and take control. He must also ensure that Starke, a brilliant man in many ways, would come up to his expectations as well as to the expectations of his subordinates. Both these men must perform as supervisors or team leaders by taking the initiative, demonstrating ambition, and making decisions. Carson knew well that there was no lack of technical knowledge on the part of these two. They had the "ability," but did they have the "will-power?" If things remained unchanged, it would not be possible for Carson to move up to the new position likely to be open soon.

QUESTIONS

1. Draw the organizational structure of the company. Indicate the problems of authority, roles, and relationships. Point out the main problems and the reasons for their occurrence.
2. How do you evaluate the performance and role of Carson as the head of the department.
3. What problems do you see in the leadership of Gilbert and Starke?
4. How would these problems affect the motivation of the Design employees?
5. What recommendations would you make in order to rectify the situation?

Robert Bart

Robert Bart had been employed with the Ministry of Consumer and Corporate Affairs for the past six months on a probationary contract; that is, Mr. Bart's contract for employment with the federal government would expire in the next few months unless he is given an offer of permanent employment. His immediate supervisor is Ellen Clark, Manager of the Commercial Practices and Investigations unit where Mr. Bart is a junior investigations officer.

When Ms. Clark initially hired Mr. Bart, she did so because her unit was short staffed with a number of pending deadlines over the next few months and also because Mr. Bart was a young, energetic, and enthusiastic university graduate with an exceptionally strong academic background — he had achieved the highest standing in his Bachelor of Commerce graduating class. However, the projects were now completed and there was no longer any immediate pressure on her unit.

Mr. Bart, to his surprise, found his job exhilarating and challenging. He had never wanted to pursue a public service career, but the ministry's offer of employment was the best he had received, and he thought it might be a useful stepping stone to get an offer from one of the top corporations in the country. His first months at the ministry not only taught him a great deal about how governments operate, but also about business-government relations. He felt that he even had a better appreciation and understanding of the world of business.

Mr. Bart was aware he would need at least a "fully satisfactory" performance review, but preferably "outstanding," rating from his manager to remain on as a permanent employee. This did not trouble him since he felt he was doing well and seemed to be fitting in with the other members of the unit. He found his work engrossing and took great pride in the quality of his investigative studies.

Ellen Clark called Mr. Bart into his office to go over his Performance Review and Appraisal Report. She gave him a copy of his performance review. Ms. Clark started by indicating that she had been satisfied with Mr. Bart's overall contribution to the unit. She stated that she thought his strengths were in research and writing and that his weaknesses, unfortunately, were in the area of interpersonal relations. This was particularly evident in Mr. Bart's dealings with the companies the ministry dealt with on an ongoing basis. Ms. Clark documented several complaints she had received from different companies about Mr. Bart's arrogant attitude and his lack of sensitivity to their circumstances and concerns. On this basis alone, Ms. Clark said, she would have to give him low scores on "Exercise of Judgement," "Tact and Diplomacy," and "Relationship with Others." As a consequence, Ellen Clark concluded, she was unable at this time to give him a rating of higher than "Satisfactory."

Mr. Bart was stunned. However, he recovered quickly and said that Ms. Clark's assessment was totally unfair and stated he would not sign the report.

QUESTIONS

1. From the evidence in the case, do you think Ellen Clark's assessment was accurate? Why?
2. What should Robert Bart do now?
3. What should Ellen Clark do now?
4. What should someone in Robert Bart's situation do during the term of his employment to maximize the possibility of a permanent job offer?

Sandra Beaumont

Sandra Beaumont was on the fifth day of her new job as the Benefits manager for the Toronto Ball Bearing Company (TBBC) when she received a letter from TBBC's insurance company. The letter outlined that the rates for TBBC's Prescription Drug Plan would have to be raised by 18% to maintain the same level of coverage — the fifth substantial raise since the plan was introduced 10 years ago.

When Sandra had been hired by the company's president, she had been told that the Benefits department had not been very well run — in fact, the manager's position had been vacant for the last six months. Normally, the company would try to hire from within; however, when the president received Sandra's application, he was quite impressed with her background and experience.

The president mentioned that, on the whole, he thought the company-funded Benefits Plan was a good one — although he wasn't quite sure whether all the employees really understood what was going on or whether some understood only too well how to use the plan. The president had made it quite clear that he cared for the individual well-being of the company's 235 employees and wanted to have the best plan that his limited resources could buy. He wondered whether he was getting the best for his money.

TBBC's employees came from various ethnic backgrounds, and many of them had been with the company for over 20 years. Even though many of them could barely speak the same language, they all got along well and were quite willing to help each other out. The managers were mostly people who had made it up through the ranks and who also felt part of the TBBC family.

Sandra had noticed that few of the managers had dropped by to welcome her to her new job. She wondered why. Perhaps the previous manager had not gotten along well with them and they were just testing her out. Or perhaps they were expecting another man to fill the position (Most of the managers were men while quite a few of the employees were women). Regardless, she certainly sensed some hostility when she approached a few of the managers to talk about the benefit plan. Equally, the few employees she had approached were not very open. Some had mentioned that if they had any problems, they could always speak to their supervisor.

After looking through the few records that were available, Sandra noticed that the Prescription Plan seemed very popular with the employees. It certainly was easy to use since the employees had to only buy the drugs and the pharmacy would then submit the bill directly to the insurance company. Since no receipts had to be submitted, Sandra couldn't even determine the kind of drugs being bought and would also find it hard to see exactly how much each employee was spending on prescriptions.

As Sandra sat down to have a cup of coffee, the phone rang. It was the floor supervisor who wanted to know how to get reimbursement for one of the employee's dental bills. Could she send him down some information?... As Sandra sipped her coffee, she thought about what she had observed over the last few days. In two hours, her first week on the job would be over. She wondered what she should do starting Monday morning and how she should go about doing it.

QUESTIONS

1. What difficulties is Sandra Beaumont likely to face in her new position?
2. What should she do to build good relationships with the other managers?
3. How should she go about reforming the benefit plan?

Victory Fashions

INTRODUCTION

Phil Mager, President of Victory Fashions, has been mulling over the same issue ever since the new shareholder's agreement was signed in January 1981. He wanted more control of the strategy of his company. He was increasingly dissatisfied with the financial progress of his company and was even more dissatisfied with his role in it. He didn't know whether to dissolve the company and strike out on his own or to continue the company in the hope of a better future.

GENERAL BACKGROUND

Victory Fashions is a manufacturer of high fashion ladies tailored clothing. In Canada, the ladies garment industry consists of over 2,000 establishments employing about 115,000 workers. Affectionately known as the "rag trade," this industrial segment represents an important economic factor in Canada. In 1990, these 2,000 establishments shipped nearly $4 billion worth of goods.

Victory Fashions was started in 1928 in Montreal by Sheldon Gerber, an enterprising immigrant who saw an opportunity to break into the apparel business which was then dominated by few major manufacturers. His strategy was to sell large quantities to major retailers. He was able to do so because of his strategy of using the most modern and efficient machinery instead of cutters, tailors, and other expensive labour. This strategy was continued into the 1960s by the new owner, Sam Greenberg, a former shipper who had worked his way up into the executive suite. Greenberg dreamed of opening an even more technologically advanced plant and closing the original plant. His dreams were realized and the old plant was scheduled to be shut down as soon as the new plant became fully operational in 1972.

However, in 1970, the clothing industry took a down turn. Changes in government regulations caused a massive influx of low-priced imports. The new modern plant which could compete with the imports was still having start-up problems, and the old plant began suffering losses for the first time in its history. The situation continued until 1975 when a creditor called a loan.

Greenberg and his executive team scrambled for funds. During a very tense month, they managed to persuade the creditors that everyone would be paid within one year, with the conditions being that the old plant would be allowed to close and that credit would be extended to the new one. The creditors agreed but required that Greenberg, nearly 65 then, get the commitment of his merchandising manager to run the business. Reluctantly, Greenberg sold one-third of the business to Phil Mager, the merchandising manager who had a "hot" reputation in the clothing industry. Mager paid for the share by mortgaging his house and releasing part of his salary. In return, he was made a vice-president.

The new plant of Victory Fashions was established in 1973. At its peak in 1981, it employed 400 workers, produced 1,000 garments daily, and had sales of $15 million. The plant was unionized, and there were strict divisions of labour between the cutters, the needle workers, the taggers, and the shippers. Within the office, approximately 20 white collar workers (non-unionized) did whatever they were told to do or saw was necessary to do. Even the cleaning lady would do clerical jobs when necessary. The four partners tended to cross functional lines quite frequently. For example, the Vice-President, Accounting would sell directly to discounters, and the President would negotiate with suppliers and work directly with designers.

The structure of Victory Fashions resists easy classification. The production department is typical of a mechanistic organization. The work to be accomplished tends to be predetermined, routine, mechanical, and repetitive. However, the merchandising department (styling and sales) tends to be market oriented and organic. There is little division of labour, no goals, little work that is predetermined or analyzed, and communication tends to be informal. The internal structure of Victory Fashions appears to be composed of disparate departments.

The nature of the environment in the fashion business is extremely important in understanding Victory Fashions. The fashion industry could be characterized as being in a turbulent environment in which governments change import quotas unpredictably, competitors produce nearly identical lines, steal logos and ideas, suppliers are unreliable in terms of delivery dates, etc. The environment is also dynamic in the sense that the product line is uncertain and unpredictable due to client demands for novelty, changing department store buyers, and the high bankruptcy rate among retailers. The environment is not complex in the sense that it requires sophisticated knowledge about the products or customers. In the fashion business, the manufacturer can easily comprehend the markets and technology, although the styles or colours are unpredictable.

Within a year, the creditors were paid off. However, this left the company seriously undercapitalized. This precarious financial position was further threatened by a new blow to the company. A recession hit in the late 70s, and consumers stopped spending on luxury items such as ladies tailored clothing.

Interest rates reached 22%. The company was scrambling for sales and money. The creditors were beginning to reevaluate the new plant.

The provincial government was approached for a loan under the Business Development Incentives Program. Government officials quickly noticed how little capital ($300,000) the company had invested on sales of $15 million. In order to approve the loan, the government demanded additional personal investment. The two owners, Greenberg and Mager, could extend themselves only so far. They were forced to ask members of the executive team to invest and thus become part owners of the company. The members of the executive team took second mortgages on their homes, and together the executives raised $250,000.

In return, Greenberg, now in his early 70s, sold all of his shares, to be paid for by profits over the next 15 years. The total sum to be paid was $300,000. Greenberg gave up his voting rights and was no longer active in the day-to-day operations of the business. He continued to come to work every day to read and talk to friends.

The new ownership agreement gave two-fifths of the company to Mager (because of his earlier investment) and three other executives received one fifth each. Mager was made President.

Sales continued to be difficult to obtain and the floating interest rates the company had previously negotiated were burdensome. During the previous five years the company had reinvested the very small profits that were generated. Two divisions which were started by Mager were profitable and were in fact supporting the divisions on which Victory Fashions had originally made its reputation.

PHIL MAGER, PRESIDENT

Mager, 38 years old, was married with two children. He had spent 10 years as a very successful merchandising manager on the retailing side. He was well known in the fashion business for his considerable talent to spot fashion trends. He had started a number of divisions since his arrival at Victory Fashions in 1973. Some proved profitable, others were phased out.

Mager had started a childrens' wear line targeted at the grandmother market. The potential profits were high, but there was little time to establish contacts with the childrens' wear retailers, and so the line slowly died. Another unsuccessful operation was the establishment of a factory outlet open to the public. This store was to act as a dumping ground for unsold merchandise and surplus fabric. However, the factory outlet had to be located at some distance from other retailers in order to avoid price conflicts. This resulted in little traffic to the outlet, which was subsequently closed.

The two most successful operations were the designer line and the import program. Even during a recession, consumers continued to spend money on designer clothing, and Phil had obtained the production and distribution licence for an important designer. Mager had approached the designer for the rights to Canada, and the contract proved to be exceptionally profitable. The import business too had been successful because the low price of these imports enabled the company to appeal to a low-end retailing clientele. Overall, these two profitable areas channelled enough money into the company to keep the company afloat in spite of losses in the other areas.

The profitability of these two divisions had convinced Mager that he had a good feel for the market. He felt restricted by the lack of capital needed to finance his other marketing projects. More importantly, he felt restricted by the new shareholder's agreement which required a majority vote for the approval of any new venture. (As will be seen later, this clause had been inserted by one partner and signed under extreme pressure and with reluctance by Mager.) Mager had felt betrayed by this clause which reduced his power in the company. He had lost control, and for him, control was critical. He hated feeling powerless — he had never wanted to work for anybody because he didn't trust others.

There was also a business reason why. Mager disagreed with this clause. He reasoned that, in the fashion business, merchandising innovations were the key to survival, and no innovations could come from a team which included an accountant and a production manager. How could Mager justify his gut feelings on a balance sheet to Carl Deacon, the accountant who was more like a bookkeeper? Deacon's idea of financial planning was to resist paying bills in order to accumulate pennies worth of interest, while in the long run antagonizing the suppliers who Mager had to then placate. Manny Kesper, VP Production, was even worse. Kesper, an old friend whom Mager had brought into the company, wanted to keep that production line moving. His idea of profitability was that "the more you make, the more your make." It was impossible to explain to him that maximizing profits was more critical than maximizing sales. Both Deacon and Kesper resisted anything new and potentially risky. The fourth partner, David Cleary, VP Merchandising, understood fashion, but Cleary had some peculiar social democratic political views on how to run a company. Cleary believed that all partners should be equal, with equal pay, equal prerequisites, and equal votes. During the last financial downturn, Cleary had persuaded Deacon and Kesper to support him.

Together, they forced Mager, who was desperate to salvage his original investment and his company, to consider a parity shareholder's agreement.

Despite 12 hour threats and protests, Phil reluctantly signed. His discomfort with the agreement persisted, particularly when he saw that his whole merchandising strategy had to be changed as a result. Previously, when he had an idea, he acted on it. He made the contact, told the designers to prepare the samples, got production moving, and, in effect, set up the entire apparatus to produce a new line or open a new division.

Now, however, when he had an idea, he would approach each partner separately, sell them on the idea from their unique viewpoints in order to obtain their vote, and then attempt to hold them in an open meeting. His success rate was very low, and he felt increasingly frustrated as he saw opportunities slip by. Phil felt that innovative merchandising ideas were the key to survival, and no innovation could come out of a group of equals. He wanted his old powers back — it was essential for the survival of the group. "It's this damn one-person, one-vote proposition that David forced on us. Not only do I own 40% of the company, but I'm President. I'm the one with the ideas that will keep this company alive...the others belong in a soap company with their traditional ideas of accounting and production. And I don't see why I should be paid the same when I have a larger investment and the top job. If I can't have control, I'll...I don't know," Mager fumed.

Mager decided to enlist the support of the external auditors and the company's lawyers in an attempt to rewrite the shareholder's agreement. The lawyers refused to unilaterally rewrite an agreement that might favour one partner. They insisted that they represented the company interest, and the company consisted of the four partners. The lawyers would be present at a meeting of the four executives and would attempt to chair it. Following is a transcript of the meeting between the lawyers, Cohen and Cohen, and the Victory Fashions management group that met to discuss the effectiveness of the present shareholders agreement.

HIGHLIGHTS OF THE TRANSCRIPT OF THE MEETING
(Executive Group Of Victory Fashions Limited, Held On June 15, 1981)

Present: Messrs Cohen, Cohen, Mager, Kesper, Cleary, and Deacon

Cohen: Phil approached me several days ago, indicating his continued dissatisfaction with the shareholders agreement. He feels that it would be to the company's benefit, and therefore to each of the partner's benefit, that the agreement be revised.

Mager: Yes, as you all know, I never liked the equal division of votes from the beginning. I only agreed to it because I was forced to make a decision within one day — you sprung it on me the day before we had to get that loan. I was very tempted to lose everything and go out on my own. I know you thought it was just that I didn't like losing power, but it was more than that. In a fashion business like ours, we have to react quickly. We're not the federal government. We can't make decisions by committees. It's too slow. I'm proposing that we create a structure whereby the president can use his 40% voting power...

Cleary: Look — we didn't force you into anything. The times have changed and you can't just follow any idea to see if it works. We need planning now, we have to work as a team, look at financial projections, determine if the idea is profitable...

Kesper: David's right. We have to look at the impact on production. Just because we're a fashion business doesn't mean that we can't have plans. Besides, we need a stable line — just to keep production moving. We can't switch lines all the time. The costs are too great and my people don't like it.

Mager: Your people are damned lucky to have jobs. If we don't meet the market demands, we go out of business. It's that simple. You two are always talking about formalizing this business, about setting objectices, doing analyses. I'll tell you what my objective is — to survive one more season. How can you plan in an environment like this — the government changes the import regulations monthly, the interest rates doubled in two years, we went from a boom to a recession in three years. Look, unless we can react quickly and not be blinded by plans made under different assumptions, we're going to die like dinosaurs.

Cleary: I think that the new partnership agreement meets all our needs. It was drawn up to reflect the fact that all of us invested the same amount of money this time around. Phil had an earlier investment, but his risk is less if the company goes under...all of us lose our houses, except for Phil. He lives in a mansion; he can afford the loss. So because we have greater risk, we should have at least equal votes. I know that in the past, Phil, you ran the company the way you wanted to, and you made a couple of good decisions that are basically keeping the company afloat. But what about your factory outlet idea...and your childrens' wear program? They both bombed. You see, if we can just tap the best of your ideas and screen out the others through our executive committee, then we'll be a better company. I'm not arguing for rigid planning, it's just our need to be more professional in our management.

Mager: But how will you know which are the good ideas and which are the bad ones until they are tested in the market? So far, you've turned down every venture I've proposed, or belaboured it so long that the economics have changed or someone else got it. Committees just don't work in this business.

Kesper: But neither do people who just follow their whims...you're great on ideas, but you don't understand production and projections and...

Cohen: Why don't we take a break? People seem to be getting a little excited. Let's reconvene in half an hour and explore this some more.

During the break Phil Mager left his partners and went back to his office. The old conflict was there, and it looked like there would be no new solutions. In his view, Victory Fashions had to be market oriented, and not a rigid organization run by MBO. "Management by Obsolescence." He mused, "Where there's a problem or a need, the company can't be handcuffed by job descriptions and memos. The market is not predictable. If we were manufacturing widgets — I'd let them win. We could have routines and schedules and goals — but, we're in fashion, and strategic plans and formal management will kill us!"

QUESTIONS

1.   Describe the structure of Victory Fashions as of the end of the case. Is it well-suited to the external environment of the firm?
2.   What are the pros and cons of a management group of four all having equal power?
3.   Describe the motivational state of Phil Mager. What are his salient needs and how can he best satisfy them?
4.   Can the disparate values of the partners be reconciled? Explain your answer.
5.   Take the role of one of the mediating lawyers and state, in detail and step-by-step, what you would do when the meeting resumed.

Case 41

Weston Tire Corporation

Weston Tire Corporation is a multinational corporation with major operations located in Canada, the United States, and Western Europe. The company employs more than 30,000 workers in all its operations. The Canadian subsidiary, majority owned by the parent, has a work force of over 5,000 employees including managerial, supervisory, and factory personnel. There are several unions covering various categories of employees in the company, but the largest number of workers is covered by the United Rubber, Cork, Linoleum, and Plastic Workers of America.

The company has been operating in Canada for more than 30 years and enjoys a high reputation for its products. The Canadian operations of the company are quite profitable. Although the products of this company are not cheap, they do have a reputation for good quality, and, because of this, they enjoy a fair share of the market.

With regard to its personnel policies and practices, the company has built a good public image. People in the community regard Weston as an excellent company to work for. Pay is above average, working conditions are quite good and employee services are excellent. The company has a record of good industrial relations, and there has not been a strike, lockout, or serious work stoppage in the past eight years.

Weston has a reputation for promoting people from within. Almost all of its 180 foremen have been internally promoted and many of the production superintendents have also risen from the ranks. The personnel director prides himself on the upward mobility of the firm's employees. The president of the company made a particular point of mentioning this aspect at the last board meeting. Three out of five corporate directors have been with the company for more than 15 years

By Anwar Rashid. Copyright © 1991, 1994 by L & S Management Publications.

and have risen to their present levels from fairly humble beginnings within the company. The R&D director is a recent recruit from outside, but the president was forced into this situation because a suitable man was not available from within the company. Besides, they needed a man with wider experience and familiarity with developments in related industries.

The company's welfare programs are beyond reproach. Weston has excellent health programs which are looked after by three medical doctors and a chief medical officer who are all trained in industrial medicine. The older employees are looked after by the company even after their retirement. The nurses from the company's medical department pay visits to ailing employees during their time of employment as well as during retirement if necessary. The firm has an excellent retirement program for its employees.

Compared with many other organizations of the same size, Weston Tire has a large personnel department headed by Mr. Jenkins, the personnel director. Mr. Jenkins enjoys a powerful position and tremendous status within the company hierarchy. He is assisted by more than 40 staff members responsible for recruitment, training, safety, welfare, security, and union affairs. In addition, he has a separate section concerned with management development programs. Mr. Jenkins is eminently qualified for the post. Over the years he has diligently and conscientiously worked toward the development of a viable and credible personnel function within the organization. He has been instrumental in getting a comprehensive set of personnel policies established and consolidated. These are now strictly followed by line management and other departments within the company. The company takes a dim view of executives who fail to follow personnel policies laid down by the board of directors. The personnel director is one of the more powerful board members and is considered by divisional heads as a formidable opponent and consequently an individual not to be tangled with.

Weston's wage levels, incentive schemes, profit-sharing plans, and welfare programs, etc., are more than impressive and far better than programs offered by other industries in the area. The company has a large number of long-service employees, and they have excellent social clubs in which they and their families participate. The present president of the company was formerly the company's director of personnel.

Jim Maloney is one of the firm's project engineers and has been with the company since he graduated from university about eight years ago. From time to time he has attended various courses organized by the company and last year was sent to the United States to attend a residential training program for potential managers. Not long ago, Jim began working closely with Dickson Chemicals, a company which received a substantial amount of subcontracting work from Weston Tire Corporation. In fact, that company depended upon Weston Tire for the largest part of its income. The chief executive of Dickson Chemicals was very impressed by Jim Maloney's work and got to know him quite well during the term of a project at Dickson's. Jim was just the man they were looking for. There was an opening as Chief Project Engineer at Dickson Chemicals and the position was offered to Jim at a very attractive salary and with the prospect of challenging work. Actually, the salary earned by Jim at Weston Tire was no less attractive, but somehow he had started to feel that he had reached a dead end, and the projects had started to become somewhat mundane. Jim was tempted by the offer as he was looking for a change of pace. The opportunity seemed to have presented itself at just the right time. Jim accepted the job offer in principle, but the contract had to be formalized. However, it was decided that since Dickson Chemicals received a substantial amount of work from Weston Tire, it would be wise for Dickson Chemicals to let the personnel director of Weston know about it in advance so that a replacement could be found for him well before he took up his new assignment. In fact, it was Jim himself who went up to see Mr. Jenkins in order to inform him about his proposed move. Jim was quite surprised at Mr. Jenkins' reaction, as he seemed very upset about it. Jim had already discussed it with his own director (production) who was reluctant but agreeable.

On the same day that he spoke to Jenkins, Jim received a note from the company president stating that he wished to see him the next morning. Jim presented himself at the president's office at 9:45 AM, and found the president to be very upset — almost in a rage. The president informed him that the company took a very dim view of those employees, particularly at professional levels, who quit the company for better prospects with a subcontracting company. The president would do everything in his power to put a stop to this move. If necessary, he would wreck Dickson Chemicals if they "poached" any of Weston's managerial personnel. As far as Jim could make out, the president had already phoned Dickson's chief executive who received the message loud and clear and he immediately washed his hands of Jim.

QUESTIONS

1. Analyze the general work environment and policies of Weston Tire, highlighting the positive and negative features.
2. Comment on Jim's action as an employee. Bearing in mind the work environment of Weston Tire, how would you have behaved with respect to the Dickson offer if you were Jim?
3. Did the president act properly when faced with the prospect of Jim's departure? What type of leadership is he exhibiting by his actions?
4. What should Jim do now?

Zimmer Engineering Limited

Howard Pearson is a management consultant located in Dartmouth, Nova Scotia and holds a faculty position with the University of Eastern Canada. During a recent social event at the Dartmouth Boat Club, he was asked to undertake a consulting project by a fellow club member, Will Browning, Senior Vice-President, Zimmer Engineering Limited.

The firm's business chiefly involved the design and sales of fluid flow equipment for industrial applications. All the required engineering was done "in-house." The supply of components such as high-capacity pumps and the fabrication of custom installations were subcontracted to outside suppliers and metal fabricators. In 1991, with a new competitor on the scene, business had slowed noticeably. Will Browning was concerned that the firm's structure and job descriptions needed change if the company was to regain its market share.

On a regular basis, Zimmer Engineering employed 11 people (see Figure 1). The staff complement could swell to 17 when the workload was heavy. Will Browning saw the firm's problem as one in which certain key people had inappropriate responsibilities for their abilities and preferences. In particular, he pointed to the Zimmer brothers, Allan and Bernard, who served as President and Vice-President, Engineering, respectively. Allan Zimmer attempted to guide all aspects of the business, even though his educational background was in finance. And Bernard, although a competent engineer, had recently acquired a time-consuming "hobby" farm that prevented him from concentrating fully on his job responsibilities. According to Will Browning, he was not effectively supervising the design and production functions. Moreover, Bernard stated that he was not interested in devoting any additional time to the firm at the present time. This meant that Allan was becoming even more involved in the technical aspects of the

FIGURE 1 ORGANIZATIONAL CHART OF ZIMMER ENGINEERING LIMITED

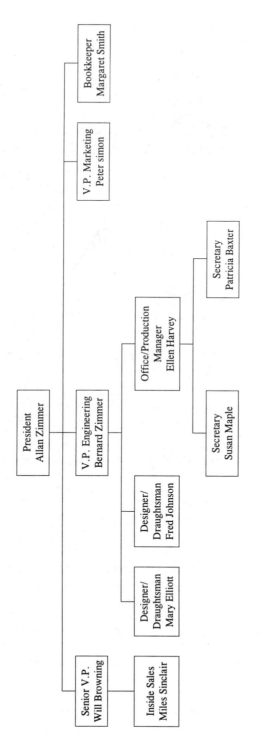

FIGURE 2   OPERATIONAL AREAS OF RESPONSIBILITY

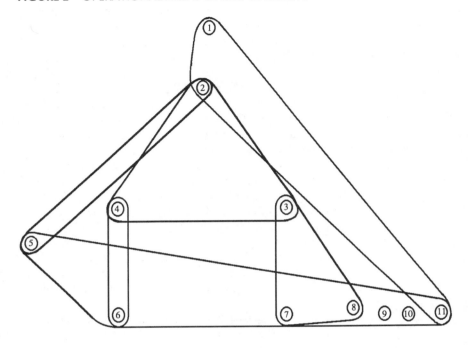

1.	President	Allan Zimmer
2.	Senior Vice-President	Will Browning
3.	Vice-President, Engineering	Bernard Zimmer
4.	Vice-President, Marketing	Peter Simon
5.	Office Manager and Manager of Production	Ellen Harvey
6.	Inside Sales	Miles Sinclair
7.	Designer/Draughtsman	Fred Johnson
8.	Designer/Draughtsman	Mary Elliott
9.	Secretary	Susan Maple
10.	Secretary	Patricia Baxter
11.	Bookkeeper	Margaret Smith

business, and expensive design and production errors were being made that generated poor customer relations. As an engineer with extensive business experience, Will Browning was usually called upon to sort out these problems after the fact. However, due to the existing structure and reporting relationships, he had no authority to prevent them from occurring and to eliminate the damage they caused. When he had suggested that Allan consult him prior to making decisions on technical matters, he was received cooly by the president. It seemed to be a matter of pride for Allan Zimmer to try to handle any sort of issue that arose.

With the quiet support of the rest of the employees, including Peter Simon and the one outside director of the company, Will Browning wanted to alter the role descriptions, authority, and responsibilities so that he would have effective control over the marketing, production, and engineering functions. The difficulty was that the Zimmers owned over 70% of the company's shares, and they certainly would not relinquish the status of their family willingly.

Howard Pearson was impressed by the work of Rensis Likert, a well-known organizational behaviourist. He decided to suggest a Likert linking pin model to reallocate responsibilities as shown in Figure 2. In this model, functional responsibilities for each job are restricted to those other positions which are also included in the same link or links that enclose that job. For example, Allan Zimmer would be involved only with Will Browning and the bookkeeper under the new plan. The revised structure would leave Allan in the position of president, but it would remove his influence over areas in which he had no expertise. Will Browning would become the buffer between the president and the technical side of the firm. Howard felt that Bernard Zimmer would probably accept the direct reporting relationship to Will Browning as long as Allan was still to be president. Bernard might even feel some relief as his responsibilities were diminished. Will would be able to step in directly to supervise design and production when Bernard was busy with his farm and to manage personally some of the more critical projects.

Howard also prepared a very brief job description for each management position (see Table 1). His intention was to involve the whole management group in filling in the details once the main thrust of the change was accepted. Will Browning totally approved of the plan, as it seemed to meet all his goals for changing Zimmer Engineering. However, he wondered how he would get Allan Zimmer to accept it.

QUESTIONS

1. Is Bernard Zimmer's attitude towards the firm irresponsible?
2. Evaluate Howard Pearson's plan. Do you think that it will be effective? What drawbacks does it have?
3. What alterations or additional measures are necessary?
4. How would you:
   (a) introduce the plan to Allan Zimmer?
   (b) implement the structural changes and new role descriptions? Answer in detail.

TABLE 1   ROLE DESCRIPTIONS

PRESIDENT

1.0   Areas of Responsibility and Reporting Relationship
   1.1   Administration and reporting for the Company Budget.
   1.2   Co-responsibility (along with Senior Vice-President) for financial planning.
   1.3   Administration and reporting for strategic planning studies.
   1.4   Bookkeeping, finance, and auditing.
   1.5   Coordinating these areas with the Senior Vice-President.

2.0   Areas for Which Objectives Should Be Set
   2.1   Company tax planning.
   2.2   Company borrowing.
   2.3   Administration costs.

3.0   Areas of Authority
   3.1   Financial statements and audit.
   3.2   Supervision of bookkeeper.
   3.3   Cheque signing authority (with Will Browning and Bernard Zimmer).

SENIOR VICE-PRESIDENT

1.0   Areas of Responsibility and Reporting Relationship
   1.1   Participation in objectives, strategies, and policies which are set and
         implemented for the functional areas of:
         (a)   Marketing
         (b)   Engineering
         (c)   Office Management
         (d)   Strategic Planning
         (e)   Production Management
   1.2   Formulation of Company Budget.
   1.3   Evaluation of performance within above functional areas.
   1.4   Definition of role descriptions as well as reporting and coordinating functions.
   1.5   Co-responsibility (along with Vice-President, Engineering) for marketing of
         engineered systems.
   1.6   Chair of the Executive Committee which will convene regularly to provide
         consulting assistance in matters of strategic and general management.
   1.7   Report to Board of Directors.

2.0   Areas for Which Objectives Should Be Set
   2.1   Return on investment.
   2.2   Net profit.
   2.3   Contribution margin.
   2.4   Development of new initiatives.
   2.5   Market areas:
         • types of customers
         • types of products
         • geographical areas

3.0   Areas of Authority
   3.1   Review of all personnel terminations.
   3.2   Final arbitration of salaries.
   3.3   Cheque signing authority (with Bernard Zimmer and Allan Zimmer) and
         review of all expenditures.
   3.4   Final authority in determining acceptance of sales and engineering contracts.
   3.5   Final arbitration of objectives, strategies, and policies that apply to individual
         functional areas of the company.

Continued...

TABLE 1   ROLE DESCRIPTIONS (Continued)

VICE-PRESIDENT, ENGINEERING

1.0 Areas of Responsibility and Reporting Relationship
  1.1 Marketing of hardware and technology.
  1.2 Co-responsibility (along with Senior Vice-President) for marketing of engineered systems.
  1.3 Job functions of draughting personnel.
  1.4 Research and development in areas of environmental control and engineered systems.
  1.5 Report to Senior Vice-President.

2.0 Areas for Which Objectives Should Be Set
  2.1 Sales of products and technology.
  2.2 Sales of engineered systems.
  2.3 Contribution margin of engineering area.
  2.4 Fixed costs of engineering area.
  2.5 Productivity of draughting personnel.

3.0 Areas of Authority
  3.1 Cheque co-signing authority (with Allan Zimmer and Will Browning).
  3.2 Supervision of draughting personnel.
  3.3 Salary review of draughting personnel.
  3.4 Engineering area budget.

VICE-PRESIDENT, MARKETING

1.0 Areas of Responsibility and Reporting Relationship
  1.1 Marketing of standard products.
  1.2 Development of new products and improvement of existing products.
  1.3 Research and development in area of industrial air handling and conditioning products.
  1.4 Report to Senior Vice-President.

2.0 Areas for Which Objectives Should Be Set
  2.1 Sales of standard products.
  2.2 Contribution margin of market area.
  2.3 Fixed costs of sales area.
  2.4 Productivity of inside sales personnel.

3.0 Areas of Authority
  3.1 Supervision of inside sales personnel.
  3.2 Salary review of inside sales personnel.
  3.3 Marketing area budget.

PRODUCTION MANAGER

1.0 Areas of Responsibility and Reporting Relationship
  1.1 Administration of outside manufacturing services relating to standard product lines.
  1.2 Purchasing of components from outside suppliers.
  1.3 Scheduling of purchased items and manufacturing priorities (for both standard products and engineered systems).
  1.4 Report to Senior Vice-President

2.0 Areas for Which Objectives Should Be Set
  2.1 Product quality/warranty expenses.
  2.2 Manufacturing costs.
  2.3 Contribution margin of manufactured products.

3.0 Areas of Authority
  3.1 Decisions as to outside manufacturers of standard products.
  3.2 Quality control.   *Continued...*

TABLE 1   ROLE DESCRIPTIONS (Continued)

OFFICE MANAGER

1.0 Areas of Responsibility and Reporting Relationship
   1.1   Office administration.
   1.2   Personnel administration
   - time keeping
   - vacation scheduling
   - absenteeism.
   1.3   Report to Senior Vice-President

2.0 Areas for Which Objectives Should Be Set
   2.1   Office efficiency.
   2.2   Personnel morale.
   2.3   Office expenses.

3.0 Areas of Authority
   3.1   Hiring and firing of clerical staff.
   3.2   Purchasing and maintenance of office equipment and supplies.

Exercises

Exercise 1

Earn Your Mark

Equity Theory

PURPOSE

To apply equity theory to a familiar situation.

PREPARATION

None required.

INTRODUCTION

You are a member of a study group which has recently submitted a major paper in your Organizational Behaviour class. Different group members took on different responsibilities in the preparation of the paper. The list below describes the different contributions that people made. For the purposes of this exercise, you will be assigned one of the following roles:

Conceptualizer: Contributed to the theoretical discussion of the issues and critiqued the drafts of the paper.

Primary Data Gatherer: Collected the raw data needed to meet the requirements of the assignment.

Data Analyst: Conducted a sophisticated statistical analysis of the primary data.

Secondary Source Analyst: Did the review of the literature and prepared the bibliography and references.

Organizer: Called the meetings for the group, scheduled the work, arranged for word processing, photocopying, and delivery of the paper. Provided the pizza.

Politician: Took charge of "professor politics" ensuring that the professor was constantly aware of the progress of the group.

Writer: Actually wrote the paper.

Ghost: Assigned to the group, attended the first meeting, announced the intention of doing an individual paper and then vanished. Received the group mark.

This is a group assignment and a group mark will be given. The exercise provides an application of equity theory and you will have the opportunity to assess the equity of your grade in light of your contribution and that of the others.

EARNING YOUR MARK — SCORE SHEET

Group Mark: _____

Roles	A	B $\left(\dfrac{\text{Group Mark}}{\text{Column A}}\right)$	C	D $\left(\dfrac{\text{Column C}}{\text{Column A}}\right)$
Conceptualizer				
Primary Data Gatherer				
Data Analyst				
Secondary Source Analyst				
Organizer				
Politician				
Writer				
Ghost				

Step 1:   In Column A give your assessment of the contribution of each member of the group including yourself. Express this as a percent. Do not consult with any other members of the group. For example, if you thought the conceptualizer did the most work, you might decide he or she deserved a high mark such as 87%. Rate each member's contribution.

Step 2:   In Column B calculate your equity ratios by dividing the mark your group earned for the assignment by your assessment of the contributions of the different members. This group mark is the mark given to you by your instructor, and can be recorded at the top of the score sheet. For example, if your contribution was 50% and your group mark was 75%, then your equity ratio is 1 ½. Your final mark was inflated by 1 ½ times as a result of the group effort.

Step 3:   Assess your feelings of equity from the group mark method of evaluating your contribution. Any ratio greater than one shows that the grade was inflated by the group mark. Any ratio less than one shows a loss associated with the group mark.

Step 4:   Hold a group discussion to assign individual marks to each member based on their contribution. The individual marks must be ordinary percentages, and the group average must remain as the original group mark. Record these new marks in Column C.

Step 5:   Calculate new equity ratios in Column D by dividing Column C by Column A. Express all marks as a percent.

Step 6:   Discuss the following issues with your group:

- How successful was your effort to achieve equity by adjusting the outcome?
- Evaluate the role of perceptual differences in achieving equity. What misperceptions occurred?
- Transfer this case to a work setting where you are involved in a team project. Imagine that you have been assigned to develop a new product for your high technology firm. Include the product manager as a team member.
  - Identify possible effort and outcome variables which would be associated with this project. Look for more than one outcome variable.
  - Develop strategies to minimize feelings of inequity amongst team members.
  - Distinguish long-term strategies which could be applied to future projects.
- A key difference between a unionized workplace and a non-unionized workplace is in method of determining pay. Non-union workplaces usually reflect the employers interest in rewarding employees individually on the basis of merit as judged by the employer. Unionized workplaces typically have a small number of "pay bands" and employees advance on the basis of seniority. Use equity theory to explain the union position on pay.

Improving Communication

Perception and Attribution

PURPOSE

To improve interpersonal communication skills through an understanding of how behaviour is perceived by other people and how individuals make attributions based on those perceptions.

PREPARATION

Your instructor may request that you complete the questionnaire prior to class.

INTRODUCTION

Read the four conclusions provided for each statement. Think of them as four points on a ruler, points numbered two, four, six, and eight. Use them to determine a score from zero to ten which you think best describes your own situation.

1. If I heard from a third party that my best friend has described my personality,

I would be quite worried about what the description would be.	2
It would be fairly likely that it would be news to me.	4
I would not mind hearing it since I rather doubt I would be surprised.	6
I am quite sure I would know exactly what they were talking about.	8

    Score 0 to 10 [ ]

2. One of the things that I think is most important about a best friend is that

I would not feel that I would have to share my thoughts or feelings. 2
The relationship would have lots of room for personal privacy. 4
We would share some things but not others. 6
We would be completely open with each other. 8

Score 0 to 10

3. If I had a performance review by my supervisor in which I was told things about how I did my work,

I would not want to hear any of it because I expect my supervisor 2
would describe things about my work that I did not know about.
I think there would be some things that I would be familiar with, but a 4
lot of it could be news.
I rather suspect I would know most of what was going to be said. 6
I look forward to my performance reviews because I want to know 8
how my supervisor sees me.

Score 0 to 10

4. I think that when I am at work it is important that,

The distinction I make between work life and private life is absolute. 2
I do not always have to tell other people what I am doing in my 4
private life.
I can share some of my personal feelings with others if I want to. 6
I not keep any secrets from my co-workers. 8

Score 0 to 10

5. If I was married and my spouse and I went on one of those TV shows where husbands and wives have to guess what their spouse is thinking or feeling,

I would dread going on such a show because I would be worried that 2
my spouse would come up with all sorts of things about me that I was
not aware of.
My spouse probably knows quite a number of things about me that I 4
don't know.
I would not expect many surprises. 6
I think that kind of experience would be very helpful as my spouse is 8
intimately familiar with me.

Score 0 to 10

6. If I was married, the kind or relationship I would like would be one where

I could still maintain a strong sense of privacy about my personal 2
beliefs and feelings.
The two of us could share a few things of mutual interest. 4
I could tell my spouse about a lot of the things that I was feeling. 6
I would be completely open and exposed to my spouse. 8

Score 0 to 10

Scores

Feedback: Add scores for questions 1, 3, and 5 = _____

Self Disclosure: Add scores for questions 2, 4, and 6 = _____

JOHARI WINDOW   (Reference: Joseph Luft, *Group Processes: An Introduction to Group Dynmamics*. Palo Alto, California: Mayfield, 1984).

Plot your scores in the window below. The upper-left corner represents a zero score. Scores rise to 30 moving to the right and downward. Draw your window and label the panes in the window.

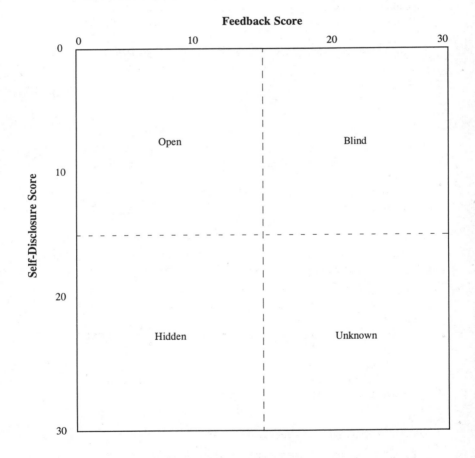

Task

After plotting your JoHari window, analyze for potential change. The area over which you have most control is that of self-disclosure. There are problems associated with both too much and too little self-disclosure.

Rate yourself using the following list of reasons for self disclosure and then identify areas for potential self improvement.

Reasons for Self Disclosure

1. **Catharsis:** Used to relieve a personal burden, ie., regretting past behaviour which was harmful.
2. **Self Clarification:** Talking things out people can sort out beliefs, opinions, thoughts, attitudes, feelings.
3. **Self Validation:** Getting others to confirm the wisdom of your thoughts or actions. Checking it out.
4. **Reciprocity:** A self disclosure by one person encourages self disclosure by others. Can be used to get others to reveal themselves.
5. **Impression Formation:** Using self disclosure to create a particular impression of yourself. Bragging.
6. **Relationship Maintenance and Enhancement:** Ongoing openness helps to maintain existing relationships.
7. **Social Control:** Telling tales about others for personal gain, includes "squealing" or "tattling."
8. **Manipulation:** When the self disclosure includes a hidden agenda which remains hidden.

Analysis
Share your findings with a partner.

Classical Conditioning in Advertisements

Learning and Reinforcement

PURPOSE

To analyse the use of classical conditioning principles in advertising.

PREPARATION

Bring at least one copy of a magazine to class. Several different magazines would be better. Scissors are useful.

INTRODUCTION

This is a small-group project. The task of your group is to find a variety of ads that illustrate classical learning theory and two of its characteristics.

Classical learning theory can be used to analyze a wide variety of modern ads. In a typical ad the viewer is exposed to an image of the product as well as to some seemingly unrelated image which provides a diverting message. The advertisers have learned that such ads help the viewer to recall the product for a longer period of time and in a more favourable light. Classical learning theory explains this benefit through the process of conditioning.

The first step involves selecting a stimulus for which the viewer has already acquired a suitable response. In the use of sex in advertising, the image of a provocative pose or exposure (the stimulus) will evoke feelings of excitement or pleasure in some viewers (the response). Since this stimulus-response pattern was not learned in the ad, the elements are called the UnConditioned Stimulus (UCS) and the UnConditioned Response (UCR). The purpose of the ad is to cause an association between a new stimulus (the product) and the existing response. Since this stimulus-response pattern is learned by the viewer, it is called the Conditioned

Stimulus (CS) and the Conditioned Response (CR). The conditioning is done through repetition of the ad, although perceptual factors such as size, location, colour, movement, novelty, etc. can affect the learning.

PART I

Look through your magazines and find five ads that employ classical conditioning. Select ads which use different UCS–UCR bonds. Identify to the members of your group the elements of the ad: the UCS, the UCR, and, of course, the conditioned stimulus. Discuss whether the UCS–UCR bond has been selected because of a real association with the product (as in the strength of the Rock of Gibraltar for the Prudential Insurance Company) or whether it has been selected on the basis of the power of the bond (as in any ad using sex when the product is not sex).

Stimulus Generalization and Stimulus Discrimination

Another aspect of classical conditioning which can be analyzed in advertisements is the related processes of generalization and discrimination of the stimulus. When people respond to a stimulus, they may in fact be capable of giving a similar response to a whole class of stimuli which are similar to the one for which the response was originally learned. This learning phenomenon has been eagerly adopted by advertisers and is most clearly apparent in the marketing of clones. The advertiser hopes that the favourable S–R bond for the original can be generalized to include the new stimulus of the clone. Sometimes the product is not a clone but nonetheless hopes to ride famous coattails. The ads vary in terms of the honesty of the pitch towards generalization because some are virtual knock-offs of the original.

Stimulus discrimination is the reverse process. In this situation, the viewer has a pre-existing S–R bond which applies to a whole class of stimuli. The advertiser wishes his product to stand out from the rest and must therefore get the viewer to discriminate and respond only to his stimulus. The popular Smirnoff Vodka ads are a good example of stimulus discrimination ("There's vodka and then there's Smirnoff!"). This is a common problem for products that don't develop strong brand loyalty, because the consumer tends to think they are all alike.

PART II

Find two ads that illustrate stimulus generalization or stimulus discrimination, and explain the elements to the members of your group.

PART I   CLASSICAL CONDITIONING WORK SHEET

NAME: _____

Ad #1   Description: _____

UCS: _____

UCR: _____

CS: _____

Relationship of UCS–UCR bond to the product: _____

_____

_____

Ad #2   Description: _____

UCS: _____

UCR: _____

CS: _____

Relationship of UCS–UCR bond to the product: _____

_____

_____

Ad #3   Description: _____

UCS: _____

UCR: _____

CS: _____

Relationship of UCS–UCR bond to the product: _____

_____

_____

Ad #4   Description: _____

UCS: _____

UCR: _____

CS: _____

Relationship of UCS–UCR bond to the product:

_____

_____

Ad #5   Description: _____

UCS: _____

UCR: _____

CS: _____

Relationship of UCS–UCR bond to the product: _____

_____

_____

PART II   STIMULUS DISCRIMINATION AND STIMULUS GENERALIZATION

Ad #1   Description: _____

General stimulus: _____

Discrete stimulus: _____

Description of generalization or discrimination: _____

_____

_____

Ad #2   Description: _____

General stimulus: _____

Discrete stimulus: _____

Description of generalization or discrimination: _____

_____

_____

Worker Monitoring

Learning and Reinforcement

PURPOSE

To examine the growing trend of worker monitoring systems and the implication of learning theory on these practices.

PREPARATION

None required.

INTRODUCTION

A growing trend in personnel supervision practice has been the use of computerized methods of monitoring the work of employees. Often these systems are a spin-off from computerization for some other purpose such as inventory control or scheduling. A typical example which is familiar to shoppers at a modern supermarket is the cashier at the checkout counter. In addition to the price, the checkout process records the item and the quantity purchased for inventory control. These records are maintained for each cashier, and, with the addition of a timer, the store is able to tell how long it takes the cashier to register the sale. Even a fairly simple system can conduct several analyses of this database: How many sales can the cashier record per hour? How many are not committed to memory and have to be looked up? How many errors are corrected? Word processing in the office provides additional methods of automated supervision. Computers can count keystrokes, words, and documents and produce a performance report based on these variables. Generally the analyses are of speed and accuracy.

Modern telephones also provide opportunities for monitoring of worker behaviour. Calls can be monitored for personal use as well as to ensure the employee is projecting the correct image on business calls.

Relatively cheap video cameras have encouraged more companies to use them for security purposes. Often the security issue is internal, and it is an easy step to move from checking for pilfering to checking for performance.

Companies using these systems cite the following benefits:

1. **Cost:** These monitoring systems usually have a low operating cost although the initial set-up may be expensive.
2. **Quantity Control:** The systems usually provide good measures of speed and accuracy.
3. **Face Validity:** The employer usually has a strong feeling of providing effective supervision.

PROBLEMS

1. **Worker Resentment:** Monitoring often leads to union grievances and reduced worker moral. Better workers may leave.
2. **Job Stress:** A typical worker complaint is that of increased job stress resulting from the monitoring.
3. **Gender Bias:** Monitoring systems are more common in female dominated jobs.
4. **Unintended Consequences:** Employers may ignore the qualitative side of employee performance, workers may be motivated to beat the system rather than to do their actual work.

EXERCISE

Objective

To apply the concept of behaviour modification to employee monitoring.

Method

Working in a group of up to six students, complete the following tasks.

Step 1: Briefly review the following concepts of employee behviour modification.

- Establish clear goals for employees
- Have the employees provide accurate information on their performance.
- Give positive reinforcement for all improvements in behaviour as well as for accurate and honest record keeping.
- Use shaping and the scheduling of reinforcement to modify behaviour toward the goals.u
- Use extinction to eliminate undesired behaviour.
- Use praise, recognition, and intrinsic rewards from the job itself as positive reinforcement; in particular, identify feedback mechanisms which serve as automatic reinforcers.
- Avoid punishment.

Step 2: Make a list of five different examples of worker monitoring. Draw upon your own experiences as a worker and as a customer.

Step 3:   Evaluate each example in terms of the effectiveness of the behaviour modification.

- outline the strengths and weaknesses of each system.
- what behaviours are being monitored?
- what behaviours are being reinforced?

Step 4:   Propose ways to improve each worker-monitoring method.

Step 5:   Evaluate each in terms of its ability to motivate towards better performance. Has it dealt with qualitative as well as quantitative methods of measurement? An ideal system of worker monitoring is one which provides the worker with the most information about their performance and thus the greatest opportunity for self-control.

Step 6:   As a group, discuss the question, "Do these worker-monitoring systems interfere with the dignity of the worker?"

The Model Boss

Learning and Reinforcement

PURPOSE

To evaluate the impact of role models on individual behaviour and in the formation of corporate culture.

PREPARATION

Your instructor may request that you complete the steps listed below prior to class.

INTRODUCTION

One of the most powerful forms of learning is through the process psychologists call modelling. According to this theory, we learn behaviours as a result of copying them from people we think are important or admirable. This is most apparent with fads and fashions where some particular celebrity will set a style for dress or mannerism or even language. With celebrities, the mass media plays an important role in communicating the new style. We also copy the behaviour of our peers, particularly those we consider to be leaders. Indeed, one useful definition of leadership is the ability to establish a fashion in a group. With peers, the contact is more immediate and intimate and as a result can be very powerful.

In each case the learning process is the same. First, we have a favourable attitude toward the person, and then we begin to associate their specific behaviours as part of their overall image. Our positive view about them as a person is carried over into what they do or say or wear or whatever. We accept these other aspects of the person uncritically and often unconsciously as part of the whole "package." Part of admiring someone involves wanting them to admire you and so we imitate their behaviour in the expectation that this admiration will be reciprocated. Since "imitation is the sincerest form of flattery," this return of admiration usually occurs and the cycle is reinforced.

We are not normally aware of the influence of modelling on our behaviour. We may think about it at the level of fashion (i.e., what people wear at the office), but otherwise the process is largely unconscious. The purpose of this exercise is to dig into this unconscious material.

Step 1:   Identify a person who you think is a model for you. To look for corporate influences, you should choose one of your supervisors managers; it need not be your immediate supervisor. Your respect for that person might be moderated by your daily work relations. It should be someone you have some interaction with, so that when you see them and hear them speak, you can observe mannerisms and other aspects of behaviour. If you do not have a current "boss," then find some other person, perhaps from a sports team you are on or a volunteer group or a friendship group or perhaps even a family.

Step 2:   Over the next two weeks, observe the behaviour of this person and those around him or her. Identify those behaviours that seem to be imitated by you and by others. You may find it easier to see the modelling in other people's behaviour rather than in your own, at least at first. List the behaviours under the following categories:

1.   **Clothing:** This is the easiest, so start here. Businesses often have a quite pronounced but unofficial dress code. The boss will set the code by personal behaviour.

   _____

   _____

   _____

   _____

   _____

   _____

2.   **Language:** Business, like any other subculture, has developed its own language, words, and expressions which relate to daily worklife. This language is in part practical because it is a shorthand reference to things normally used in the business. Some of it is faddish in that it is a popular expression, but you could get along very well without it because there is a plain English word that would do just as well. Sometimes it is just an inappropriate overuse of a particular word or expression. Taken together, special language serves to identify who is in the know and who is not.

   _____

   _____

   _____

   _____

   _____

   _____

3. **Routine Behaviours:** The official work day might be nine to five, but there will be some additional norm about how early you should be and exactly when you can leave. If you punch a time clock, this might not vary a lot, but in a white collar office this is often quite important. Also check out routines about coffee breaks, lunch hour, etc. Employees who do not model their behaviour correctly may learn of their error.

---

4. **Mannerisms:** This category includes the little pieces of personal behaviour which we all have but are not very conscious of. They include the behaviours we have which others might think are funny or eccentric. Sometimes these become quite stylish in the sense that everyone does them. They can include our non-verbal communication patterns which we use to supplement our verbal communication. This one is trickier, so you will have to look harder.

Step 3:   Report your findings to your discussion group. How similar are the different observation people have marked? How strong was the modelling?

Cognitive Learning in Trade Journals

Learning and Reinforcement

PURPOSE

To apply the principles of cognitive learning to advertising.

PREPARATION

Your instructor may request that you analyze five ads prior to class. In any event, you will be asked to get access to a copy of a trade journal. Your library may be willing to provide an old issue for this purpose.

INTRODUCTION

Commercial advertisements are designed to shape our attitude about particular products and services. One of the methods used by advertising agencies involves what psychologists call cognitive learning. This is learning that involves our ordinary thought processes and is the kind of learning you most frequently use. When you read a text book or listen to a lecture and your brain processes the information it receives, this is cognitive learning. Along with this cognitive processing of information, our brain also undertakes an evaluative processing of the information being received. Is this information worthwhile or not? This may occur at various levels of awareness.

In cognitive oriented ads the message at the front is quite clear: here are the features of our computer, these are the advantages of our credit card as compared to others, and so forth. Typically the ad contains a lot of information. The image of the product might be quite obscure or even absent.

At another level the ad provides a different message: Are you computer literate? Ours is a technological society, are you part of it? How up to date are you?

This second level of ads can be very powerful when ads are looked at within a particular category. For example, the Toronto Star runs a regular section of computer ads. The main products are personal computers and business software. This market is still dominated by a large number of small suppliers, each of whom can only afford a small ad in a large circulation paper like the Star, so the paper groups the ads together. The effect of this is twofold: to display the competition amongst the companies and encourage technical advertising of their features, and to convey an overall positive image of the relevance of computer applications to modern business. The ads themselves rarely focus on the image theme that you need computers to be in business today.

For this exercise, use trade journals as a source of data. Pick one trade journal. For the purpose of this exercise, a trade journal could include something outside of business, i.e., a magazine for a particular sport such as running or sailing or some specific hobby. The idea is to get a focused journal. Collect at least five cognitive ads and analyze them at the two levels: first for the overt content and then for the underlying attitude or value set being conveyed. Compare the ads looking for common sets of values and attitudes.

Your instructor will direct you to either hand in this exercise or to provide a verbal report.

JOURNAL: Name the journal and briefly outline its target market.

NAME: _____

TARGET MARKET: _____

AD #1: Content of Ad _____

_____

_____

_____

AD #2: Content of Ad _____

_____

_____

_____

AD #3: Content of Ad _____

_____

_____

_____

AD #4: Content of Ad _____

_____

_____

_____

AD #5: Content of Ad _____

_____

_____

_____

Underlying Attitudes and Values of the Ads:

_____

_____

_____

_____

_____

Exercise 7

What's the Use
— Innovation

Creativity

PURPOSE

To experience the "creative" demands of business.

PREPARATION

Your instructor may request that you complete the questionnaire prior to class.

INTRODUCTION

Your supervisor has given you a very strange job. After a corporate merger and restructuring, there are some leftovers, and she has sent you a list of this "stuff" for your input. She expects that you will make good use of these "things."

PART I

Look over the list and come up with as many possible uses as you can think of. Be creative in your ideas and don't censor your own work. Your supervisor will think any idea is worth looking at right now.

The "Stuff"

1.   Fifty gross, black rotary dial telephones.

_____

_____

_____

_____

_____

_____

2. Seventy-five office sets including large, double-pedestal oak desks (Empire style) as well as chairs, credenzas, etc.

_____

3. Approximately 3,000 copies of annual reports from past years. All are printed on glossy paper in full colour. All refer to companies which no longer exist.

_____

4. Complete fixtures for two company cafeterias. One seating 100 using cafeteria service and the other seating 20 with full dining room service.

_____

5. Approximately 10,000 hub caps for assorted cars of various ages.

_____

6. One corporate art collection of 400 pieces, but of little appraised value.

_____

7. A remote fishing camp used by executives. Completely equipped and ready for the next season. The staff were not advised of the restructuring.

_____
_____
_____
_____
_____
_____

8. The public goodwill of a now disbanded furniture company.

_____
_____
_____
_____
_____
_____

9. One hundred and thirty-five employees.

_____
_____
_____
_____
_____
_____

PART II

Compare your ideas with the others in your group. There are no right or wrong ideas, but you are looking for ideas that go beyond the conventional use. Try to grade them in terms of conventionality: i.e., strictly conventional, same use but very different target, very different use, off the wall.

Use your group to add to the lists. Follow the brainstorming technique of avoiding judgements about ideas; just list them all.

Look for combinations of ideas from the different items. Synthesis is a higher form of creativity. List the combined ideas below.

_____
_____
_____
_____
_____
_____
_____

PART III

Evaluate the process in terms of the creativity achieved. What were the major barriers to creativity? What were the major stimulants of the creative process?

Exercise 8

Self-Esteem Inventory

Personality and Attitudes

PURPOSE

To analyze the concept of self-esteem and to examine various elements of that overall concept.

PREPARATION

Your instructor may request that you complete the questionnaire prior to class.

INTRODUCTION

Self-esteem is the term popularly used to describe positive feelings of self worth and a belief in personal ability to perform effectively and to cope in a variety of situations. It is not a measure of actual ability, but rather a measure of personal attitude. Such attitudes can have a powerful effect on personal performance since behaviour is the result of a combination of ability and motivation. Of the two, motivation may well be the more important. A key ingredient of motivation is a personal belief in one's own potential. Self-esteem inventories measure that belief system.

The following questionnaire is easy to use and is self-scoring. Each of the following 45 words and phrases relate to aspects of self-esteem. Decide how well each of them fits you. Be as honest as you can with yourself. Rate them as they apply to you. A common problem with instruments like these is that people put down the answer that they think the examiner wants to hear or that they think is the most socially desirable. Try to avoid this bias when picking your answer.

The original version of this self-esteem inventory was developed by Keitha Davey, Gail Higginson and Barbara Learn.

After you have filled out the questionnaire, use the scoring key to tabulate the results. Meet with your group to analyze the instrument, compare your results, and discuss the questions found at the end of this activity.

Rate as follows:

A	NEVER describes me
B	RARELY describes me
C	SOMETIMES describes me
D	MOST OF THE TIME describes me

1	helpful	_____	24	achiever	_____
2	easily discouraged	_____	25	cooperative	_____
3	makes decisions easily	_____	26	dependent	_____
4	likes to succeed	_____	27	problem solver	_____
5	tries hard	_____	28	capable	_____
6	pleasant	_____	29	sets own goals	_____
7	easily embarrassed	_____	30	agreeable	_____
8	leader	_____	31	pessimistic	_____
9	shy	_____	32	assertive	_____
10	practical	_____	33	high aspirations	_____
11	cheerful	_____	34	peacemaker	_____
12	timid	_____	35	follower	_____
13	persistent	_____	36	skilled	_____
14	self-confident	_____	37	popular	_____
15	ambitious	_____	38	feels inferior	_____
16	likeable	_____	39	analytical	_____
17	self-doubting	_____	40	creative	_____
18	shows initiative	_____	41	blaming	_____
19	intelligent	_____	42	flexible	_____
20	accepts new ideas	_____	43	realistic	_____
21	confused	_____	44	independent	_____
22	planner	_____	45	enduring	_____
23	competent	_____			

SELF-ESTEEM SCORE SHEET

This self-esteem inventory has five sub-scales. Transfer your answers from the above sheet and circle the score for each choice. The item number is provided to help in transferring the score. Do NOT change any of your answers. Notice that the responses in the second factor score in a different direction to the others. Add up the score for each sub-scale and then combine the two for a total self-esteem score. Compare your score to the norms provided.

	AMIABILITY				
#	Item	A	B	C	D
1	helpful	1	2	3	4
6	pleasant	1	2	3	4
11	cheerful	1	2	3	4
16	likeable	1	2	3	4
20	accept new ideas	1	2	3	4
25	cooperative	1	2	3	4
30	agreeable	1	2	3	4
34	peacemaker	1	2	3	4
37	popular	1	2	3	4
40	creative	1	2	3	4
42	flexible	1	2	3	4
45	enduring	1	2	3	4
	TOTAL SCORE =		+	+	+
	=				

	CONFIDENCE				
#	Item	A	B	C	D
2	easily discouraged	4	3	2	1
7	easily embarrassed	4	3	2	1
9	shy	4	3	2	1
12	timid	4	3	2	1
17	self-doubting	4	3	2	1
21	confused	4	3	2	1
26	dependent	4	3	2	1
31	pessimistic	4	3	2	1
35	follower	4	3	2	1
38	feels inferior	4	3	2	1
41	blaming	4	3	2	1
	TOTAL SCORE =		+	+	+
	=				

ACHIEVEMENT					
#	Item	A	B	C	D
4	likes to succeed	1	2	3	4
15	ambitious	1	2	3	4
24	achiever	1	2	3	4
29	sets own goals	1	2	3	4
33	high aspirations	1	2	3	4
	TOTAL SCORE =		+	+	+
	=				

CONTROL					
#	Item	A	B	C	D
3	makes decisions easily	1	2	3	4
8	leader	1	2	3	4
13	persistent	1	2	3	4
18	shows initiative	1	2	3	4
22	planner	1	2	3	4
27	problem solver	1	2	3	4
32	assertive	1	2	3	4
36	skilled	1	2	3	4
39	analytical	1	2	3	4
43	realistic	1	2	3	4
	TOTAL SCORE =		+	+	+
	=				

COMPETENCE					
#	Item	A	B	C	D
5	tries hard	1	2	3	4
10	practical	1	2	3	4
14	self-confident	1	2	3	4
19	intelligent	1	2	3	4
23	competent	1	2	3	4
28	capable	1	2	3	4
44	independent	1	2	3	4
	TOTAL SCORE =		+	+	+
	=				

SUB-SCALE FACTOR	SCORES
Amiability	
Confidence	
Achievement	
Control	
Competence	
SELF-ESTEEM	

Interpretation

1. **Amiability:** Amiability refers to a positive attitude about getting along with others. Personal values stress the importance of interpersonal processes rather than on a task orientation.
2. **Confidence:** Confidence relates to a positive belief in one's own ability and is the result of a feeling of emotional security.
3. **Achievement:** The need to achieve has long been recognized as a hallmark of business success. It is usually defined in terms of a person who gets positive reinforcement from achieving recognized goals. A corollary of this value is that the person is not motivated by unachievable or unrealistic goals.
4. **Control:** This factor is most closely aligned to the values associated with a manager. The control referred to involves the control of others.
5. **Competence:** The value factor is a subjective rating of personal competence. Positive self-esteem requires a strong belief in one's own ability.

DISCUSSION QUESTIONS

1. Analyze the items in each sub-scale to broaden your understanding of the factor. Was there a relationship in your score between the items?
2. Describe the kind of "organizational persons" who would score highest in the different factors, i.e., who would you find in top management, personnel, marketing, research and development, etc. Is there a fit between your score and your career plan?
3. Attitude and motivational factors are subject to personal development; indeed, a large part of management training would fall in this category. Prepare a personal development plan and present it to your group.
4. Discuss any minority group bias you suspect may exist in the concept of self-esteem. To what extent is self-esteem an ethnocentric concept of western, industrialized, male culture?

NORMS

PROFILE CHART

Percentile

	0	10	20	30	40	50	60	70	80	90	100
Amiability		36 37	38	39	40	41 42	43	44	45	47 48	
Confident		20	24	25	26 27 28	29	30	31	32	35	
Achievement		15	16		17	18	19	20		21	
Control	25		30	31	32	33 34	35	36	37	39	
Competence	21	22	23	24		25	26		27	28	
Self-esteem	130		135	140		145	150	155	160	165	

Exercise 9

Risk Taking

Personality and Attitudes

PURPOSE

To measure individual differences in risk taking.

PREPARATION

Your instructor may request that you complete the questionnaire prior to class.

INTRODUCTION

See Part II.

PART I

Complete and score the following questionnaire. Score each item as True or False as it pertains to you and your past behaviour.

_____ 1. I am a smoker.

_____ 2. At least once in the past I have quit my current job before finding a replacement for it.

_____ 3. Over the past two years I have received two or more traffic tickets.

_____ 4. My recreational activities over the past three years have included at least one that could be considered risky, such as downhill skiing, water skiing, motor vehicle racing, mountain activities, sky diving, hunting, white-water sports, etc.

_____ 5. At least once in the past I have disagreed with my supervisor about a business issue in a private meeting.

_____ 6. At least once in the past I have disagreed with my supervisor about a business issue in a group setting which included my supervisor's peers and supervisor (i.e., the next level of management).

_____ 7. I have been a passenger in a motor vehicle when the driver was clearly impaired by drugs or alcohol.

_____ 8. I have driven a motor vehicle when I was clearly impaired by drugs or alcohol.

_____ 9. I have critically evaluated the work of my peers knowing that my comments would get back to them.

_____ 10. I never buy trip or flight cancellation insurance.

_____ 11. In a business venture I have risked the equivalent of at least one year's income.

_____ 12. I regularly eat high cholesterol "junk food."

_____ 13. I have applied for a transfer or promotion to another department knowing that my supervisor will resent what I am doing.

_____ 14. I have appplied for a transfer or promotion to another department without discussing it with my current supervisor.

_____ 15. When driving on a crowded street I never leave room in front of my car for another car to get in.

16. I would not mind a sales job that had good earning potential but involved a very large proportion of "cold calls" (i.e., no previous contact with the potential customer).

_____ 17. I wager at least $20 per week in various forms of gambling including lotteries and office pools.

_____ 18. When planning a vacation I much prefer to visit someplace new, someplace that neither I nor my friends have previously been to.

_____ 19. Most of my personal investments are either in the stock market or are directly invested in my own business.

_____ 20. In the past year I have been asked by at least one friend or acquaintance to join them by investing in a business venture.

[   ]   TOTAL NUMBER OF "TRUE" ANSWERS

GROUP SCORE: Record the number of people with each score		
0 =	7 =	14 =
1 =	8 =	15 =
2 =	9 =	16 =
3 =	10 =	17 =
4 =	11 =	18 =
5 =	12 =	19 =
6 =	13 =	20 =

PART II

A modern psychological theory has evaluated the usefulness of risk taking behaviour in people. The theory assesses Risk Utility and evaluates the way in which individuals will give a positive evaluation to risk taking by crediting certain benefits such as unloading stress, showing aggression, impressing others, showing independence, taking self-control, opposing authority, coping with anxiety, gaining acceptance into a peer group, etc.

The theory further states that people vary in the level of their need to take a risk and will even deliberately undertake risky behaviour if they perceive things as being too safe. This process is called risk homeostasis.

In your study group, examine the question of risk taking as a personality style. Compare people's scores looking for categories. Can you distinguish the risk takers from the risk avoiders? Let these individuals discuss how they see this label fitting themselves.

This risk-taking scale includes items from a wide variety of activities. This is based on the concept of cognitive dissonance, which states that individual belief systems should be internally consistent. Therefore, people are unlikely to be risk takers in one part of their life and risk avoiders in another. How does this fit with your experience?

Take a few minutes in your group to evaluate the theory and the questionnaire.

What Matters in a Job?

Drives and Needs

PURPOSE

To measure individual differences in needs.

PREPARATION

Your instructor may request that you complete the questionnaire prior to class.

INTRODUCTION

Think about your future career. Think about the ideal job you would like to have. What matters the most to you? What matters the least to you? Listed below are the same three groups of characteristics about jobs. Rank each group separately from 5 for the most important to 1 for the least important. Do this on your own.

CAREER	
#	**Rank this Group from 5 (Most) to 1 (Least)**
1 _____	My co-workers will be very friendly
2 _____	The company will protect me from harassment by customers, fellow employees, and supervisors.
3 _____	The working conditions will protect me from bad weather.
4 _____	The work will be creative and challenging.
5 _____	My supervisor will recognize the value of my work and praise me for it.

CAREER (Continued)	
#	**Rank this Group from 5 (Most) to 1 (Least)**
6 _____	I will be able to participate in decision making.
7 _____	The company will sponsor social activities both on and off the job.
8 _____	The pay and fringe benefits will be good.
9 _____	There will be good opportunities for promotion to a higher status job.
10 _____	The company will work hard to maintain safe working conditions.
#	**Rank this Group from 5 (Most) to 1 (Least)**
11 _____	I will get along well with my supervisor.
12 _____	There will be a merit pay system based on performance.
13 _____	The company will provide a cafeteria for its employees.
14 _____	The work itself will have a flexible schedule and I will have a lot of autonomy.
15 _____	There will be excellent job security.

Think about your current job (or if you don't have one right now think about the last job you had). What are the best things about that job? What are the worst things about the job? Listed below are three groups of characteristics about jobs. Rank each group separately from 5 for the best thing to 1 for the worst thing. Do this on your own.

CURRENT JOB	
#	**Rank this Group from 5 (Best) to 1 (Worst)**
1 _____	My co-workers will be very friendly
2 _____	The company will protect me from harassment by customers, fellow employees, and supervisors.
3 _____	The working conditions will protect me from bad weather.
4 _____	The work will be creative and challenging.
5 _____	My supervisor will recognize the value of my work and praise me for it.

CURRENT JOB (Continued)	
#	Rank this Group from 5 (Best) to 1 (Worst)
6 _____	I will be able to participate in decision making.
7 _____	The company will sponsor social activities both on and off the job.
8 _____	The pay and fringe benefits will be good.
9 _____	There will be good opportunities for promotion to a higher status job.
10 _____	The company will work hard to maintain safe working conditions.
#	Rank this Group from 5 (Best) to 1 (Worst)
11 _____	I will get along well with my supervisor.
12 _____	There will be a merit pay system based on performance.
13 _____	The company will provide a cafeteria for its employees.
14 _____	The work itself will have a flexible schedule and I will have a lot of autonomy.
15 _____	There will be excellent job security.

Scoring

The items in this list represent the five levels of need found in Abraham Maslow's Hierarchy of Needs. Each of the groups of five has an item which refers to one of Maslow's needs as applied to the workplace. Use the number in the left-hand column to sort out the items. Add the scores together for each level of the hierarchy.

The instrument also differentiates between your needs as they exist as an ideal and the way in which your current employer is meeting your needs. These are also scored separately.

YOUR CAREER: WHAT IS YOUR HIERARCHY OF NEEDS?

Self-actualization: Add together the ranks for items 4, 6, and 14

(4) _____ + (6) _____ + (14) _____ = _____

Self-esteem: Add together the ranks for items 5, 9, and 12

(5) _____ + (9) _____ + (12) _____ = _____

Social: Add together the ranks for items 1, 7, and 11

(1) _____ + (7) _____ + (11) _____ = _____

Security: Add together the ranks for items 2, 10, and 15

(2) _____ + (10) _____ + (15) _____ = _____

Physiological: Add together the ranks for items 3, 8, and 13

(3) _____ + (8) _____ + (13) _____ = _____

CURRENT JOB: HOW ARE YOUR NEEDS BEING MET?

Self-actualization: Add together the ranks for items 4, 6, and 14

(4) _____ + (6) _____ + (14) _____ = _____

Self-esteem: Add together the ranks for items 5, 9, and 12

(5) _____ + (9) _____ + (12) _____ = _____

Social: Add together the ranks for items 1, 7, and 11

(1) _____ + (7) _____ + (11) _____ = _____

Security: Add together the ranks for items 2, 10, and 15

(2) _____ + (10) _____ + (15) _____ = _____

Physiological: Add together the ranks for items 3, 8, and 13

(3) _____ + (8) _____ + (13) _____ = _____

TABLE OF RESULTS		
Hierarchy of Need	**Your Career**	**Current Job**
Self-actualization		
Self-esteem		
Social		
Security		
Physiological		

TASK

Analyze your results and compare them with those of the other members of your discussion group.

1. What is your strongest need? Is it being met in your current job?
2. Where differences exist between your needs and your current job, discuss ways of redesigning the job to better meet your needs.
3. In your group, analyze the 15 job characteristics and categorize them in terms of their relationship to the job. Are they an integral part of the job or are they external to the job? For example, being able to participate in decision making is intrinsic to the job, whereas the existence of a company cafeteria is external to the job.

Exercise 11

Occupational Values

Motivation

PURPOSE

To analyze Frederick Herzberg's two factor theory of worker motivation.

PREPARATION

Your instructor may request that you complete the questionnaire prior to class.

INTRODUCTION

Step 1:   Read the list below, it describes 16 characteristics you are probably looking for in the job you are in or the one you will seek after graduation. They will not all be of equal importance to you. For the purposes of this exercise, you are to rank them in your order of importance.

It is difficult to rank order a long list. Try this method, place a 1 beside the most important characteristic, then place a 16 beside the least important characteristic. Follow this with the second most important, then the 15th, and so forth.

Step 2:   Frederick Herzberg distinguished between those characteristics of a job which could lead to job dissatisfaction (hygiene factors) and those which could lead to satisfaction (motivational factors). The hygiene factors are usually related to job context and are external to the job itself, whereas the motivational factors are related to job content and are internal to the job. Return to your previous list and, in the column headed H\M indicate whether you think the job characteristics are hygiene or motivational factors.

Step 3:   Tabulate the frequency of your factors according to the listed ranges of ranks.

242

Rank	G	Job Characteristic	H\M
		The pay is good	
		The boss provides lots of direction	
		The job provides a chance to use your mind	
		The work environment is very attractive	
		You are free to decide how to do your own work	
		The company is an "equal opportunity employer"	
		The job has well-defined responsibilities	
		"Voluntary overtime" is NOT expected	
		Your professional development is supported	
		You find the work itself to be very interesting	
		The job provides very secure job tenure	
		You can achieve your career path	
		Individual achievement is formally recognized	
		Workers participate in decisions regarding work	
		Your co-workers are very nice	
		The job title reflects its importance	

YOUR RANKINGS		
Rank Range	**Hygiene Factors**	**Motivational Factors**
Ranks 1 to 4		
Ranks 5 to 8		
Ranks 9 to 12		
Ranks 13 to 16		

Step 4: In your discussion group of six to eight students, compare your findings:

1. How much agreement did you have on the rankings? A good way to do this is to attempt to come to a group consensus on the value of the different job characteristics. Record the group ranking in the column headed G.

2. Discuss the Herzberg categories and review your decisions about them. Herzberg's most controversial hygiene factor is pay. If it means pay as in the money you use to live on, then it is clearly external to the job, but if it means pay as a symbolic recognition of your achievement by your employer, then it is internal to the job. Record your group rankings below:

GROUP RANKINGS		
Rank Range	Hygiene Factors	Motivational Factors
Ranks 1 to 4		
Ranks 5 to 8		
Ranks 9 to 12		
Ranks 13 to 16		

3. Discuss whether there is a relationship between job factor and ranking. What conclusions can your group reach regarding age- or gender-related preferences about job characteristics?

Job Enrichment

Motivation

PURPOSE

To evaluate the job enrichment possibilities of a variety of modern workplace systems.

PREPARATION

Your instructor may request that you complete part of the work prior to class.

INTRODUCTION

A great deal of attention has been placed in recent years on reorganizing work. These efforts fall under the general name of job enrichment, but their effect goes beyond the job itself. While the overall purpose has been to improve worker productivity, there are other goals of maximizing the long-term use of the work force, of treating all members of the work force equitably, and of improving the corporate image. Modern companies typically adopt goals that stress the need to help their employees reach their highest potential. They are often employed by Quality of Work Life programs.

The list below is a fairly comprehensive set of these modern alternatives. For each of them, discuss the goals which the alternative will best achieve and how they will be achieved. Use this framework:

1. **Classical Job Enrichment:** Use Herzberg's two factor theory to evaluate the alternatives as to their emphasis on hygiene and motivation factors.
2. **Long-term Work Force Development:** The most successful companies really do believe that their work force is their most valuable asset and will take steps to develop and maintain this resource over a longer period than the current financial statement.

3. **Corporate Values:** Do these alternatives represent certain statements about the value system of the corporation? These can include moral and ethical values which do not have any immediate bottom-line consequences.

4. **Corporate Image:** For some organizations, this might be related to the previous item, however, you may identify some alternatives that have a high value as corporate image builders.

5. Discuss any personal experience you may have had with some of these alternatives. A major issue with any planned change is the implementation process. What implementation strategies would you recommend?

THE NEW SYSTEMS

1. **Compressed Work Week:** Fewer days per week, each day is longer. Many hospital nurses work 12-hour shifts, also common is four days at 10 hours. Firefighters work a two-shift day with 8:00 AM and 6:00 PM shift changes.

2. **Councils:** Communication groups composed of a cross section of employees of the organization. Often used as a means of downward communication, but the real benefit is upward communication. Replaces some management functions.

3. **Cross-training:** Training people in skills beyond their immediate job area, sometimes at quite a distance, with office workers trained for shop work, etc.

4. **Fast-track:** Employees selected on the basis of either their ability and/or their membership in some targeted group (such as a minority) are given extra assistance in gaining promotion. The extras can include special training, a managerial mentor, and preferential selection. It is often combined with cross-training. The designation itself is usually valued.

_____

_____

_____

_____

_____

_____

5. **Flex Time:** Any system which gives employees some control over their starting or ending time during the day. Flex time does not usually refer to compressed or split schedules.

_____

_____

_____

_____

_____

_____

6. **Gain Sharing:** Any of a wide variety of systems which return part of the savings from improved productivity to the employees.

_____

_____

_____

_____

_____

_____

7. **Job Rotation:** Employees are moved through a group of similar jobs on a regular schedule. It usually replaces seniority as the basis of job assignment and helps alleviate boredom and some aspects of fatigue.

_____

_____

_____

_____

_____

8. **Job Sharing:** One job is shared by two people.

_____

_____

_____

_____

_____

_____

9. **Labour-Management Committees:** Formal union-management group which attends to matters outside the contract. It recognizes that many union grievances have nothing to do with the contract, but the union and its contract is the only vehicle available for workers to deal with management on an equal footing.

_____

_____

_____

_____

_____

_____

10. **Leaderless Work Groups:** The normal duties of a first line supervisor are turned over to the work group. The group sets its own schedules within general goals and objectives.

_____

_____

_____

_____

_____

_____

11. **Matrix Organization:** A reporting system where employees are responsible to two parts of the organization at the same time. It calls on greater self-management skills by the employee.

_____

_____

_____

_____

_____

_____

12. **Pay-for-Skills:** A pay system by which employees are paid for their skills and ability whether currently used or not rather than their actual job assignment. It encourages personal growth and development.

_____

_____

_____

_____

_____

_____

13. **Permanent Part-time Jobs:** Full-time benefits with part-time work.

_____

_____

_____

_____

_____

14. **Quality Circles:** Similar to the leaderless work group. Employee groups are given responsibility for their own quality control.

_____

_____

_____

_____

_____

Exercise 13

Feedback in Communication

Interpersonal Communication

PURPOSE

To demonstrate the need for feedback in developing effective communication.

PREPARATION

None required.

INTRODUCTION

In this exercise, you will experience one of the fundamental principles of communication, namely that feedback increases accuracy. In this example, we will use the communication of spoken language. This is an appropriate application for the business world where most communicating is done face-to-face. The concept being applied is that if you have the opportunity to check out what you are hearing, the speaker will be able to modify the message to increase its accuracy.

Three different members of your class will be called to describe an object to you. They will use different methods to describe these three objects to you. The objects are similar but are not identical. After you have drawn them, you will score your accuracy.

Method One: One-way communication with no spoken or visual feedback.

Method Two: One-way communication with no spoken feedback but with visual feedback permitted.

Method Three: Two-way spoken and visual communication.

Method One
Use this page to draw the first object described to you.

Number of correct shapes. Score one point for each correct shape in the correct order.	
Number of correct intersections. Score one or two points for each intersection.	
TOTAL _____	

Method Two
Use this page to draw the second object described to you.

Number of correct shapes. Score one point for each correct shape in the correct order.	
Number of correct intersections. Score one or two points for each intersection.	
TOTAL _____	

Method Three
Use this page to draw the third object described to you.

Number of correct shapes. Score one point for each correct shape in the correct order.	
Number of correct intersections. Score one or two points for each intersection.	
TOTAL _____	

ANALYSIS

Your teacher will collect the results from the classroom for the three methods and put them in a table on the board. Transfer the classroom results into the blank graph shown below. The scale for the Y-axis will depend on your class scores. Find the biggest score in the table, round it off, and make it the top of that axis.

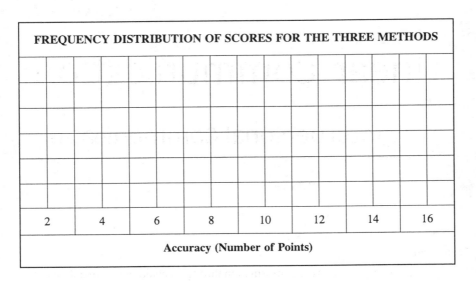

FREQUENCY DISTRIBUTION OF SCORES FOR THE THREE METHODS

| 2 | 4 | 6 | 8 | 10 | 12 | 14 | 16 |

Accuracy (Number of Points)

TASK

1. How accurate are the three methods of communication? What happens to accuracy when feedback is added to the communication. Pay particular attention to differences between Methods One and Two.
2. What effect does class size have on the three methods? What do you think would be an optimum size for each method?
3. What implications can you draw from this exercise for the workplace? What would it mean if you were trying to communicate a new operating procedure for a machine? What if you were trying to communicate the companies new anti-harassment policy to all employees?

Exercise 14

Linear Communication

Interpersonal Communication

PURPOSE

To evaluate the impact of passing information through a chain of command on the accuracy of communication.

PREPARATION

None required.

INTRODUCTION

This exercise is a scientific version of the game you played as a child, when a story was passed down the line in whispers, and the final version was compared to the original. Usually the discussion afterward centred around where the story went wrong. That childhood game is of considerable value to modern business communication because most communicating at work is done through spoken communication. It is important to have realistic knowledge about the accuracy and sources of error in oral communication.

You will listen to a group of your fellow classmates pass on a story, and you will record the parts of the story they get correct. Use the score sheet below for that purpose. The first time you hear the story, it will be read to a student and should be completely correct. Each successive telling will be based on the recall of the previous student. It is not unlike receiving a series of instructions from your supervisor about how to perform a particular job.

255

SCORE SHEET

#	Story Item	1	2	3	4	5
1	Alice Bigelow worked for the Beaver Basket Company					
2	newest member of their sales department and the first woman					
3	an old and established Canadian company					
4	manufacturing wooden baskets					
5	used by the fruit and vegetable industry					
6	used in the home as laundry baskets					
7	switched to more modern packaging methods					
8	serve the growing manufacturing industry of Southern Ontario					
9	from Minesing which had an abundant forest					
10	to Ajax which was close to major highways					
11	visited manufacturers and helped them package their product					
12	make the packages and ship them to the manufacturer					
13	importers who required domestic packages for their products					
14	current packages made of paper and plastic					
15	still privately owned by the original family					
16	corporate culture was filled with the traditional rural values of the founders					
17	they no longer manufactured any wooden laundry baskets					
18	problem was with her expense form for her first sales trip.					
19	for a week her actual expenses came to $730					
20	one of the older salesmen asked to see it					
21	far too low and ought to be padded the same way as the men					

#	Story Item	1	2	3	4	5
22	he showed her how to do this by faking receipts and adding charges					
23	past average for her trip was around $800–$850.00					
24	put in that much or the accountants would wonder about the previous expense forms					
25	if she wanted to be one of the boys she had better play ball on their team					
26	her great grandparents were from Minesing and had founded the Beaver Basket Company					
27	first member of her family in a generation to actually work for the business					
28	had not told anybody that she was a part of the family that owned it					
29	whether to blow the whistle on the salesmen or choke on it					
30	she decided to save it for a rainy day					

Consolidate your results in the following table:

Items	1	2	3	4	5
1 – 5					
6 – 10					
11 – 15					
16 – 20					
21 – 25					
26 – 30					
TOTAL					

Your instructor will assemble class data which you should copy into the table below. You will use it to analyze the results of the exercise.

Items	1	2	3	4	5
1 – 5					
6 – 10					
11 – 15					
16 – 20					
21 – 25					
26 – 30					
TOTAL					

ANALYSIS

1. Describe the accuracy of the story as it was passed from person to person.
2. What points caused the greatest difficulty?
3. Compare the accuracy in the six groupings, was there improved accuracy at the end of the story over the middle? If so, why might that be?
4. Did the novelty of the "fact" have any effect on accurate recall? Why might that occur?
5. Describe the major barriers to accurate recall of the story.

Bidding Exercise

Group Decision Making

PURPOSE

To investigate different modes of resource allocation and the effect of communication on these modes.

PREPARATION

Divide into groups of 7 or 9 students each. One person in each group acts as "banker," the others divide into subgroups of two persons each.

INTRODUCTION

Decision making in competitive circumstances occurs when there is a limited amount of resources to be distributed among individuals, groups, or entire organizations according to the strategies and tactics employed by all the decision makers. Among firms, such competition is a necessary and desirable facet of a private-enterprise-based economy. Regulatory measures are employed by governments to help maintain these competitive activities as well as to protect the public interest against monopolistic practices.

Within organizations, the various divisions and work groups must also often compete for finite resources in order to carry out desired and necessary programs. Sometimes hostility and lack of cooperation among managers predominate during negotiations for the allocation of these resources. In other situations, conflict is avoided and a mutually acceptable allocation of the resources is achieved. In this simulation, the class is divided into units of seven to nine students. These units are further divided into three or four groups of two students each who act together, and the remaining student takes the role of "banker." The simulation is carried out by each group of two students competing for resources with the other two or three groups within their unit. There is no interaction between units, all of which operate separately.

INSTRUCTIONS

1. Each group of two students is issued $200 in simulated funds by the banker.

2. The simulation consists of a series of rounds, all of which begin by each group paying in $20 and the bank paying in $30 to a central "pot" (managed by the banker). No group still participating can avoid this payment.

3. Then, each group in turn bids for the total in the pot in an auction run by the banker. All bids must be in multiples of $5. There is no maximum. A bid is accomplished by handing the amount to the banker who retains it permanently.

4. When a bid is received that no other group wishes or is able to surpass, the round ends. The group who submitted the highest bid wins only the amount originally put in the pot. That amount does not include any of the bid funds which are all forfeited to the bank (including the winning bid) when the bids are made.

5. The simulation ends when:
   (a)   A pre-selected number of rounds has been played.
   (b)   All groups except one have gone bankrupt. This occurs when a group possesses less than $20.

6. The winning group is the one possessing the largest amount of funds when the simulation ends.

7. Members of each group of two may discuss their bids with each other quietly. Your instructor will inform you whether any communication **between** groups within the units is allowed. Under no condition are payments permitted between groups.

8. The banker also has the role of referee. His or her word is final concerning enforcement of the rules of the simulation.

9. The banker must record the number of rounds played, the total amount taken in by the bank in forfeited bids, the amount paid out by the bank to the pot, and the amount held by the winning group at the end of the simulation.

Span of Control

Leadership

PURPOSE

To determine differences in the number of people that a supervisor can effectively control.

PREPARATION

Your instructor may request that you complete the questionnaire prior to class.

INTRODUCTION

An important issue in administration in organizations is the question of how many people a manager can effectively supervise. This question is usually described by the term "span of control" when referring to an individual supervisor, and, when referring to an organization, the distinction will be made between tall (and narrow) structures as opposed to wide (and short) structures. In this activity, you will rate your own span of control if you are a supervisor, or of that of your supervisor if you are not one yourself. The premise on which this scale is based is that a supervisor's core activity is to manage the personal aspects of working with employees, that is to say, understanding them as individuals, determining how best to motivate their performance, etc. Any time that a supervisor spends on other aspects of management detracts from this core tasks, and therefore reduces the time available for the personal aspects of management and as a corollary reduces the number of people who can be effectively supervised.

The criteria used for determining span of control, therefore, are those which have an impact on the managerial workload and include the following:

1. **Similarity of the Jobs Being Supervised:** The more alike the work of the people being supervised, the less the time that will be required by the supervisor in learning and keeping up-to-date on the activities being

performed. If all those being supervised do the same thing, then more can be supervised than if the employees all do totally different jobs.

2. **Physical Proximity:** Does the supervisor need to spend a lot of time travelling between those people being supervised? If so, this will reduce the amount of time available for direct contact with the employees.

3. **Complexity of the Work Being Supervised:** Simple, repetitive work requires less training than complex tasks and less supervisory time being spent on the training function.

4. **Direction and Control of the Work:** Can the work run itself or does it require close supervision? Will the manager be frequently called upon to solve task problems as opposed to focusing on personal aspects of the supervision.

5. **Coordination Outside the Department:** Does the supervisor spend a lot of time coordinating the work with other parts of the organization or with other external organizations? If so, the span will be reduced owing to the competition for the supervisor's time.

6. **Planning of Work:** Does the supervisor have responsibility for planning and scheduling or for developing and interpreting company policies? How well-formulated are these policies?

Rating Scale

Supervisor's job being rated: Give the job title and describe the nature of the work. Are you the supervisor?

_____

_____

_____

_____

_____

_____

For each of the six factors, pick the one choice that most closely fits the job being evaluated. Write the accompanying score in the column.

Similarity of Jobs

_____ 1 Fundamentally distinct jobs. Not just different tasks but also different work routines. No transfer from one job to another.

_____ 2 Inherently different. Some slight possibility of transfer between jobs.

_____ 3 Similar jobs. Fairly common hiring pool. Transfers routine.

_____ 4 Essentially alike. Job rotation common.

_____ 5 Identical jobs.

Physical Proximity

_____ 1   Dispersed, more than one city or region. Overnight or full-day trips required to visit locations.

_____ 2   Separate locations, one urban region.

_____ 3   Separate buildings, one location.

_____ 4   All located in one building, but separate rooms.

_____ 5   All together.

Complexity of Work

_____ 2   Extremely complex and varied, requiring constant supervision of the tasks being performed. Supervisor is the task expert.

_____ 4   Complex but less varied.

_____ 6   Less complex.

_____ 8   Routine.

_____ 10   Simple and repetitive.

Direction and Control

_____ 3   The workers require constant, close supervision with frequent re-training.

_____ 6   Frequent and continuing supervision.

_____ 9   Moderate, periodic supervision.

_____ 12   Limited supervision.

_____ 15   Minimum training and supervision.

Coordination

_____ 2   Extensive relationships with other organizations which are non-repetitive in nature. Constantly making new arrangements.

_____ 4   Considerable, close relationships.

_____ 6   Moderate number of relationships which can be easily controlled.

_____ 8   External relationships are limited to defined courses of action.

_____ 10   Almost an autonomous department.

Planning

_____ 2   Extensive planning function. New policies and missions are developed as a regular part of the work. No "book" to follow.

_____ 4   Policies are developed as guided by mission statements.

_____ 6   Feedback is expected on policy development. Supervisor is "consulted" on policy changes.

_____ 8   Planning only in strictly local applications.

_____ 10   Minimum planning. Follow the "book."

_____   TOTAL SUPERVISORY SCORE

Use this guide to determine the span of control. Circle the score and then read the number below it. This is the ideal number to be supervised.

SUPERVISORY SCORE												
10	15	18	21	24	27	30	33	36	39	42	45	50
1	2	3	4	6	8	10	12	14	16	18	20	22

Suggested Span of Control

Actual number of employees supervised.

The suggested span of control should be interpreted as a range rather than as a specific number. Other factors not included above would have an influence on the number of employees a supervisor could manage.

DISCUSSION QUESTIONS

1. How does the suggested span of control compare to the actual number of employees supervised?
2. If there is a strong difference between the two, discuss how that difference is reflected in supervisor effectiveness.
3. Evaluate the supervisor's job and determine ways of improving any difference between the actual and the suggested span of control. Would this be best accomplished through changing the number of people supervised, or could it be done by changing the supervisor's job? Discuss.
4. As the manager at the next level, how would you increase this supervisor's span of control?
5. Discuss the reasons why you would normally expect different spans of control at different levels of management in an organization.
6. Use the span of control evaluator to measure and evaluate the span of control of a supervisor found in one of the cases in this book.

Exercise 17

Sources of Power

Power and Influence

PURPOSE

To understand some of the different ways in which others can influence your behaviour.

PREPARATION

Your instructor may request that you complete the questionnaire prior to class.

INTRODUCTION

Beginning with the work of Max Weber, social scientists have analyzed power in terms of its various sources. The following is a fairly typical current list of these sources:

1. **Charisma:** This source of power is within the personality of the leader. We will do as they wish because we respect or admire them and want them to respect us.

2. **Expertise:** An expert can correctly manipulate and interpret data. This special skill can be of benefit to others and as such puts the expert in a position of power over those dependent on that expertise.

3. **Force:** Compliant behaviour can be gained through fear of punishment, whether actually used or not. Punishment is anything the subject of the power would like to avoid.

4. **Information:** Any person who has accurate information that is of use to others has power over those people. It is the desirability of the information which provides the power.

5. **Networks:** People with good connections have power. The strength of the power is directly related to the influence of the people in the network. Compliance is based on a desire to have a favourable evaluation in the network.

6. **Position:** Formal positions carry formal powers which are accepted as right and proper by all those who are subservient to that position. This power is legitimate in that it is well understood and agreed upon by all parties to the relationship.

7. **Reward:** Just as force is based on the fear of punishment, rewards can be used as a basis of gaining compliance. The leader must have the ability to deliver a reward. A reward is anything desired by the subject of the power.

PART I

Think about the bases you believe the ideal manager should have for his or her power. Should it largely be from one source, or should it be spread over several? Which ones should be the most important?

Rate each of the seven power sources on a scale of 0–20.

- Give it a zero if you think this source of power is of no value whatsoever in business management.
- Give it a 20 if you think that this is the absolute apex and one need not look any farther for a source of management power.
- Give scores that are in between for less extreme sentiments.
- Give each source a different score.
- Consult the definitions if you need help with the meaning of the words.

IDEAL MANAGER	
	Score 0 – 20
1. Charisma	
2. Expertise	
3. Force	
4. Information	
5. Networks	
6. Position	
7. Reward	

PART II

Now rate yourself. How do you respond to different kinds of power?

- Give it a zero if you absolutely reject the use of a particular type of power on yourself.
- Give it a 20 if you think you would follow this person anywhere.
- Give it an intermediate value for less extreme positions.
- Give each source of power a different score.

YOURSELF	
	Score 0 – 20
1. Charisma	
2. Expertise	
3. Force	
4. Information	
5. Networks	
6. Position	
7. Reward	

PART III

Plot these two profiles on the graph below.

	0	**5**	**10**	**15**	**20**
1. Charisma					
2. Expertise					
3. Force					
4. Information					
5. Networks					
6. Position					
7. Reward					

Analysis
1. Where are the major disagreements?
2. Why are they there?
3. Where are the major agreements?

PART IV (Optional)

Rate your supervisor using the same scales. Look for trouble spots in your relationship. Identify possible opportunities for improvement. Would you really like to have your supervisor know how to exercise more power and influence over you? What could be done to improve trust in your relationship?

SUPERVISOR	
	Score 0 – 20
1. Charisma	
2. Expertise	
3. Force	
4. Information	
5. Networks	
6. Position	
7. Reward	

Exercise 18

Let's Make a Deal!

Conflict

PURPOSE

To identify isues involved in developing cooperative strategies of conflict resolution.

PREPARATION

None required.

INTRODUCTION

You are an employee of Canramco, a modest-sized automobile parts manufacturer located in the industrial heart of Southern Ontario. Like much of the auto industry, your company is unionized and is represented by local 10822 of CAW. As the expiry of each contract approaches, the company and the union select negotiating teams to work out a new deal. In this simulation, you will be assigned to either the management or the union negotiating team.

Each team has its own power base. The union can either decide to settle, or it can go on strike. The decision to strike will be influenced by the union strike fund and the support it receives from other locals. This information is their secret and is not available to the management team. In effect, they can decide to strike or settle at will. The management position is similar. They can either settle or lock out their workers. The decision to lock them out would in part depend on their orders and inventory. This information is their secret and not available to the union team.

Most of the contracts are for one year, but three of them are for more than one year. The negotiating process has been greatly simplified for the purpose of this simulation. The teams can either choose to settle or not. After an opportunity to discuss strategy in caucus (the members of each team privately), the teams meet to air their views and to agree on a strategy for this contract. At a pre-determined

269

time, the conciliator will call for the teams to show their intent for the current contract. The team leaders will then show a card indicating whether they will settle of not. The round will then be scored and the next round of negotiations will begin. A large part of the challenge is to build trust so that agreed-upon deals will in fact be carried out.

The overall goal is the long-term growth and health of the company and its work force.

CANRAMCO ECONOMICS

The basic structure is that both parties will agree to settle when the deal conforms to the industry norm. As a small company, they do not want to be very different from their competition. For the sake of simplicity, this norm is given to be 6%. If the union gets more than the norm, then the company will cut back on the size of the work force growth to cover the increase in wages. Similarly, if management steals a contract, it will have more money to hire more workers but end up with a disgruntled work force which will lower product quality at a cost in quality bonuses to the company.

THE PAYOFF SCHEDULE		
Union	**Management**	**Payoff**
Settle	Settle	6% increase in wages, sales
Settle	Lock Out	2% wage, 8% work force
Strike	Settle	8% wage, 2% work force
Strike	Lock Out	6% decrease in wages, sales

Contract Length	The Choices		The Changed Status		
	Union	Management	Wages	Sales	Work Force
			Starting positions		
	Circle the Decisions		$16/hr.	$10 million/yr.	100
1 year	Se St	Se LO			
1 year	Se St	Se LO			
2 years	Se St	Se LO			
1 year	Se St	Se LO			

Contract Length	The Choices		The Changed Status		
	Union	Management	Wages	Sales	Work Force
3 years	Se St	Se LO			
1 year	Se St	Se LO			
3 years	Se St	Se LO			
1 year	Se St	Se LO			
1 year	Se St	Se LO			
1 year	Se St	Se LO			

DEBRIEFING

After you have negotiated the ten contracts, meet as a whole group to evaluate the outcome.

1. How has Canramco thrived as a company?

2. What were the major barriers to sticking with the win-win solution?

3. Were there key personality interactions that particularly helped or hindered the process? Discuss these.

4. Give your evaluation of this simulation.

_____

_____

_____

_____

_____

_____

Mediating Conflict

Conflict

Mediation is a process which helps people resolve disputes. It differs from arbitration in that arbititration involves a judgement by a third party as to what the resolution to the dispute should be. An arbitrator is a judge of the facts and renders a decision. A mediator helps the parties to the dispute find their own solution.

A key difference between the two processes is in terms of this outcome. An arbitrated dispute may well leave one or the other or both parties quite unhappy with the result. This can lead to an appeal or to continuing conflict between the parties. It is often a solution of the win/lose variety.

The successful mediation of a conflict leads to a satisfactory solution for both parties. It is a win/win solution. Although each may not get what they originally preferred, they will both be satisfied with the result. The conflict ends with a successful mediation. The result will NOT be appealed to a higher authority.

One of the primary methods used by the mediator to help the parties find their own solution is to work with them to improve their communication. By the time an independent mediator arrives on the scene the conflict has probably gone on for some time and the communication process will be clogged with a lot of history that impedes the process. A key mediator function is to get the parties communicating in a clear and rational manner. This may involve establishing rules for fair communication, especially if there is a power imbalance between the parties to the dispute.

This exercise was originally developed by Fred Ruemper, Kate Beattie and Wendy Ruemper for the purpose of staff training at Georgian College.

Effective mediator behaviour involves:

1. **Neutrality.** Nothing ends the mediation process faster than the belief by one of the parties to the dispute that the mediator is biased against them. Lack of trust leads to feelings of anxiety, reluctance to disclose and share, and hostility.
2. **Careful attention to verbal and non-verbal communication.** Good mediators attend to what people are saying and how they say it. They take many notes, show a keen interest in their comments and seek clarification of needs and wants.
3. **Communicate very little themselves.** Mediators avoid saying or doing anything judgemental. They restate things, ask for clarification, keep things moving, unblock firm positions. They keep things in the present.

Stages of mediation:

1. **Entry.** The ground rules for the mediation are agreed to by the parties. The mediator develops a relationship with the parties which is based on trust.
2. **Fact finding.** Through a question and answer process the mediator helps the parties identify and confront the issues about which they disagree. Often a dispute will be a mixture of facts and values. Value conflicts are beyond the scope of easy change but issue conflicts can be resolved. The mediator can help the parties separate the issues and get them on the table. Real positions can be separated from irrelevant power plays.
3. **Option building.** The mediator helps the parties discover the options they have to resolve the dispute. This involves an invitation to be as creative as possible about options.
4. **Bridging.** Once the options are clear the parties need help in moving toward accepting one of them. At this stage it is important that the parties to the dispute take ownership of their ideas for resolving it since they must ultimately accept them as a solution.
5. **Closing.** The deal is struck and the details are worked out. The parties agree on how to sell it to others who have a stake in the outcome. The mediator has a role in selling the deal once it is struck.

TASK

In groups of four, work through one of the following cases. In addition to the three roles identified in the case, there is a fourth role of Coach. The coach is the advisor to the mediator and observes how the mediator is doing. The coach can call time-outs to meet privately with the mediator and give advice.

A. The Profane Professor

Complainant: You are Janet, a twenty-five year old student who has decided to return to school after 'stopping out' for a few years while experiencing teenage marriage and parenthood. Neither experience was easy and you are now a single parent and sole support of two youngsters in Kindergarten and Grade Two. Your youthful pregnancy and marriage caused you to drop out of high school prior to graduation even though you had always been a good student.

A year ago you started to pull your life together. The first step was to rid yourself of an immature and dependant spouse. The next step was to take upgrading to prepare yourself for post secondary education. Your plan has been on track and things are going well. You are now enroled in first year in the Music Technology Program. Prior to returning to school you had supported your children and husband with some part-time work as a discjockey. You found that you liked it and were quite successful. You hope to work at a more technical level and are confident of your future success.

Right now you are really upset with your Popular Music Professor, Jefferson Smith. You can't believe that the college would tolerate such behaviour from one of its faculty members. He uses profanity in class and never misses an opportunity to talk about sex. His sexual references seem to centre on his own fantasies and life experiences. He seems to want to impress the younger people in the room with his liberated approach to life and his widespread experiences. You don't see how any of this has any relevance to the course content. You checked the course outline and read the book. There is no sexual or profane comment or reference in either of them. You want him to stick to the course and stop his in-class sexual and profane diversions. You aren't a prude but you haven't made this major investment in your education to be diverted by this teacher. As far as you know you are the only student to complain; but you know you aren't the only one to be unhappy with him.

Respondent   You are Professor Jefferson Smith and you are a professor in the Music Technology Program. You have been a popular member of the faculty for the past twenty years and have basically been doing things the same way ever since you first arrived. Your speciality was in popular music at university and you have always seen yourself as a pretty with-it guy.

Your student evaluations have always seemed excellent. Your self esteem is strong and you feel good about your ability to relate to the young people of today.

You were very surprised when the Human Rights Officer asked you to make an appointment to receive a complaint. The complaint is from one of the women students in your Popular Music Course and she is upset with what she says is your inappropriate use of profanity in class and she further says that you never miss an opportunity to talk about sex. The complaint has you mystified. You never had a complaint before and this one seems really harsh. The student has taken everything out of context. You don't think you dwell on sexual matters, but it is a theme in popular music and a topic of interest to young people.

Mediator   Your name is Martha and you are a long standing member of the student counselling services at the college. A student by the name of Janet has filed a complaint with the Human Rights Officer about a Professor by the name of Jefferson Smith. The complaint is that he uses profanity in class and makes sexual references about most of the subject matter in his course.

You have been selected as mediator because of your participation in a recent mediator training workshop and your background in the student counselling department. You don't know the complainant but the respondent is well known to you. For years there has been talk about him around campus and you have heard student complaints in your counselling role, however there are no previous formal written complaints on record.

B. The Group Mark

Complainant   Your name is Raj and you were assigned by your teacher to a team to complete a major assignment for your course in Management Practices. The project counts for thirty percent of the final grade in the course and it is important to you that you get an A in the project and the course. Your group received only a C+ and you are quite unhappy about it. Your goal is to make the Dean's List and the poor mark you received in this project will make it hard for you to keep up your class average.

For the most part you blame the other members of the team because of their lack of interest in getting an A in the project, but you are also upset that the teacher deliberately structured the groups such that the good students were spread around and didn't have a chance to work together. The teacher said she was replicating the real world of work.

Doris and Herb are the two other members of the team and it is your view that they didn't make enough of a commitment to the project to warrant an equal share of the mark. Both of them have stated that a C+ is just fine and completely within their personal expectations. Neither are strong students and have stated that it was an extremely educational experience working with you on this assignment.

Your request is that you be granted an A for your major contribution to the assignment. You don't care what happens to the others. They can keep their C+ or take a lower mark so that a C+ average for the group is maintained.

You made this request to your professor but she rejected it out of hand. You can't understand her inflexibility on this issue.

Respondent   You are Prof. R. B. Ramcharan and you were approached by Raj who was the member of a group doing an assignment in your Management Practices Course. Raj didn't like his mark on the assignment which is the group mark and appealed to you for a different mark than that given to the other members of the group. His case was based on his belief that he had contributed more than the other group members and ought to be given a greater reward. You rejected Raj's request for a separate evaluation of the group project. Your goal was to teach teamwork and in your view Raj didn't demonstrate much learning. You are most displeased that he has made a 'federal case' out of it by appealing the grade to the Academic Director. If Raj thought you were inflexible earlier, he will have lots to learn as you take him through advanced studies on this one.

You have already had several conversations with your colleagues in the faculty lounge and they all agree that this is a key issue of academic freedom and integrity.

Mediator   You are Dr. Sandy, the Academic Director, and it is ordinarily your duty to arbitrate marks appeals that come up from the faculty. Recently the Vice-President, Academic took you to a workshop on conflict mediation and announced to you at the end of the workshop that she didn't want any more appeals settled by arbitration, but rather that they should be settled by mediation. You were told that the difference between arbitration and mediation is that an arbitrator is like a judge who makes a decision, whereas, a mediator helps the parties to resolve the dispute themselves. As she saw it, mediated settlements wouldn't be appealed and that it would mean happier students and less acrimony in the department. You suspect that the real attraction is that mediated settlements will mean a lot less work for her since she is the next step in the appeal process.

Your first opportunity to try this out will be with Prof. Ramcharan and one of his students who is unhappy about his mark on a group project.

C. Who Needs Professional Development?

Complainant   You are Juan and you are a relatively new faculty member of the business program of your college. For the past year you have had your heart set on attending the upcoming annual conference of the Professional Market Research Society (PMRS) in Ottawa. You have prepared and submitted an important paper, and it has been accepted for presentation at a workshop. This is the first time anyone from the program has had a paper accepted for presentation at this meeting and you believe it will bring much prestige to you and to the program. The cost of the conference is about $1000 including: conference fees, air fare, single accommodation at the hotel and a few incidentals. This represents the balance of the money in the business program conference pot. As far as you are concerned this is a just and fair reward for all of the effort you have put into upgrading the level of academic excellence in the program which frankly is desperately in need of all the upgrading it can get. It seems to be top heavy with tired old business types.

Unfortunately you may not get the money. Meng-Che, the Academic Director, has recommended that the money go to Henry, one of those 'tired old business types', a crony of his from the old days. In your view the only useful contribution Henry could make would be to apply for early retirement. He still teaches from the same notes and overheads he developed twenty years ago.

You have appealed to Meng-Che to reconsider his decision or at least offer a satisfactory explanation for his lack of support for your initiative. While he said he was pleased that your paper was accepted for presentation he nonetheless wants Henry to go and he won't explain his support for Henry. Your personal finances are such that you cannot afford this on your own as you are the father of a young family and have been stuggling with the burdens of a sick child.

You and Meng-Che have agreed upon contacting Anthony from the Benefits Department to see if he can mediate the dispute and avoid an unappealing choice.

Respondent   You are Meng-Che, the Academic Director for the Business Programs. For some months now you have been trying to revive a rather moribund department. The problem, as you see it, is that you have an aging and somewhat tired group of faculty who lack enthusiasm for the job. Some of these old cronies of yours seem to spend their days watching their investment portfolios shift with the market tide and count down the years until they can retire on a decent pension. Unfortunately, most of them are too far from retirement for that to be a viable option. Recently, you have been working on Henry and have convinced him to get involved with the Professional Marketing Research Society just as he was some years ago and see if it will fire up his juices. Your inducement was to supply him with funding to attend the annual conference in Ottawa.

Juan then applied for money to attend the same conference. Apparently, he will be presenting a paper on his recent innovations. You would really like to encourage Juan's initiative. He is a resourceful and enterprising young faculty member who is a key element in your plan to renew the program. Unfortunately you only have $1000 left in the budget and you have been working on Henry for quite a while and feel committed to your renewal plan with him.

Mediator   You are Anthony from the Benefits Department and you have been asked to mediate a dispute between Juan of the Business Program and Meng-Che his Academic Director. The issue has to do with the allocation of professional development resources for an upcoming conference in Ottawa. You know that Meng-Che wants to allocate the money to Henry, a very senior faculty member.

You know Juan because he is the father of a young family who has been having some financial struggles lately with a sick child. You know Henry because he is one of the old timers who is part of the 'burned out burden' that senior management has been talking about lately.

D. The After Pub Class

Complainant   You are Professor Viola Lopiccolo and you have had a struggle with students attending class after lunch in the student pub. The lunch seemed to feature too many glasses of beer. The only problem is with the Wednesday afternoon class. The other two classes are in the morning. You have already had two sessions with the students about this problem. At first the issue was that the students were skipping the Wednesday class and when you dealt with this in class, the result was that several of them came to class when they were intoxicated. When you then dealt with the drinking, it seemed to clear up the problem except for Tom.

Tom has insisted on his "right" to drink and to attend class afterward. He denies that he is impaired and is quite aggressive about this. His aggressive behaviour has you worried for your own safety. Last week when you asked him to leave the class he refused and started waiving his arms in your direction.

You have filed a complaint about Tom's behaviour and have asked that he be permanently removed from your class.

Respondent   You are Tom, a senior student at the college. Professor Viola Lopiccolo has filed a complaint against you and has asked that you be permanently removed from her class. She claims that on several recent Wednesday afternoons you have come to class while intoxicated.

This is an extension of an earlier issue of attendance at the Wednesday afternoon class. You and several of the students in the class had developed the routine of going to the campus pub at lunch prior to Professor Lopiccolo's class. When she found out what was going on she "raised the roof" and so you started showing up with beer on your breath. She didn't like that either.

None of your other Professors care what you do at lunch. All they care about is that you do the work. They don't seem to mind if you don't show up all the time.

You believe that as a mature student you can do what you want with your life. Professor Lopiccolo isn't a morality cop, its none of her business whether you drink. Besides, you can handle your own booze.

You would be in serious trouble if you were barred from her class. It is the only section of this course and you need it to graduate.

Mediator   You are Kevin Kralik a student and member of the Student's Advisory Council. You has been called on to mediate a dispute between a student and a faculty member. Professor Viola Lopiccolo has filed a complaint against Tom, a senior student and has asked that he be permanently removed from her class. She claims that on several recent Wednesday afternoons he came to class while intoxicated and exhibited threatening behaviour.

One reason you have been selected as mediator is because you are the President of Bacchus, the student organization for responsible drinking. You know that there is a problem with on-campus pubs and that some students don't always exercise the best judgement. You also know that not all faculty see the pub as a problem. You were a student of Professor Lopiccolo and know that she sets high standards for her students.

Mechanistic or Organic

Organizational Design

PURPOSE

To measure individual preferences in organizational design.

PREPARATION

Your instructor may request that you complete the questionnaire prior to class.

INTRODUCTION

How well does each of the following statements describe your views about an ideal place to work?

Score 5 if it is a perfect description. Score 0 if it is totally wrong. Score 4, 3, 2, or 1 if it fits somewhere in between.

_____ 1. I get most of my motivation to work from the job itself rather than from the rewards the company gives me for doing it.

_____ 2. I respect my supervisors for what they know rather than for the fact that the company has put them in charge.

_____ 3. I work best when things are exciting and filled with energy. I can feel the adrenalin rushing through me and I like it.

_____ 4. I like it best if we can play things by ear. Going by the book means you do not have any imagination.

_____ 5. People who seek security at work are boring. I don't go to work to plan my retirement.

_____ 6. I believe that planning should focus on the short term. Long-term planning is unrealistic. I want to see the results of my plan.

_____ 7. Don't give me a detailed job description. Just point me in the general direction and I will figure out what needs to be done.

280

_____ 8. I don't expect to be introduced to new people. If I like their looks, I'll introduce myself.

_____ 9. Goals should be set by everyone in the organization. I prefer to achieve my own goals rather than those of someone else.

_____ 10. One of the things I prefer most about a job is that it be full of surprises.

_____ 11. I like a job that is full of challenges.

_____ 12. Organization charts are only needed by people who are already lost.

_____ 13. Technology is constantly changing.

_____ 14. Supervision and control should be face-to-face.

_____ 15. If organizations focus on problem solving, the bottom line will take care of itself.

_____ 16. I would never take a job which involved repetitive activities.

_____ 17. Organizations are constantly in a state of change. I don't worry about how the players line up.

_____ 18. Every decision I make is a new one. I don't look for precedents.

_____ 19. When people talk about efficiency, I think they really don't want to do a good job.

_____ 20. The people who know the most about the work should be put in charge.

Scoring

Total scores of less than 50 suggest a preference for mechanistic or formal organizations, scores above 50 suggest a preference for organic or informal organizations.

TASK

1. Within your group compare scores and discuss the kinds of work which you think goes with your preferred organizational style.
2. Describe in general the kinds of jobs most characteristic of an organic and mechanistic design.
3. Rate the following organizations in terms of whether you would expect them to be mechanistic or organic.
   - a fast food chain
   - a business college
   - a car factory
   - a car design centre
   - a beauty parlour
   - a pollution control plant
   - the maintenance department in a factory
   - a bus company
   - a taxi company
   - a computer programming department
   - a data coding department

- ◦ a summer camp
- ◦ the management team for a large company
- ◦ an army combat unit
- ◦ a police detective department
- ◦ the editorial staff of a newspaper
- ◦ the creative department of an advertising agency
- ◦ this class

Enriched Job Design

Organizational Design

PURPOSE

In this exercise you will design an enriched managerial job.

PREPARATION

None required

INTRODUCTION

An enriched job is one that incorporates a fair degree of autonomy and participative power sharing between the job holder and her or his supervisor. The key problem to be faced is what aspects of the duties and the responsibilities of the position need to be specified by the hierarchy, and what aspects should be delegated to the job holder. The assumption for this exercise is that this is a newly designed position. The hiring exercise that follows uses the job design you create.

In an enriched job, the job holder has significant delegated and/or shared power over at least one and possibly all three of the following components:

1. Objective-setting where targets for key-result areas will be formulated by the job holder alone (delegated power) or with a direct supervisor (shared power).
2. Resource budgets which specify what resources may be employed in meeting the targets.
3. Work plans or procedures which specify what work methods will be employed.

With the high degree of autonomy attached to enriched managerial positions, the organization must ensure that sufficient control is still maintained so that the diminishment of authoritarian control over individual employees does not result in an uncoordinated and ineffective structure. If that occurs, the motivational advantages of job enrichment are lost to organizational inefficiency. Following are four categories over which upper management may exercise relatively complete control even when managing an enriched position.

1. **The performance responsibilities of the job** as defined by key-result areas in which the job holder will be expected to set and achieve objectives. For example, instead of telling a production supervisor what the quota should be, the job description may state "the production supervisor will (perhaps in consultation with the general manager) establish the production targets which are to be met." This establishes the key-result area of production volume as critical without removing the authority for target-setting from the job holder. The key-result areas may also be listed in order of their priority to organizational effectiveness.

2. **The custodial responsibilities of the job.** That is, which organizational resources the job holder must maintain, protect, and replenish.

3. **Overall budgetary allocations** to the position that still allow the individual to make the division of suballocations within the overall budget.

4. **Any universally applicable organizational policies** such as compensation packages, vertical and lateral communication responsibilities to other organizational units, etc.

THE PROBLEM

You are the Mid-Canada District Sales Manager of Hi-Tech Corporation with 4 branch offices under your supervision in Manitoba, Saskatchewan, and soon, Northwestern Ontario. With head office in Calgary (where you are located), Hi-Tech supplies computerized instrumentation to a variety of industrial plants across Canada. The company has decided to open a new branch office in Thunder Bay, Ontario, to serve industrial customers from Kenora to Sault Ste Marie. You must now design, as an enriched job, the branch manager's position. This is the most junior management position in the field sales group. The following information forms part of the job description:

- The only activity of the branch office will be the solicitation of sales to industrial customers and directly associated activities. All promotional activities, order processing, and service arrangements are performed by head office.
- There will be sufficient funds allocated to maintain the branch manager, a maximum of five salespersons, and one secretary.

Each group of students is to draft the rest of the job description containing:

1. A set of from six to eight key-result areas listed in order of priority for which the branch manager must set and attain objectives. Give your reasons for each one selected.

_____

_____

_____

_____

_____

_____

_____

_____

2. A list of from five to seven custodial responsibilities for which the branch manager must also develop policies and work procedures.

_____

_____

_____

_____

_____

_____

_____

_____

_____

Remember to avoid over defining work procedures. This is to be an enriched job in which the branch manager must develop his or her own methods of fulfilling the job requirements. When you have performed the two steps above, refer to the three components of individual control listed at the beginning of this exercise. Will the branch manager have an enriched position? Will Hi-Tech Corporation and the district manager still have sufficient control over the Thunder bay branch?

Exercise 22

Personnel Selection

Organizational Design

PURPOSE

To learn principles of personnel selection in the challenging context of an enriched job.

PREPARATION

The job design exercise preceeding this one must have already been completed.

INTRODUCTION

Modern management theories support the notion that human behaviour is context or situationally specific. It is not practical to describe behavioural traits or patterns for any individual unless the situation in which the individual is placed is also specified. The same person might behave quite differently in an altered environment. In personnel selection, it is necessary to first identify the behavioural patterns that would facilitate high performance on the job. These should be quite specific. For example, when attempting to hire an accountant, instead of simply saying "should act intelligently," it would be better to state, "should be capable of rapid and accurate quantitative analysis even when under stress." This defines the desirable behavioural pattern in much more detail. The former statement could apply to almost any job — the latter is targeted at the requirements derived from the task environment of an accountant.

Once the appropriate behavioural patterns have been decided upon, a strategy for selecting a person who is likely to display those patterns when on the job must be devised. In the High-Tech Corporation example, you have already defined the task environment. Assume that the educational and experiential backgrounds have already been defined for the branch manager position and you are to carry on from there.

286

1. From the prioritized list of key-result areas, define a set of from six to eight behavioural patterns that would likely lead to successful performance. Concentrate on those pertaining to the leadership of the branch. Be as specific as possible and be realistic. Remeber that this is a junior management position which will not be filled by a senior executive.

2. From Job Application (A), Job Interview (I), Previous Experience (E), Testing (T), and Dynamic Assessment (D) indicate which mode(s) would be useful to evaluate whether each job applicant would be likely to exhibit the selected behaviour patterns if she or he was hired. Note separately the reasons for selecting each mode, any disadvantages or biases that mode might have, and how they might be overcome.

Desirable Behaviour Pattern	Mode of Personnel Selection

Measurement Scale

Quality of Work Life

PURPOSE

To measure those aspects of job satisfaction which are enclosed by the concept of Quality of Work Life and to measure five core dimensions of jobs of this scale.

PREPARATION

Your instructor may request that you complete the questionnaire prior to class.

INTRODUCTION

Use the following instrument to evalute a job you have recently held. How well do each of the statements describe the job? Score 5 if it is a perfect description. Score 0 if it is totally wrong. Score 4, 3, 2, or 1 if it fits somewhere in between.

_____	1.	My job provides me with different tasks to perform throughout each hour.
_____	2.	The other workers depend on the job I do to accomplish their work.
_____	3.	The different jobs I do require different skills.
_____	4.	I know right away if there is a problem with the way I am doing my job.
_____	5.	My employer has a mission statement, and I am familiar with how my job supports it.
_____	6.	In my job I hear back about how people react to what I do.
_____	7.	I know at the end of each week whether I have had been successful on the job or not.
_____	8.	My supervisor provides me with accurate production reports on a frequent basis.
_____	9.	Everyone who works where I do is aware of how all the jobs fit together to achieve our company goals.

	10.	I am my own boss.
_____	11.	I get to control my own work.
_____	12.	My employer arranges that we are given different tasks on different days.
_____	13.	On my job I know exactly why I perform each task.
_____	14.	Our work is mostly custom work with each project being unique.
_____	15.	I feel responsible for getting my whole job done.
_____	16.	I get regular information on how well my work is going.
_____	17.	My supervisor only checks up on me when something really goes wrong.
_____	18.	I get to try out different ways of doing my job.
_____	19.	My supervisor likes it if I figure out a better way of doing my job.
_____	20.	When I go to work each day, I do not really know for sure what we will be working on.
_____	21.	One good thing about my job is that I know what it is that I have accomplished.
_____	22.	At the end of my career I will be able to look back and identify what I achieved through my work.
_____	23.	When people ask me what I do for a living, I am able to tell them exactly what I have done.
_____	24.	Our work is organized so that each of us does a complete job.
_____	25.	My work is monitored so that I have daily reports on my progress.

The questions above are each related to one of the core dimensions of a job a described by Hackman and Oldman (J. Richard Hackman and Greg R. Oldman. "Development of the Job Diagnostic Survey." *Journal of Applied Psychology* Vol. 60 1975.) Use the table below to add up your score for each of the core dimensions. The numbers in the cells identify the questions which are related to each dimension.

CORE DIMENSIONS OF JOBS: HACKMAN AND OLDMAN						
1. Task variety	1 =	6 =	11 =	16 =	21 =	
2. Task identity	2 =	7 =	12 =	17 =	22 =	
3. Task significance	3 =	8 =	13 =	18 =	23 =	
4. Autonomy	4 =	9 =	14 =	19 =	24 =	
5. Feedback	5 =	10 =	15 =	20 =	25 =	

QWL PROFILE

The Quality of your Work Life is best viewed as a snapshot at a particular point in time. The result is that it is usually presented as a profile graph of the scores. Plot your QWL profile on the graph outline below.

QUALITY OF WORK LIFE PROFILE									
Core Dimensions	5		10		15		20		
Task Variety									
Task Identity									
Task Significance									
Autonomy									
Feedback									

Interpretation

The five core dimensions that Hackman and Oldman have identified provide a useful basis on which to analyze jobs. They represent core dimensions of a job and should not be taken to be a complete basis for job analysis. All should be present to provide a job which is psychologically satisfying and will motivate employees to greater performance.

1. **Task Variety:** Task variety involves performing different tasks which require different talents. Workers typically see jobs which require more of their talent to be more challenging and as a result more motivating. Variety relieves monotony and can also help avoid the muscle strain caused by repetitive movements.

2. **Task Identity:** One of the keys to effective worker motivation is the satisfaction which comes from being able to identify that they have done a whole job, that they can point out what it is they have built or achieved. This is best exemplified in the problem of extreme job division where the work has been divided into so many parts that each has lost all meaning to the worker. To extend the old analogy, while working on a twig, they have trouble seeing the tree, let alone the forest.

3. **Task Significance:** Not only must the task be identifiable, it must be seen as important or worthwhile. This is a particular problem with routine work, especially if there is a widespread worker belief that whatever they do will be checked and repaired by someone else later on.

4. **Autonomy:** How much responsibility is the employee given for their own work routines? Are employees given specific detailed instructions about

their work, or are they given broader goals and invited to share in their achievement? While autonomy is usually associated with the managerial level of work, there have been major breakthroughs in achieving autonomy in jobs on the factory floor.

5. **Feedback:** Workers need information about their performance, and they need it before their exit interview. Misunderstandings about performance expectations are easily avoided. Frequency of feedback varies with the job, but the lessons of psychology are that feedback should be provided at almost the same instant as performance and that its impact diminishes with time. Feedback must be positive as well as negative. "No news" is not "good news," it is simply no news.

TASK

1. After drawing your QWL profile, do an analysis of your job and determine its strengths and weaknesses.
2. Identify areas needing improvement and develop ways to improve your job. Use the five core dimensions as the basis of this job redesign.
3. If you are working in a study group, share this with the members of your group to get their feedback.

Measure and Evaluate

Organizational Culture and Values

PURPOSE

To measure and evaluate employee values as an aspect of corporate culture.

PREPARATION

Complete Steps 1, 2, and 3 prior to class.

INTRODUCTION

This is a group activity. The purpose is to develop a picture of one aspect of corporate culture, namely, the value system of the ideal employee as seen from the company point of view. We will measure this using a ranking of a list of typical human values. A value is any trait that people believe is important and is used as the basis of behaviour. If people think it is important to be helpful, then they will act on this value by providing assistance to others. Norms are based on values.

Step 1: Rank the values on the sheet on the next page in the order you think they are important for employees in a corporation. Use one of the score sheets. You may find it easier to fill this out with a particular company in mind; if so, read the case called Mason Electric and analyze the corporate values found their. View them from the perspective of the company or its management. Try to avoid thinking about a specific manager. Use a generalized ideal.

Long lists are hard to rank, so use this method: Place the number 1 next to the value you think is most important and the number 16 next to the one you think is least important. Then number the second and the fifteenth and so forth.

Step 2: Get three people to give you their rankings. The previous sheet can be folded in four or cut into four rectangles so that people will not be influenced by how other people responded. Explain to these people how they should rank the items.

	Ambition		Ambition
	Broadmindedness		Broadmindedness
	Competence		Competence
	Cheerfulness		Cheerfulness
	Cleanliness		Cleanliness
	Courage		Courage
	Helpfulness		Helpfulness
	Honesty		Honesty
	Imagination		Imagination
	Independence		Independence
	Intelligence		Intelligence
	Obedience		Obedience
	Politeness		Politeness
	Responsibility		Responsibility
	Self-control		Self-control
	Tolerance		Tolerance
	Ambition		Ambition
	Broadmindedness		Broadmindedness
	Competence		Competence
	Cheerfulness		Cheerfulness
	Cleanliness		Cleanliness
	Courage		Courage
	Helpfulness		Helpfulness
	Honesty		Honesty
	Imagination		Imagination
	Independence		Independence
	Intelligence		Intelligence
	Obedience		Obedience
	Politeness		Politeness
	Responsibility		Responsibility
	Self-control		Self-control
	Tolerance		Tolerance

Step 3:   Compile your results and calculate a rank order based on the four sets of data that you have. Do this by first adding up the ranks that the four sheets give for each value. Use this total for each value and assign new ranks from one to sixteen.

Step 4:   Meet with your group and repeat this procedure with the your group data. You should end up with one list of the values with ranks from one to sixteen.

Step 5:   Discussion questions for your group:

1. What agreement was there among the members of your group about the importance of these corporate values? How much agreement was there about the most important? the least important?
2. What does your list reveal about corporate culture? What value judgments would you make about it? Make predictions about behaviour based on these values.
3. Compare your list of corporate values to the list below of values held in general society. Discuss similarities and differences. There are norms for both males and females. Discuss the extent to which values are related to gender or perhaps other minority group status.

RANK ORDER OF VALUES FOR GENERAL SOCIETY		
Male	**Female**	**Value**
2	4	Ambition
4	5	Broadmindedness
8	11	Competence
12	9	Cheerfulness
9	8	Cleanliness
5	6	Courage
7	7	Helpfulness
1	1	Honesty
16	16	Imagination
11	13	Independence
14	15	Intelligence
15	14	Obedience
13	12	Politeness
3	3	Responsibility
10	10	Self-control
6	2	Tolerance

Census and Climate

Organizational Culture and Values

PURPOSE

To become familiar with the concept of a "corporate census" which measures minority group composition in the organization and with the related concept of corporate climate which measures the "atmosphere" as it exists for the different members of the corporate community.

PREPARATION

Your instructor may request that you complete the questionnaire prior to class.

INTRODUCTION

Record the number of your choice in the column on the left-hand side of the page. After completing the questionnaire, turn to the scoring key to calculate your census and climate index scores.

CENSUS QUESTIONS

_____ 1. What is your sex?
    (a) Female
    (b) Male

_____ 2. Are you a member of one of the Aboriginal peoples of North America (North American Indian, Inuit, Métis)?
    (a) Yes, I am a North American Indian
    (b) Yes, I am Inuit
    (c) Yes, I am Métis
    (d) No, I am not an Aboriginal person

_____ 3. Are you a member of a visible minority? Members of visible minority groups are persons of colour or race who are identifiable minorities in Canada. Please note that this question does not refer to the country in which you were born, your citizenship, or your religion.
   (a) Yes, I am Black (including African Black, American Black, Canadian Black, West Indian Black)
   (b) Yes, I am East Asian (including Chinese, Japanese, Korean, Polynesian)
   (c) Yes, I am South Asian (including Indian, Pakistani, Bangladeshi, Sri Lankin)
   (d) Yes, and I am of another visible minority
   (e) Yes, and I am of mixed race
   (f) No, I am not a member of a visible minority

_____ 4. Do you have a disability? Please include your disability even if it does not preclude your employment. Do not include temporary disabilities such as those caused by injury that will heal. The World Health Organization defines disability as "a major limitation that substantially limits an individual from performing one or more of the major life activities in a manner considered normal."
   (a) Yes, I am blind or visually impaired (do not include problems correctable with lenses)
   (b) Yes, I am deaf or hard of hearing
   (c) Yes, I have a medical disability (including arthritis, diabetes, epilepsy, hemophilia, heart condition, multiple sclerosis, muscular dystrophy, psychiatric illness)
   (d) Yes, I have a mobility disability, such as the need to use a wheelchair
   (e) No, I do not have a disability

_____ 5. What is your native language, that is, the language you first learned to speak and still understand?
   (a) English
   (b) French
   (c) Chinese
   (d) Italian
   (e) Portuguese
   (f) Other

_____ 6. Do you believe that the variety (dialect) of English or French that you speak limits your employment opportunities?
   (a) Yes
   (b) No

_____ 7. Do you have any children?
   (a) Yes
   b) No

_____ 8. Age at present time:
   (a) 17–20
   (b) 21–24
   (c) 25–30
   (d) 31–40
   (e) 41 or more

_____   9.   Citizenship:
        (a)   Citizen of Canada
        (b)   Not a citizen of Canada

SCHOOL CLIMATE QUESTIONS

Answer these questions with reference to the class you are now attending.

_____   10.   This course is:
        (a)   A core course for my program
        (b)   A general education or elective course

_____   11.   Does your instructor know you by name?
        (a)   Yes
        (b)   No
        (c)   Don't know

_____   12.   How often do you voluntarily answer questions or contribute to class discussions in this class?
        (a)   Never
        (b)   One to three times during the course
        (c)   An average of once a week
        (d)   An average of two to three times a week
        (e)   An average of one or more times a day

_____   13.   How often does the instructor call on you or ask you to respond to a question or comment?
        (a)   Instructor does not call on anyone
        (b)   One to three times during the course
        (c)   An average of once a week
        (d)   An average of two to three times a week
        (e)   Never

_____   14.   How does the instructor most frequently call on you?
        (a)   By name
        (b)   By pointing with hand
        (c)   By eye to eye contact/looking at me
        (d)   Instructor never calls on me

_____   15.   Are there times when you raise your hand to ask a question or make a comment but do not get called on by the instructor?
        (a)   Once or twice
        (b)   Three or more times
        (c)   I am called on when I raise my hand
        (d)   I never raise my hand

_____   16.   Why do you think the instructor does not call on you when you raise your hand? (Select the **one** answer which best reflects your opinion.)
        (a)   Too many students want to respond
        (b)   Others beat me to it
        (c)   Instructor does not see or hear me
        (d)   Instructor ignores me
        (e)   This situation never occurs

_____ 17. Are there times when you want to participate in class by asking a question or making a comment but choose not to do so?
   (a) Once or twice
   (b) Three or more times
   (c) Nearly every class
   (d) No, because I participate when I want to
   (e) I do not want to participate

_____ 18. If you have wanted to participate in class by asking a question or making a comment but did not do so, what was your reason for not doing so? (Select the **one** response that most closely corresponds with your feelings.)
   (a) Felt insecure, inadequate, or uncertain
   (b) Another student asked question or commented first
   (c) Too many students in class
   (d) Disagreed with instructor, but chose not to speak out
   (e) This situation never happens

_____ 19. In your opinion, which students most frequently participate in class? (Select the **one** answer that best represents your opinion.)
   (a) Those who are most knowledgeable or most interested in the subject
   (b) Those who are seeking clarification or want more information
   (c) Those who are trying to show off or get attention
   (d) I have not noticed

_____ 20. In your opinion, which students ask the most questions and make the most comments in class?
   (a) Male students
   (b) Female students
   (c) Male and female students equally
   (d) Have not noticed

_____ 21. How does the instructor react to the questions you make in class?
   (a) Encourages me to question or comment again
   (b) Discourages me from commenting or asking a question again
   (c) Neither encourages nor discourages me
   (d) I never participate

_____ 22. In your opinion, how does the instructor react to opinions and comments given by other students in the class?
   (a) Respects the opinions of students in this class
   (b) Does not respect the opinions of students in this class
   (c) Embarrasses or "puts down" students for their opinions
   (d) I did not notice

_____ 23. Does your instructor use humour or make humorous references that you feel are offensive, embarrassing, or belittling to any individuals or groups?
   (a) Never
   (b) One time
   (c) Occasionally
   (d) Frequently

_____ 24. How often do students participate in this class by asking questions or making comments?
   (a) Never
   (b) Rarely
   (c) Occasionally
   (d) Frequently

_____ 25. Sex of instructor
   (a) Male
   (b) Female

_____ 26. Class Size _____

WORK CLIMATE QUESTIONS

Answer these questions with reference to your current place of employment. If you are not currently employed, make reference to your most recent job. Use either full-time or part-time work.

   If you have more than one supervisor, pick the one with which you have the most frequent contact, that is, the one who is most regularly involved in overseeing your work.

_____ 27. How well does your supervisor know you?
   (a) Not at all
   (b) Knows my name
   (c) Knows my work
   (d) Understands my personality

_____ 28. How often do you voluntarily answer questions or make suggestions about work routines?
   (a) Never
   (b) Every month or so
   (c) An average of once a week
   (d) An average of two to three times a week
   (e) An average of one or more times a day

_____ 29. How often does the supervisor call on you or ask you to respond to a question or comment?
   (a) Supervisor does not call on anyone
   (b) Every month or so
   (c) An average of once a week
   (d) An average of two to three times a week
   (e) Never

_____ 30. How does the supervisor most frequently call on you?
   (a) By name
   (b) By pointing with hand
   (c) By eye to eye contact/looking at me
   (d) Supervisor never calls on me

_____ 31.   Why do you think the supervisor does not call on you for help? (Select the **one** answer which best reflects your opinion.)
   (a) Too many workers want to help
   (b) Others beat me to it
   (c) Supervisor does not see or hear me
   (d) Supervisor ignores me
   (e) This situation never occurs

_____ 32.   Are there times when you want to offer suggestions but choose not to do so?
   (a) Once or twice
   (b) Three or more times
   (c) Nearly every day
   (d) No, because I participate when I want to
   (e) I do not want to participate

_____ 33.   If you have wanted to participate by offering a suggestion or making a comment but did not do so, what was your reason for not doing so? (Select the **one** response that most closely corresponds with your feelings.)
   (a) Felt insecure, inadequate, or uncertain
   (b) Another worker spoke first
   (c) Too many workers
   (d) Disagreed with supervisor, but chose not to speak out
   (e) This situation never happens

_____ 34.   In your opinion, which workers most frequently participate? (Select the **one** answer that best represents your opinion.)
   (a) Those who are most knowledgeable or most interested in the work
   (b) Those who are seeking clarification or want more information
   (c) Those who are trying to show off or get attention
   (d) I have not noticed

_____ 35.   In your opinion, which workers offer the most suggestions and make the most comments?
   (a) Male workers
   (b) Female workers
   (c) Male and female workers equally
   (d) Have not noticed

_____ 36.   How does the supervisor react to what you have to say?
   (a) Encourages me to question or comment again
   (b) Discourages me from commenting or asking a question again
   (c) Neither encourages nor discourages me
   (d) I never participate

_____ 37.   In your opinion, how does the supervisor react to opinions and comments given by other workers?
   (a) Respects the opinions of workers
   (b) Does not respect the opinions of workers
   (c) Embarrasses or "puts down" workers for their opinions
   (d) I did not notice

_____ 38. Does your supervisor use humour or make humorous references that you feel are offensive, embarrassing, or belittling to any individuals or groups?
  (a) Never
  (b) One time
  (c) Occasionally
  (d) Frequently

_____ 39. Sex of supervisor
  (a) Male
  (b) Female

_____ 40. Is this a part-time or full-time job?
  (a) Up to 24 hours per week
  (b) More than 24 hours per week

CENSUS QUESTIONS		
Q#	Response	Score
1	a =2 b =1	
2	a =8 b =9 c =5 d =1	
3	a =5 b =4 c =6 d =7 e =8 f =1	
4	a =9 b =8 c =3 d =7 e =1	
5	a =1 b =3 c =6 d =5 e =7 f =8	
6	a =2 b =1	
7	a =2 b =1	
8	a =1 b =1 c =1 d =2 e =3	
9	a =1 b =3	
TOTAL CENSUS SCORE =		

SCHOOL CLIMATE QUESTIONS		
Q#	Response	Score
10	a =1 b =2	XXXXX
11	a =1 b =3 c =2	
12	a =5 b =4 c =3 d =2 e =1	
13	a =0 b =4 c =3 d =2 e =1	
14	a =1 b =2 c =3 d =4	
15	a =2 b =3 c =1 d =4	

Q#	Response	Score
SCHOOL CLIMATE QUESTIONS (Continued)		
16	a =1 b =2	XXXXX
17	a =1 b =3 c =2	
18	a =5 b =4 c =3 d =2 e =1	
19	a =0 b =4 c =3 d =2 e =1	
20	a =1 b =2 c =3 d =4	
21	a =2 b =3 c =1 d =4	
22	a =1 b =2 c =3 d =0	
23	a =1 b =2 c =3 d =4	
24	a =4 b =3 c =2 d =1	
25	a =4 b =1	
26	XXXXX	
TOTAL SCHOOL SCORE =		

Q#	Response	Score
WORK CLIMATE QUESTIONS		
27	a =4 b =3 c =2 d =1	
28	a =1 b =2 c =3 d =4 e =5	
29	a =0 b =4 c =3 d =2 e =1	
30	a =1 b =2 c =3 d =4	
31	a =1 b =2 c =3 d =4 e =0	
32	a =2 b =3 c =4 d =1 e =0	
33	a =3 b =2 c =1 d =4 e =0	
34	a =1 b =2 c =3 d =0	
35	a =3 b =2 c =1 d =0	
36	a =1 b =3 c =2 d =0	
37	a =1 b =2 c =3 d =0	
38	a =1 b =2 c =3 d =4	
39	a =3 b =1	
40	a =2 b =1	XXXXX
TOTAL WORK SCORE =		

SCHOOL / WORK SCORE									
CENSUS SCORE									

Plot the status and climate scores for your group on the graph paper. Use separate sheets for school and work scores. If you have only a small number of group members, you may wish to combine your data with that of other groups.

DISCUSSION QUESTIONS

1. Describe the relationship if any between status and climate.
2. What variables other than status might contribute to a chilly or a warm climate?
3. What corporate costs would be associated with a chilly climate?
4. What strategies might be undertaken to warm up too chilly a climate?

The Merger Task Force

Organizational Change and Development

PURPOSE

To play a role as a participant in a task force given the mandate to merge a smaller organization into a larger one.

PREPARATION

Read The Limerick Arena Association case.

INTRODUCTION

You will role play one of the members of the Mayor's Task Force on Parks and Recreation in the City of Limerick. This role will be assigned to you in advance of the first meeting of the task force so that you can prepare your own analysis of the situation and your strategy for the planning to be done.

TASK FORCE GOALS (as stated by the mayor)

1. Prepare a plan for the integration of the arenas into the current Parks and Recreation department. The plan could include a new organization chart, list of new positions, reassignment of resources, etc.
2. Develop an implementation strategy for the plan which could include contingency planning.
3. Develop a proposal to suitably recognize the past achievements of the LAA and the vital past contributions of the board members.

PERSONAL PLAN FOR THE TASK FORCE (for your eyes only)

Position Title: _____

My Agenda: _____

_____

My assessment of the others on the task force.

1. Director of Parks and Recreation

   _____

   _____

2. Director of Public Works

   _____

   _____

3. Deputy Treasurer

   _____

   _____

4. Personnel Director

   _____

   _____

5. Union President

   _____

   _____

6. Manager of the Public Utilities Commission

   _____

   _____

7. Librarian

   _____

   _____

8. Manager/Coordinator of LAA

   _____

   _____

9. User-Group Representatives

   1. _____

      _____

   2. _____

      _____

   3. _____

      _____

Alice's Expense Account

Ethics

PURPOSE

To discuss the question of ethics in business.

PREPARATION

None required.

INTRODUCTION

The following mini-case introduces a fairly common example of situational ethics in business. Use it to stimulate a discussion of the broader issues which are involved.

The Case

Alice Bigelow worked for the Beaver Basket Company. She was the newest member of their sales department and the first woman. The Beaver Basket Company was an old and established Canadian company which got its start manufacturing wooden baskets. These were used by the fruit and vegetable industry, but they also manufactured a line used in the home as laundry baskets.

They kept abreast of the times, and, when technology changed, they switched to more modern packaging methods and expanded their product line to serve the growing manufacturing industry of Southern Ontario. They moved their offices and plant from Minesing, Ontario, which had an abundant forest, to Ajax, which was close to major highways.

Members of the sales team visited manufacturers and helped them package their product in a visually pleasing manner. The Beaver Basket Company would then make the packages and ship them to the manufacturer. Many of their customers were importers who required domestic packages for their products.

Most of their current packages were made of paper and plastic. Despite this modernization, the Beaver Basket Company was still privately owned by the original family. The corporate culture was filled with the traditional rural values of the founders even though they no longer manufactured any wooden laundry baskets.

Alice had a problem with her expense form for her first sales trip to Western Ontario. She had been away for a week, and her actual expenses came to $730. She was about to hand it in when one of the older salesmen asked to see it. He said that it was far too low and that she ought to pad it the same way all the men did. He showed her how to do this by faking restaurant receipts, adding mileage, parking charges, and customer entertainment. He suggested that the past average for her trip was around $800–$850 and, if she didn't put in that much, then the accountants would start to wonder about the previous expense forms. He made it clear that, if she wanted to be one of the boys, she had better play ball on their team.

The problem that Alice had was that her great grandparents were from Minesing, Ontario, and had founded the Beaver Basket Company. She was the first member of her family in a generation to take any interest in actually working for the business, and she had not told anybody that she was a part of the family that owned it.

She did not know whether to blow the whistle on the salesmen, choke on it, or to save it for a rainy day.

TASK

1. List the options which Alice had and identify the pros and cons of each option. Consider all aspects of her situation, including her immediate circumstances as well as her long-term plans to work at the Beaver Basket Company.

2. Discuss the morality of the salesmen, in particular, the older salesman who undertook to teach Alice the tricks of the trade. Expense account padding is a fairly institutionalized practice. How is it justified by the participants? What rationalizations would they give for their unethical behaviour? How deviant is it?